Magic and Witchcraft in the West

Magic and Witchcraft in the West

Sabbats, Satan and Supersitions

Frances Timbers

First published in Great Britain in 2019 by
Pen and Sword History
An imprint of
Pen & Sword Books Ltd
Yorkshire - Philadelphia

Hardback ISBN 9781526731814
Paperback ISBN 9781526757630

A CIP catalogue record for this book is available from the British Library.

Typeset in India by Vman Infotech Private Limited

Printed and bound in the UK by TJ International Ltd.

Pen & Sword Books Ltd incorporates the Imprints of Pen & Sword Books Archaeology, Atlas, Aviation, Battleground, Discovery, Family History, History, Maritime, Military, Naval, Politics, Railways, Select, Transport, True Crime, Fiction, Frontline Books, Leo Cooper, Praetorian Press, Seaforth Publishing, Wharncliffe and White Owl.

For a complete list of Pen & Sword titles please contact

PEN & SWORD BOOKS LIMITED
47 Church Street, Barnsley, South Yorkshire, S70 2AS, England
E-mail: enquiries@pen-and-sword.co.uk
Website: www.pen-and-sword.co.uk

or

PEN AND SWORD BOOKS
1950 Lawrence Rd, Havertown, PA 19083, USA
E-mail: Uspen-and-sword@casematepublishers.com
Website: www.penandswordbooks.com

For all my familiars: Spic and Span, Potlicker and Puddin'head, Spritzy, Misha and Kifi, Buffy, Nicodemus, Cassiopeia, Andromeda, Ollie, Lizzie Lizzie Elizabeth, Marley, Mr T, Chico, Chiquita, Scruffy, Little Frere, Valiente, Kali, Gizmo, and Mamasita. With honorary mention to Zepher, Tinker, and Rigby. They taught me that life is brief. Take time to cuddle and sleep in the sun.

Contents

List of Illustrations

Introduction

Information is often circulated in popular culture for so long that it is taken as 'truth'. General opinion, even if it is incorrect, is accepted as a source of authority. I get frustrated every Halloween when the TV or radio announcer tells me that the 'witch-craze' happened in Europe in the middle ages, when in actual fact, most of the trials occurred in the early modern period. The middle ages refers to the period in the West between the fall of the Roman Empire and the Renaissance, from approximately the fifth century to the end of the fifteenth. The early modern period is defined as the years after the Renaissance and before the French Revolution, roughly between 1500 and the late 1700s. When I use the term 'premodern' in the following text, I am referring to the middle ages and the early modern period combined. The so-called 'witch-craze' is associated with the middle ages because of a general perception that medieval Europe was a time of ignorance and superstition, which is also incorrect. While it is true that the majority of the population were still illiterate peasants living in villages, the high middle ages was the period when the first universities were founded and cathedrals such as Paris's Notre Dame were built. And anyway, it was not in the so-called 'Dark Ages' that executing witches became popular. The era of burning witches at the stake was in the early modern period from 1550 to 1660. Just to put things in perspective, this is the same era when Galileo was arguing for heliocentrism, Descartes was giving birth to analytical geometry, and Francis Bacon was establishing empiricism. In other words, during the so-called scientific revolution.

Another erroneous idea that is circulated in popular culture is that nine million women were executed during a paranoid witch-hunt designed to search out female social deviants. The Roman Catholic institution of the Inquisition is usually held to blame. As we will see in Chapter 7, the Inquisition was one of the more lenient vehicles of witchcraft persecution. And historians have proven beyond a doubt that prosecuting witches was not a programme of genocide, but rather a concern over the enemy within. The situation is more comparable to the twenty-first century practice of managing terrorists than it is to the twentieth-century Holocaust. There was no systematic persecution of witchcraft in early modern Europe by the church or state. Yes, there were many trials in the period from 1428 to 1782 — between 90,000 to 100,000 — but they were sporadic rather than a routine occurrence. During the height of the persecution, there were occasional outbreaks of large witch hunts, but these were also aberrations to the norm. In total, between 40,00 to 50,000 women, men, and children were executed in all of Western Europe, most of them in Germany.

It is true that most of the victims were female. But in some areas, especially where shamanism was an element of the culture, there was a much larger percentage of men executed. A related misconception is that the majority of victims were midwives, healers, and wise women. Yes, occasionally midwives got caught up in accusations, but as a group, they were under-represented demographically. Midwives were well-respected members of the community and were more often employed to help identify a witch than they were accused as being witches.

Contemporary critics of the witchcraft persecutions believed that the women who were being accused, and were often confessing, must have been suffering from mental instability, or experiencing menopause or melancholy. Post-Freudian commentators blamed repression and hysteria, especially in cases of possession allegedly caused by bewitchment. Various other rationalisations have been offered to explain away this seemingly barbaric episode in history. The alleged flying of witches was attributed to the use of hallucinogenic ointments smeared on the body or the broomstick. Incidents of apparent possession, especially in relation to the Salem episode, have been blamed on ingesting ergot, a fungus that grows on rye, which can cause delusions. But these efforts to explain away the impossible do not put the phenomenon of witchcraft into cultural context. Anthropologically speaking, witchcraft gave early modern people a way to explain the inexplicable. Witchcraft accusations served a purpose in the community, which could help deal with grief and anger. In the face of repeated outbreaks of plague, constant war, bad weather that affected crops, the subsequent diseases associated with famine and malnutrition, and religious rivalry, the idea of a satanic conspiracy made sense. God was allowing the Devil to wreak havoc because of human sin and social disorder.

One more misconception. Since before the birth of modern Wicca, discussed in Chapter 8, there was a theory floating around that the people being accused of witchcraft were actually practising the remnants of a pre-Christian fertility cult, which had been driven underground by the church. No evidence supports this idea. The meeting of witches that demonologists called a sabbat was the invention of the judges, lawyers, and clergy who were writing about this phenomenon.

So what is this phenomenon we are discussing? One of the biggest challenges in writing about magic and witchcraft is defining the subject. The terminology has changed over time and from one culture to another. The definition and connotations of the word witch are especially ambiguous and constantly shifting. The modern twenty-first century Western witch, discussed in Chapter 8, is a completely different entity to the classical Greek and Roman witches portrayed in Chapter 1, or the persecuted premodern witch in the rest of the book. Since the bulk of this volume is about the witchcraft persecution era in Western Europe, I will limit my discussion of the definition of witchcraft to that period. The most important difference between witchcraft and magic, as discussed herein, is that witchcraft was a cultural construction, an imagined crime.

Let's start with magic. The following description of magic is by the sixteenth-century scholar, theologian, and magician, Henry Cornelius Agrippa:

> 'Magic is a faculty of wonderful virtue, full of most high mysteries, containing the most profound contemplation of most secret things, together with the nature, power, quality, substance, and virtues thereof, as also the knowledge of whole nature, and it doth instruct us concerning the differing, and agreement of things amongst themselves, whence it produceth its wonderful effects, by uniting the virtues of things through the application of them one to the other, and to their inferior suitable subjects, joining and knitting them together thoroughly by the powers, and virtues of the superior bodies.'[1]

The ritual or ceremonial magic that Agrippa is discussing in this passage was mechanical and rooted in natural philosophy, the precursor of modern science. The power of magic was occult, that is, hidden, but it was not demonic. The magician just had to know how to tap into the powers of nature and the heavens. My use of the term magic largely agrees with Agrippa. Magic was a set of practices designed to produce 'wonderful effects' that were outside of what was considered normal or natural. Magic was an art, engaged in by mostly elite males for the purpose of manipulating the natural world and invoking spirits. Magic could be learned; it was not dependent on any innate ability. The magician used his knowledge and skill in an effort to achieve magical results. This does not mean that I believe that magic worked, but it was definitely attempted. Officials of the church and state did not always agree with Agrippa's definition; nevertheless, very few of these practitioners were caught up in the witchcraft net.

If magic is an art, what is witchcraft? As the name implies, it is a craft engaged in by a witch. So what is a witch? First, let's take a look at the origins of the term itself. The word witch is derived from the Old English word *wicce*, which denoted a female sorcerer, and *wicca*, for a male sorcerer. The plural was *wiccan*. By the time of the prosecution era, the word witch was gender neutral. The double 'c' indicates that it was pronounced as 'ch' rather than a hard 'c'. The term was in use since at least the ninth century. The current spelling became standardised sometime in the sixteenth century. Sometimes the term wizard, from Old French, was used, but usually in reference to a wise man rather than a male witch causing harm. Warlock was not a common appellation for a male witch.

Modern witches use the term Wicca to describe their religion, pronounced with a hard 'c'. In order to present the idea of witchcraft in a favourable light, Wiccan leaders have suggested alternative explanations about the root of the word witch. Gerald Gardner, the founder of Wicca, claimed the word meant 'wise people'. Starhawk, the American star of modern witchcraft, promoted the idea that it meant 'to bend or shape', as in wicker furniture. However, the word wicker is derived from the Swedish word *vika* meaning 'to bend'; it has no association with witchcraft. The confusion may arise from the Anglo-Saxon term *wícan*, with one 'c', meaning to give way or yield. Yielding, a passive action associated with weakness, is not quite the same as bending, an active undertaking, and rather loses the meaning Starhawk was attempting to convey, which was that the witch could bend or shape reality.

During the witchcraft persecution era, witchcraft was defined as *maleficium*, the Latin term for the act of causing harm by supernatural means. The witch could either employ practical or technical charms and rituals, or she could cause harm with her innate ability or power, such as the evil eye. Both methods of causing harm were redefined as devil-worship in the sixteenth and seventeenth centuries. The early church fathers converted classical and pagan gods into demons, which were considered the source of the witch's supernatural power. Intellectuals who wrote about magic and witchcraft believed that both the magician and the witch must have made pacts with the Devil, whether explicitly or implicitly, in order to achieve their goals. The witch was constructed as a member of a diabolical cult that worshipped Satan, usually in a parody of Christian ritual. In a society that was ubiquitously Christian, at least from the official standpoint of both church and state, witchcraft was considered heretical, since it flew in the face of the orthodox doctrines of the church.

Although there were probably some folk who had negative thoughts about their neighbours and wanted to cause misfortune, as far as historians can determine, no one was overtly worshipping the Devil. Certainly, there were some people who were bending the rules of Christian dogma, but most of the people accused and executed for witchcraft were not actually performing any magic, witchcraft, or sorcery. Some may have been using simple spells or charms, a practice that was referred to as witchcraft only when misfortune occurred. There was a very broad use of charms and natural magic employed by the general population, which was not considered malevolent. In fact, people frequently resorted to 'white magic' for cures, protection, fertility, and love. The accusation of witchcraft occurred when something bad happened, which required an explanation and there was a likely suspect to blame. In any case, the techniques allegedly or actually used by those who were accused of witchcraft were not capable of causing the harm for which they were employed. So when I refer to someone as a witch, I mean the person was suspected or accused of witchcraft, not that she was casting spells or worshipping demons. The most important difference between witchcraft and magic, as discussed in this book, is that witchcraft was a cultural construction, an imagined crime.

Historians have spilled a lot of ink trying to determine the reason for the rise and decline of witchcraft persecution in the sixteenth and seventeenth centuries. There were many contributing factors but no single primary reason. The bottom line is that the persecution of witchcraft can only happen in a witch-believing society. Nowadays, in the West at least, if your neighbour thinks you put a spell on his dog, he is not going to get very far with reporting you to the authorities, secular or ecclesiastic. He is more likely to be considered eccentric or a little mad. Yes, there are many people who still believe in supernatural powers, but society as a whole does not support this view. Empiricism has won out in the courtroom. The premodern world, however, was inhabited with a multitude of spirits. Gods, angels, demons, ghosts, sprites, brownies, fairies, goblins, werewolves, and vampires: the belief in the supernatural world was ubiquitous. Before the advent of Christianity, the relationship between humans and the spirit world had been somewhat ambiguous. After Christianity gained ascendency in Europe, the spirit world was divided into good and evil on a much more black and white basis than it had been before. God and angels were good; all the rest were agents of Satan. The belief in original sin, based on the biblical Adam and Eve story, meant that all humans were potentially corrupt. This concept was combined with the idea that Satan, the leader of the fallen angels and God's archenemy, was active in the world on a daily basis. Witchcraft became configured as a sect of devil-worshipping heretics, who threatened society as a whole, as well as individuals. The fear surrounding Satan and witchcraft was further exacerbated by the Protestant Reformation and the Catholic Counter-Reformation. Zealous reformers were quick to label their opponents as servants of Satan. The pope was the anti-Christ and Martin Luther was the Devil's spawn. Both sides of the divide attacked popular culture and the 'superstitions' held by the masses in an effort to educate them in theology, as well as the ideology of the various sects. The persecution of people considered witches was possible because almost everybody, including church, state, and the general population, was onboard with the concept of the witch.

Alongside the power of the Christian churches was a 'magical world-view'. The medieval and early modern eras had inherited the belief that humans and the rest of the cosmos, including the earth, the heavens, and the plants and animals, were interconnected. Premodern people had a social and emotional relationship with Nature, which granted mystical and magical powers to elemental aspects. Power was inherent in the natural world and could be drawn on for both good and bad purposes. A vast wealth of rituals, recipes, and techniques were available to manipulate the natural world for specific ends. In both the Christian and the magical world-view, things did not happen randomly, but as a result of a chain of causation. Both misfortune and good luck had causes, perhaps on account of bad behaviour on the part of the person or as a result of malevolent actions of an enemy.

Witchcraft and magic are perennial topics that are as relevant today as they were in the persecution era. The concept of magic and witchcraft existed long before the so-called witch-craze and continued long after. The examination of magic and witchcraft offers a window into the past, in which we can examine the mental, social, and religious ideas of our forefathers. The study of witchcraft illuminates the lives of ordinary people in the past and shines a light on the fascinating pop culture of the premodern world. Witchcraft is a metaphor for oppression in an age in which persecution is an everyday occurrence somewhere in the world. Fanaticism, intolerance, prejudice, authoritarianism, and religious and political ideologies are never attractive. Beware the witch hunter!!

***

This book grew out of the lectures and tutorial discussions on magic and witchcraft that I have been giving for several years at Trent University in Peterborough, Canada. As such, it is designed as a broad overview of the subject for the novice. After looking at some of the ancient and classical contributions to the formation of the witch figure, I trace the development of witchcraft as heresy, beginning in the early middle ages and continuing into the early modern era. The influence of elite males, who discussed magic and witchcraft in terms of demon-worship and attendance at the sabbat, is balanced with an examination of the beliefs at the lowest end of society, from where the majority of the accusations arose. Before turning to the legal aspects of the prosecutions, which included torture and interrogation by the Inquisition as well as secular authorities, I explore the ritual magic engaged in by elite men, who were influenced by the Renaissance humanists. All of these historical manifestations of magic and witchcraft were influential in the development of modern pagan witchcraft.

Chapter 1

By Seed and Root, Classical Beginnings

When Medea first laid eyes on Jason, she was so aroused by his beauty that she felt an overwhelming passion for him. Jason, the leader of a group of heroes known as the Argonauts, had arrived at the kingdom of Medea's father, King Aeëtes of Colchis, to retrieve the Golden Fleece, which was a symbol of his kingship. Medea's father had agreed to relinquish the Fleece if Jason could perform a series of daunting tasks. Although it meant betraying her father, Medea chose to aid Jason, using magical herbs and spells, so that he could overcome the challenges her father had set before him. In return, Jason swore by the sacred rites of Hecate to take her as his wife. After Jason gained the Golden Fleece, he asked his new bride to use her magical skills to extend the life of his elderly father, Aeson. At the next full moon, Medea proceeded barefoot, dressed in flowing garments with her hair unbound, to a sacred grove at midnight. She extended her arms to the starry night sky; three times she turned herself about; three times she sprinkled her hair with water taken from the stream; three times she cried out; and then she knelt on the earth to pray to Hecate, the Triple Goddess of the Underworld. She invoked the powers of earth, air, water, and fire to aid in her request. She tells the reader of her powers to control the weather, raise the dead, and draw down the moon:

> 'all ye Deities of the groves, and all ye Gods of night, attend here;
> through whose aid, whenever I will,
> the rivers run back from their astonished banks to their sources,
> *and* by my charms; I disperse the clouds, and I bring clouds *upon the Earth*;
> I both allay the winds, and I raise them;
> and I break the jaws of serpents with my words and my spells;
> I move, too, the solid rocks, and the oaks torn up with their own *native* earth,
> and the forests *as well*.
> I command the mountains, too, to quake, and the Earth to groan,
> and the ghosts to come forth from their tombs.
> Thee, too, O Moon, do I draw down.'[1]

Medea then flew through the night sky in a chariot drawn by winged dragons to collect herbs for her spell. When she returned, she put the ingredients into a cauldron that was bubbling over the fire. On an altar to Hecate, she sacrificed a black-fleeced sheep and mixed its blood with milk and honey. After purifying Jason's father with this mixture, she replaced the old man's blood with her herbal concoction and rejuvenated him.

***

The foundation of Western culture lies in the philosophy, literature, and religions of ancient Greece and Rome. Both Greek and Roman sources reflect deep-seated beliefs in magic and witchcraft, most of which have survived or reappeared in the present. That is not to say that the presentation of magic and the construction of the witch in the classical era have been handed down to the twenty-first century in one continuous line. Rather, the later periods have looked back to the ancients for models from which to form their own versions. Then, as now, there was no single image of the witch, nor one unanimous opinion concerning magic. An author might even present various viewpoints on the subject. However, it is safe to say that the figure of the witch, as it developed in the premodern period, drew heavily on the portrayals of magic and witchcraft in the period before the decline of the Western Roman Empire (*c.* 476 CE). The classical literary construction of the evil witch, who brewed up concoctions to cause harm, became entangled with the actual practices of magic and witchcraft by both professionals and amateurs. Charms, spells, curses, and herbal craft added further elements to the stereotypical witch. Two other major events influenced the construction of magic and witchcraft in Western Europe. At the same time that Christianity was developing as an institution, the Roman Empire was making contact with the other cultures of Europe such as the Goths and Vandals. Elements of these pagan cultures were incorporated into the beliefs about witchcraft at the same time that witchcraft was being redefined as a sin, not just a crime.

The story of Medea is a good example of how magic deteriorated into witchcraft. The Greek sorceress has stood the test of time. Centuries before the Roman poet Ovid recounted the tale of Jason and the Golden Fleece in Book VII of *The Metamorphoses*, Medea was known in Greek mythology as the granddaughter of the sun god Helios and a priestess of the chthonic goddess Hecate. She was not originally a witch, but rather a minor goddess in the Greek pantheon of deities. In the original Latin version of the poem, Ovid says that Medea uses *cantusque artisque magorum* (line 195), which translates as: the incantations and arts of the magicians or wise men. However, English translations of the text often use the word 'witch' to describe Medea, with all the negative connotations that handle implies. Certain aspects of Medea's performance of magic became associated with witchcraft: flying through the air, brewing potions, and chanting incantations. One can even see aspects of modern Wicca in her behaviour, as she proceeds barefoot to the sacred grove and calls on the four elements. According to Ovid's version of the tale, Medea used her magical talents as a priestess for good rather than casting spells to cause harm, which defines the evil witch. Nonetheless, the figure of the night witch and the power of women were more fascinating subjects for authors and playwrights. As a result, Medea became the stereotypical witch. In the play *Medea*, the Roman tragedian Seneca portrayed her as an evil witch with unlimited powers, who could curse her enemies with potions brewed up in her cauldron.

Similar to Medea, the figure of Circe gets a bad rap in history. Predating Ovid and Seneca's portrayals of Medea, Circe was described in Book X (lines 274–566) of Homer's *Odyssey*. The epic poem had been a traditional oral poem until it was written down in the late eighth or early seventh century BCE. On his way home from the fall of Troy, Odysseus (also called Ulysses) encountered Circe on the island of Aeaea. Homer described her as a goddess, the daughter of the Titan sun god Helios. Circe turned Odysseus's crew into swine by feeding them food laced with drugs, followed by a wave of her magic wand, not an unreasonable course of action for a woman living alone on a remote island. Sailors do not have the best reputation. Odysseus was able to resist her magic because he had been given a preventative magic herb by the god Hermes. Following some negotiations, Circe turned Odysseus's comrades back into men, younger and more handsome than before. Sounds like a good deal. She also fed and entertained the crew for a year, until they had recovered from the weariness of their previous adventures. When it was time for Odysseus to leave, Circe instructed him on how to safely enter the house of Hades to consult with the spirit of the blind seer Tiresias about how to find his way back home. In spite of her efforts to help Odysseus, Circe is frequently portrayed as an evil witch rather than a helpful goddess. Note that the god Hermes never gets transformed into a witch, even though he used a magical herb for counter-magic.

Odysseus also comes out as a hero, in spite of his necromantic dabbling. Historically, he is the first recorded necromancer. The contrast between Circe's performance of magic and Odysseus's tells us more about the gender ideals surrounding magic and witchcraft than they do about actual magical practices. In Book XI of *Odyssey*, Odysseus, following Circe's instructions, performed necromantic rites to raise the dead in Hades. The ritual was very similar to Medea's efforts to increase the life of Jason's father. Odysseus dug a pit and cut the throats of a pair of black sheep over the trough, which had been blessed with milk, honey, wine, and barley. With vows and prayers, he called upon the spirits of the dead to arise. Many ghosts were attracted by the blood, which would have given them the power of speech. But finally the spirit of Tiresias appeared and offered his advice on the subsequent voyage. Odysseus's actions are usually interpreted as religious rites for the purpose of divination or prophecy, as opposed to magical spells.

The stories concerning Medea, Circe, and Odysseus raise the issue of what constitutes magic. The line between religion and magic was, and still is, often very blurry. In ancient Greece and Rome, religious rites had magical overtones, especially to the modern observer. The traditional rites performed at grave sites to appease the dead were similar, if not identical, to the rituals performed to summon up the dead for divination. Elaborate rituals were also performed to gain the favour of the gods. Prayers, exorcisms, ablutions, animal sacrifice, suffumigation, invocations, and the use of complicated paraphernalia were just some of the elements of these magico-religious ceremonies. Religious procedures were performed in a temple setting. These public rituals not only appeased the gods but also served an anthropological purpose in society. Religious rituals drew the community together. Similar rituals performed in secret, however, raised suspicions about the magicians' motives and separated the magician from the mainstream society. Although the magus, like the priest, was attempting to attain supernatural aid, magic was not usually condoned.

The Greeks did not claim to be the founders of magic. They attributed magic to the Persian prophet Zoroaster (also referred to as Zarathustra), who founded the religion of Zoroastrianism, which is still practised in parts of India, Iran, and elsewhere. The wise men portrayed in the story of the birth of Jesus are believed to be Persian Magi or disciples of Zoroaster. The Persian practices were seen as magic because foreign practices are often viewed as 'superstitious' by the dominant culture. One culture's religious practices can be another culture's magic. For example, the transubstantiation of the host during the Eucharist in Roman Catholic mass is viewed as superstitious by the Protestant faction of Christianity. But for the Catholic follower, the transformation of the host is orchestrated by the divine. One method of distinguishing between religion and magic is to examine the intent of the practitioner. The religious officiant offers prayer and sacrifice to the gods submissively, in the hope that the gods will be pleased and smile kindly on him or her. The magician, on the other hand, tries to manipulate and control the supernatural spirits to obtain his desires. But this still leaves the question of why Circe is considered a witch but Odysseus is not.

In some cases, there was no doubt about an author's opinion concerning witchcraft. The Romans, more than the Greeks, promoted the idea of the wicked female witch in literary venues. The Roman poet Horace presented a fully developed concept of the evil witch in Ode V of his *Book of Epodes.* The witch Canidia, with her uncombed hair woven with snakes, used toads, owl feathers, poison herbs, and bones to make a love charm. The centrepiece of her concoction was a young boy, whom she had buried up to his neck. Delicious food was placed within his sight to intensify his desire as he starved to death in the pit. Canidia intended to extract his liver, which would be filled with desire, to add to her potion. She called upon Night and the goddess Diana to witness her proceedings. Horace may have been taking a satirical approach to the subject of witchcraft by emphasising the grotesque aspects of Canidia's spells. Whatever his motives, his contribution to the genre of literary witches has had a long lasting effect. That is not to say that there is a direct line of descent from the Greek and Roman understandings of magic and witchcraft to the present day, or even into the middle ages. Nonetheless, later constructions of the witch, such as those portrayed by Shakespeare, were drawn from these classical literary sources. Hollywood is only the most recent player in this game. The classical texts were continually rediscovered and reinterpreted by Christian theologians as well as playwrights. The concept of the female witch, making nasty potions to seek love or revenge, became widely accepted. And the classical witches were often aligned with goddesses of the Underworld, which would become the Christian Hell.

In addition to the configuration of witches and witchcraft, the classical era contributed a philosophy that would later have a profound effect on both early modern magic and modern paganism. The Greek philosopher Plato developed the idea of the *anima mundi* or world soul, through which there is a connection between all living things. Almost all of the Greek philosophers embraced the notion that the natural and supernatural worlds were alive and intelligent, having both soul (*psyche*) and reason (*nous*). Plato argued that 'everything is full of gods'; in other words, the divine is immanent.[2] Not only the four elements of the physical world (fire, air, water, and earth) shared in the world soul, but also the stars and planets in the heavens. The ability of the heavenly bodies to affect earthly human ones was what underwrote the power of astrology. The virtues of the heavenly bodies could be accessed by employing the earthly materials that resonated with that particular planet or star. This combined concept of innate divinity and cosmic consciousness is what later magicians used to justify their experiments. Plato's doctrine of macrocosm and microcosm was used extensively after the Renaissance to explain how magic worked, a subject to which we shall return in Chapter 6.

Written sources from the classical age inform us about elite beliefs and practices, but what about the popular culture of the common people? Archeologists have unearthed material evidence of a thriving belief in magic in Greek and Roman culture, including curse tablets, love spells, 'voodoo' dolls, amulets, and charms. Curses were not limited to the lower levels of society. They were employed in legal and political battles, competitions such as horse races, and love affairs gone awry. Curse tablets were frequently constructed of lead, which had sympathetic magical attributes, but could also be made of other metals, such as gold, silver, or iron. [See image #1, London Curse Tablet] After being inscribed with the curse, the metal was rolled up or folded over to further bind the intended victim. The tablet could then be placed in a grave, a well, or the sanctuary of an earth god or goddess, such as Demeter or Hecate. The resident spirit of the grave site or the underground deity would hopefully aid the execution of the curse. Binding spells were often a form of love magic, designed to limit the activities of the desired person and bind her or his affections to the practitioner. Alternatively, the spell bound the person's rivals.

Greek literature leads us to believe that women were the main practitioners of love magic. However, the Greek Magical Papyri indicate that it was actually more the preserve of men. The manuscripts known as Greek Magical Papyri were recovered from the sands of Egypt in the nineteenth century. They were written down between the first and fourth centuries CE, when Romans ruled Egypt, but probably originate from before that time. They are a blend of Greek, Egyptian, Jewish, and Near Eastern material, reflecting the synthesis of cultures that took place in Alexandria. They indicate that Greek men used love magic to reverse impotence and to enhance sexual performance, as well as to arouse desire in another person, either male or female. Erotic binding spells could have been aimed at respectable young women who were inaccessible, because they were protected by their families. In that case, the purpose of the spell would have been a socially beneficial marriage rather than a romantic encounter or simple lust. In other cases, the spells appear to be directed at more sexually available women. A typical spell calls on a demon helper to go to every street and every house and every tavern to bind the intended woman. The woman would not be able to enjoy vaginal or anal intercourse or fellatio with any other lover. These spells discuss love as a form of erotic infatuation or madness. Once the woman is delivered into the hands of her lover, she would be tamed and settle into the new relationship.

There were also formulae for women to attract men. Rather than erotic love, women's spells were designed to obtain or regain the affection of a lover. They were also used to reduce the anger of a husband toward his wife and other aspects of marital discord. They were often employed in conjunction with herbs, ointments, amulets, and knotted cords. Some spells were for increasing a person's charisma in general. Male commentators frequently criticised the use of love spells and aphrodisiacs by women. There was a fear of loss of autonomy and control by a subordinate person (the wife), which was a form of emasculation. Male anger and male sexuality were closely related to a Greek man's sense of masculinity. One can see how the female practitioner of love magic became the evil witch, subverting power and gender relations.

In general, men used erotic love spells to instil uncontrollable passion and women used milder spells to induce affection. One exception to this general pattern was the wealthy courtesan and the prostitute, who engaged in love magic more typical of male techniques. Prostitutes used spells to gain new clients, to eliminate competition, and to maintain ongoing relationships. The woman took the role of seducer, the traditional role of the man. This is not surprising when one considers that Greek courtesans were more like men in both their education and autonomy. Rather than inciting lust for the spell maker, the purpose was to restrain the victim from having sex with other women or any boys. The other reason for a prostitute to use love magic on her clients was revenge. It seems that romantic or idealistic love was rarely the purpose of love magic.

Love magic could also take the form of a curse. In this case, the spell was intended to make the victim fall in love with someone inappropriate. When Homer was rejected by a priestess, he allegedly caused the woman to lust after old men. This trope was used by Shakespeare in *A Midsummer Night's Dream*. Oberon, the partner of Titania, the Queen of the Fairies, instructed his servant Puck to put a curse on her. As a result of the enchantment, she fell in love with the weaver Bottom, who (temporarily) had the head of an ass.

Love magic also employed figurines. The Greek Magical Papyri contain instructions about using a pair of wax dolls entwined in an embrace. The female was to be pierced with needles through the brain, eyes, ears, mouth, hands, feet, bowels, and vagina, then both of the figures were to be laid on the grave of someone who had died a violent or premature death. A long invocation to Persephone and other gods requested that the object of the magician's affection be bound to him and that she should have 'no pleasurable intercourse with any other man' nor 'be strong nor well' nor have 'sleep except with me'.[3] Figures like this are commonly referred to as 'voodoo' dolls, which is a relatively modern designation. The word voodoo is derived from the Haitian religion known as *vaudun*, a synthesis of indigenous African practices and Roman Catholic religion, which developed during New World slavery. The ancient Greeks referred to the dolls as *kolossoi*. They were most commonly constructed of wax, clay, bronze, or lead. Sometimes hair or other personal material was incorporated into the figure to strengthen the magic. Occasionally, the intended victim's name was inscribed on it. The figurines could be used for the purpose of inspiring love or cursing an enemy. Wax dolls could be melted to activate the curse. Metal dolls were sometimes twisted or mutilated to intensify the results. In a terracotta vase in Egypt, a nude female figurine made of unbaked clay was discovered along with a lead tablet on which a binding spell was engraved. The spell was intended to bring a woman to a man to love him 'for the whole time of [his] life'.[4] As per the description in the Greek Magical Papyri, the figure is in a kneeling position with her hands bound behind her back. Thirteen pins pierce her body: one in the top of her head; one in her mouth; one in each ear, eye, hand, and foot; one in the solar plexus; one in the anus; and one in her vagina. This so-called Louvre doll (currently housed in the Louvre Museum) dates from the fourth century CE. [See Image #2, Clay and bronze 'Voodoo' Doll] The use of such 'poppets' would eventually get firmly linked with witchcraft.

To protect oneself against a curse, a person could wear an amulet or talisman. Technically, amulets were natural objects that did not require further magic to make them efficacious. Talismans, on the other hand, were imbued with magical power by constructing them at astrologically beneficial times, inscribing them with symbols, and consecrating them. Both could be used to protect against specific diseases, to gain love or power, or for general protection. They could be made from organic substances, such as wood, wax, or leather, or from more durable substances, such as lead. The amulet could be very simple, but the talismans that have survived are frequently complex. For example, a verse or incantation could be inscribed on a roll of papyrus or on a sheet of gold or silver foil. The material would then be rolled up and inserted in a copper tube, which could be hung around the neck. Gemstones, sometimes mounted in a ring or pendant, were also inscribed with magical letters and shapes. The Greek Magical Papyri contain a recipe for constructing a magic ring that grants amazing powers to the wearer, including controlling a person's mind, inflicting harm, exorcising demons, summoning ghosts, and prophesying. The stone that was set in the ring was a bloodstone, engraved with an image of the sun, represented as a snake swallowing its tail: the *ouroboros*. The rituals that empowered the ring included incantations said every day for two weeks at dawn, marinating the ring for a day in the guts of a live (soon to be dead) rooster, and inscribing a hieroglyph of the name Helios (Sun) on the back of the ring. Medical amulets required diagnoses of the illnesses so that the appropriate materials and incantations could be employed. Sometimes amulets were applied in combination with a verbal charm or the tying of knots. After the influence of Christianity, prayers and biblical verses were used as well.

Curse tablets, love spells, voodoo dolls, and talismans could be commissioned from professionals or constructed by amateurs, which made them accessible to all levels of society, even slaves. Even when the curse tablet was intended for the use of a woman to attract or bind a man, they were usually written by a professional male practitioner. The lower classes also made use of the magical practices of the village wise men and wise women, who learned their craft orally from a family member or a mentor. Usually illiterate, wise folk made charms, healed sick cattle, used herbal remedies, and recited simple incantations. Divination or prediction might also be one of the services they offered. A category of healers known as 'root-cutters', who were more often literate, specialised in gathering and preparing herbs and other plants, both medicinal and poisonous. The application of herbs for medical purposes was sometimes combined with written or oral charms or incantations, thereby making them more magical than medical (at least in modern eyes). Wise folk and root-cutters had many customs concerning the collection and preparation of plants, drawn from traditional beliefs concerning the powers of particular herbs and the influence of the stars. Leaving offerings in the place of plants or harvesting only at night may appear 'superstitious', but such practices were drawn from a long magico-religious heritage. When Nature is viewed as divine, the gathering of plants necessarily takes on a religious character. Due to their extensive knowledge, wise folk and healers could do either good or harm. Knowledge of poisonous plants contributed to the eventual elision of herbalists with witches. In Greek, the term *pharmakon* could mean a drug used for curing or for poisoning, but also referred to magical knowledge, in that the person had the expertise in how to use drugs. The term *pharmakis* came to mean a wise woman or a witch. The Greek and Roman poets combined the skills of the healers with the activities of the night witch. As detailed above, Medea, Circe, and Canidia all used herbal lore for magical purposes. These fantasies concerning the knowledge and power of women should not be interpreted as reflecting an exclusive female expertise concerning drugs or the practice of witchcraft in the classical era. Evidence reveals that there were plenty of male aficionados in the field.

The popularity of magical practices does not mean that they were acceptable in society. In Plato's opinion, binding curses should have warranted the death penalty. Binding spells, harmful magic, charming crops, and simple poisoning were all frowned upon. But in general, the ancient authorities were more concerned with the restitution of damages than the punishment of magical practices. Laws protected individual interests, such as safety and property, and also supported the authority of the state. If it could be proven that a person harmed livestock by magical means, the person would have to pay for that livestock. Even the use of a love potion was only problematic if the person died from it. The practice of illiterate folk magic was only a concern when it caused personal harm. The power that underwrote magic was not as important as the resulting crime.

Roman law followed the Greek pattern. A few highlights will demonstrate. The Twelve Tablets, laws from the fifth century BCE, forbade a person from enchanting his neighbour's crops so that they were magically transported into his own field. In the second century BCE, some 5,000 Romans were executed for using *veneficium* to cause harm, a somewhat ambiguous term that referred to both poison and malign witchcraft. All aspects of magic were gradually prohibited in an attempt to suppress the development of private or cult religions, whose secret rites were viewed as threats to conventional religious beliefs. Magical divination, astrology, and necromancy were all sanctioned as competition to traditional forms of divination. The prohibitions were linked with the learned magic that had infiltrated from Egyptian and Jewish sources. The Emperor Augustus ordered that any books on the magical arts were to be burned.

Enter Christianity

Christianity survived as an underground, persecuted cult for almost 400 years after the crucifixion of Jesus. As Christianity became legalised and institutionalised, the early Church Fathers had to come to terms with the beliefs already in place in Roman society. One topic that would have serious repercussions on the understanding of the practice of magic was the role of demons. Christian theologians built on the ambiguous nature of the spirit world to effectively demonise both Roman and pagan belief systems. Fear was a key emotion in the propagation of Christianity, especially toward the end of the Roman Empire. The fear of involvement with bad spirits helped to convert the masses to the new sect. At the same time, the burden of guilt could be lifted from any wrongdoing by blaming evil spirits: the Devil made me do it!!

The concept of demons existed in the Greek and Roman world long before Christianity embraced the concept of Satan. *Daimones* were intermediary supernatural entities, which could relay information between man and the divine. Similar to fairies or witches' familiars, they could interfere in human endeavours. These spirits might be benign or malignant. In *Symposium*, the philosopher Plato described them as having passions the same as humans, which made them unreliable. Plutarch, another Greek philosopher and a priest at the temple of Apollo, agreed that *daimones* could work for good or for evil. They could be helpful, like a guardian spirit, or act against a person to cause harm. He believed that a person possessed by malevolent *daimones* required exorcism, a practice that was later adopted by Christianity. Understandably, the ancient Greeks had an ambivalent relationship with *daimones*. The classical understanding of the spirit world paved the way for Christian theologians to exploit the fear of demons as evil-doers in league with Satan. The problem, in the eyes of the new church, lay in the fact that *daimones* were devious and could play tricks on the soul. Raising the spirits of the dead, as the witch of Endor did so Saul could speak to Samuel and as Odysseus did in order to speak to Tiresias, were traditional techniques of divination. But what if the spirits were not Samuel and Tiresias, but just evil demons pretending to be them?

Christianity was an outgrowth of Judaism. Jewish traditions were inherited directly when Christianity adopted the Old Testament as part of the Bible. Angels, made by God at the time of Creation, became an element of the Christian cosmos. Jewish tradition also contributed the idea of fallen angels as demons. The demon Azâzêl is mentioned in both *Leviticus* 16: 8–10 and the non-canonical *Book of Enoch* 6:1–8:4. In *Enoch* 6:1–2 and 7:1–2, he is one of the leaders of the angels that lusted after human women and got thrown out of heaven for his efforts. The fallen angels were doomed to reside in the air until the day of judgement, which situated them in the same airy realm as the *daemones.*

> 'And it came to pass, after the children of men had increased in those days, beautiful and comely daughters were born to them. And the angels, the sons of the heavens, saw and lusted after them, and said one to another: 'Behold, we will choose for ourselves wives from among the children of men, and will beget for ourselves children.' And they took unto themselves wives, and each chose for himself one, and they began to go in to them, and mixed with them, and taught them charms and conjurations, and made them acquainted with the cutting of roots and of woods.'

The offspring born of these unusual relationships were bound to the earth as evil spirits. Another damning aspect of this story was that the fallen angels taught their human wives the art of 'charms and conjurations' as well as 'the cutting of roots', which would contribute to the allegations of witchcraft against women. Of course, the unfallen angels remained good spirits, similar to the good *daimones*, which contributed to the dichotomy of good versus evil that is an integral part of Christianity.

The other element of demonology that came from the Judaic tradition was Lucifer or Satan as the Devil with a capital D. The term 'lucifer' is only mentioned once in the Hebrew Bible (*Isaiah* 14:12). It means 'shining one' or 'morning star' and was possibly referring to the planet Venus. By the time of the English King James Version of the Bible, Lucifer was understood as the angelic name of the Devil before his fall from heaven. Satan was also named in the Old Testament. In Hebrew, the word means 'accuser' or 'adversary'. Satan was one of 'the sons of God' (*Job* 1–2), in other words, an angel. The abridged version of the story is that Satan presented himself along with other 'sons of God' and said that Job, who was an extremely reverent and wealthy man, would not be so pleased with God if God had not blessed every aspect of his life. God took up this challenge and told Satan he could test Job. Job's servants, oxen, sheep, camels, and children were all destroyed, but still Job worshipped God. So God told Satan to go ahead and afflict Job's body as well. Job was covered with boils from head to toe and was reduced to skin and bone. Satan lost the bet, since Job's faith never wavered. God rewarded him with twice as much as he had before. Satan was also mentioned in the New Testament. Jesus went into the desert after being baptised by John the Baptist and was tempted by the Devil. Over time, Satan was transformed into the leader of the fallen angels and the chief antagonist of Christianity. Beelzebub, originally a Philistine god, was later demonised as the prince of demons in the *Testament of Solomon*, a work attributed to the biblical King Solomon but probably written between the first and fifth centuries CE.

If the demonic spirits of the ancient world were going to be defeated, they needed to be replaced with another type of supernatural power, a role conveniently filled by the angels. How else could the Christians explain the acts of magic that were already included in the Judaic tradition? For example, Moses and his brother Aaron had competed with the Egyptian magicians in their efforts to escape Egypt (*Exodus* 7–8). Aaron threw down his staff and it turned into a snake. The Egyptian magicians did the same. But Aaron's snake-staff swallowed up the other magicians' snake-staffs. (It is all so phallic, isn't it?) Using the same staff, the brothers changed the water of the Nile to blood, covered the land with frogs, turned dust to gnats, and much more. The Egyptian magicians could never surpass them. The Church Fathers explained that the Egyptian magicians were sorcerers who employed demons, whereas Moses and Aaron were performing miracles in the name of God and had the assistance of the angels. How convenient. Nevertheless, Moses would later be viewed as schooled in the Egyptian arts. Manuscripts discovered in the nineteenth century, dating from the fourth century, were considered to contain occult knowledge that God had dictated to Moses along with the Ten Commandments. The *Eighth Book of Moses* instructed the reader on how to meet God so that he could reveal the future.

This type of magical battle continued in the Christian tradition. In the new church's struggle for supremacy, only supernatural activities connected with Jesus and his disciples were acceptable. This was made clear in the story of the magical battle between Peter the Apostle and Simon the Magus (*Acts* 8: 9–24). Simon, a recent convert to the Christian faith, was impressed with Peter's ability to lay his hands on a person with the result that the person received the Holy Spirit. He approached Peter and offered to buy the ability for himself, which earned him Peter's wrath. The request also got Simon's name permanently associated with simony, the buying of ecclesiastical privileges, such as benefices. The brief encounter mentioned in the gospel passage was elaborated on in later church stories recorded in the fourth century, such as the *Clementine Recognitions*. Both men performed astounding feats, but what Simon did was termed magic, while Peter's accomplishments were considered miracles. The final competition between the two men was a flying display. Simon flew with the help of evil demons, which allowed Peter to bring him to ground by calling on the aid of the heavenly angels. Stories such as this were told as homilies or mini-sermons, as the Catholic church spread its doctrines to the masses. The link between magic and demons became firmly cemented in the mind of the ordinary person.

If there was any doubt about the power that demons had over humans, the mid-fourth century *Life of Anthony* would have dispelled it. According to his biographer, the Egyptian monk Anthony gave up his property and went into the desert to follow an ascetic life. There he was tempted and tormented by myriads of evil spirits. When sexual temptation failed, the demons beat him mercilessly. The devils sometimes took the form of wild beasts, snakes, and scorpions, in an attempt to frighten him into giving up his faith. [See Image #3, Copper engraving of the 'Temptation of St Anthony'] Anthony's conviction and the sign of the cross caused the demons to disappear. The average person could understand from this account that even the monastic life was not protection against the workings of the Devil and his minions, only Christian belief and symbols were effective. This rhetoric of fear was used to convert the masses to the new religion.

The effect that Christianity had on beliefs concerning magic and witchcraft was aided and abetted by secular authorities. For the first three centuries after the crucifixion, the cult of Jesus was persecuted. Free and open worship was not allowed until 313 CE when the Western Roman Emperor Constantine I passed the Edict of Milan, which announced that Christianity would be tolerated in the Empire. Constantine was not necessarily a Christian himself, but he sought social stability and possibly the appeasement of the Christian God for the good of the Empire. He condemned magical arts that were used to harm or to turn minds and hearts to lust. However, he specifically excluded punishment in the case of magic for the purpose of healing or for the protection of the crops. The intention of the magic was the issue not the practice. But his son Constantius II condemned astrologers, soothsayers, prophets, and other magi in 357 CE. Christianity later became the official, and only, church of the state under the Emperor Theodosius I. In 380 CE, he effectively outlawed the old gods of Rome. He dissolved the college of the Vestal Virgins, an order of priestesses who served Vesta, the goddess of the hearth, and who maintained a sacred fire that protected Rome. Theodosius closed or destroyed many other temples as well. Along with the promotion of the Christian God was the condemnation of all things magical. In the fifth century CE, the emperor Theodosius II ordered the various Roman laws to be collected into one code, known as the *Theodosian Code*. Future imperial decrees contained laws against all forms of magic, and there were many provisions concerning heresy. Divination, necromancy, and owning occult books were also forbidden. One contemporary author lamented that consulting a soothsayer, using an old wife's charm to relieve pain, or wearing a protective amulet could all result in the death penalty. The Roman Empire already had a history of implementing severe laws against the practice of magic that caused harm. What was new about the post-Theodosian legislation was the move from concern about social issues to emphasis on the moral issues of magic. By legislating Christianity as the only acceptable religion, conversion and salvation came under the purview of the secular authorities. As a result, there were legal repercussions to heretical issues.

Against this background of increasing support for Christianity from the Roman state, entered Augustine, the Bishop of Hippo. He played a huge role in the formation of doctrine during the process of Christian institutionalisation. He interpreted what he considered to be 'superstitions' of the classical religions into a theology concerning demons. Considered the most influential of the Church Fathers, Augustine discussed his views on demons and magic in *The City of God* (fifth century). He rejected the idea that *daimones* were intermediaries or interpreters of divine will in favour of the belief that the airy spirits were evil demons determined to do harm. Demons were equated with the fallen angels and their offspring, who deserved all the wrath of mankind. In his efforts to undermine any authority that the soothsayers and magicians might have had, he attributed all the results of their practices to demons. In the classical Roman era, both good and bad spirits could be harnessed by priests, soothsayers, and magicians. For the new church, the danger lay in the possibility that the demons were deceiving the person by pretending to be angels. In Augustine's opinion, all magic was demonic and a result of a pact with devils. He belittled what passed for magic as merely illusion produced by 'lying angels'. Nonetheless, the delusions produced by the Devil were no less evil for not being real. He argued that demons could do harm in two ways: 'either by pretending to bring us benefits — in which case they harm us all the more, because they deceive us all the more — or by openly doing evil'. He immediately went on to say that both ways were only possible 'when permitted by the deep and hidden providence of God'.[5] The problem was that people were fooled by demonic tricks and, therefore, moved away from God. Augustine attempted to repudiate the power of demons at the same time as he warned against their evil. Augustine's influence on church opinion continued into the early modern era. In the late middle ages, several Inquisitors used his work to justify their views on witchcraft. His writings would continue to be used during the height of the witchcraft persecution era to condemn 'white magic' as vehemently as 'black magic'.

Despite its best efforts, the conquest by Christianity did not result in the destruction of the magic of the ancient world, but rather guaranteed its survival. The need to defeat the evil spirits of the Roman world would, ironically, result in the adaptation by the new church of some of the magical aspects of the old pagan religions. Some elements were adopted by the new church as part of its conversion programme. Others were condemned as demonic and would surface time and time again in relation to accusations of witchcraft. As we have already seen, good *daimones* were transformed into winged angels, who could act as messengers to and from God. They were also soldiers of God, interceding against the fallen angels. Bad *daimones* were labelled as demons and agents of Satan.

Jesus had not needed any ceremonies or props to perform his miracles, but as the church was established as an institution, the Catholic priesthood developed many rituals that were similar to the Roman priesthood. Aspects of Roman religion that were adapted for Christian use included: the smoke of sacrifices, which was imitated in the burning of incense; the popularity of statues, particularly of saints and the Virgin Mary, to which people lit candles and offered prayers and petitions; processions and sacrifices for protection of the crops, which became Rogation Days; and magical amulets, which were continued in the form of healing charms that used gospel verses. The modern practice of wearing a cross, a crucifix, or a Saint Christopher medal appears to be a continuation of the practice of wearing an amulet to protect against evil. The sign of the cross, as we saw in the case of Saint Anthony, replaced the many pentacles and images that had been used by magicians to control the spirit world. Complex formulae and prayers in Latin mimicked the incantations of previous magicians.

Another element of Greek and Roman religion that was incorporated into the later beliefs of witchcraft was the concept of the Devil as a goat or a man with goat parts. During the height of the witchcraft persecutions, confessions by accused witches and depictions by artists often portrayed Satan or demons with goat-like feet and horns. Other representations included clawed feet and hands, a long dragon-like tail, and wings like a bat. As early as the fifteenth century, the heretical group known as Waldensians, which would become a model for Satan worshipping witches, was illustrated paying homage to a goat. [See Image #4, Miniature illustrating Waldensians worshipping the Devil in the form of a goat and flying through the air in *Traité du crisme de Vauderie*] The most obvious model for the half-man/half-goat configuration is the Greek god Pan, who was the god of shepherds and the wild nature of the mountains. His buttocks, legs, and horns were similar to a goat's. Roman fauns and Greek satyrs were also half human and half animal. All of these figures were associated with virility and fertility in the classical era. The premodern English woodcut of Robin Goodfellow in *Robin Good-Fellow, His Mad Prankes, and Merry Iests* illustrates how these ideas were adapted to witchcraft. [See Image #5, Woodcut on title page of *Robin Good-Fellow*] One pamphlet described the spirits as 'lusty Satyrs'.[6]

The spread of Christianity followed the path laid down by the Roman Empire, travelling around the Mediterranean and making contact with Germanic and Celtic societies in the north. The religious and cultural practices of the 'barbarian hordes' were considered demonic by both the Romans and the Christian theologians. Romans documented the worship of the Celtic 'Horned God', Cernunnos. Archaeological discoveries have also been cited as evidence of a Horned God. A silver cauldron, dating from the second century CE, was unearthed near the village of Gundestrup, Denmark. Amidst the rich repoussé work is a horned figure, which has often been identified as the same Celtic god. [See Image #6, Detail of silver Gundestrup Cauldron] The Egyptologist and folklorist Margaret Murray used this sort of evidence to argue that early modern witchcraft was the remnants of a pre-Christian fertility cult, in continuous operation from the time of the hunters and gatherers until medieval Christianity drove the cult underground. In *The God of the Witches* (1931), she points out that various horned creatures had been revered across Europe since the palaeolithic era, as evidenced in cave drawings and inscriptions. However, there is no incontrovertible evidence that all of these figures represented the same god, nor if the figures were even considered gods. They could have been anthropomorphised representations of the hunt. The historian Ronald Hutton, in *The Triumph of the Moon* (1999), argues that the Greek god Pan and the Celtic figure of Cernunnos were not ancient influences on the configuration of the Devil, as has often been promoted, but that they were more recent borrowings in the Victorian era when neopaganism began to thrive. In any case, Murray's theory about the survival of a pre-Christian fertility cult has been thoroughly debunked by historians. Nonetheless, it was very influential during the formation of Wicca as an earth-based spiritual movement, a topic to which we will return in Chapter 8.

The Horned God as the Devil was not the only borrowing from older traditions to make its way into premodern ideas about witchcraft. It would take centuries of Christianisation to convince the common people to give up their pagan practices. Some aspects of pagan belief would become key elements in the configuration of the witch, such as the Wild Ride. By the sixteenth century, the Greek and Roman deities, Hecate of the Underworld and the goddess of the hunt Diana, were transformed into leaders of witches who flew through the night sky to the sabbat, a phenomenon we shall explore in Chapter 4. The concept of demonic flight was based on a combination of the airy *daimones* and the fallen angels.

The subtleties of dealing with spirits may not have been obvious to the masses undergoing conversion to Christianity. What the new church wanted to make evident was that it had access to superior forms of the supernatural. For example, exorcism had been a magician's tool prior to the advent of Christianity. Exorcism became an element of the new church following Jesus's example of driving demons out of the possessed. The scriptures point out that the difference between the old method of exorcism and Jesus's method lay in the fact that Christian exorcism replaced the demonic spirits with the Holy Spirit (*Luke* 11:14–20). This prevented evil spirits from re-entering the individual. Exorcism became a standard part of the Christian baptismal ritual, as well as a method of dealing with demonic possession.

Christianity inherited many aspects of magic and witchcraft from the classical world, which were combined with the groundwork of Judaic traditions. All of this happened at an intellectual level while Christianity was finding its feet amidst a rich blend of Greek and Roman heritage and several pagan cultures. The result was a synthesis of Greco-Roman culture, Judaism, and Celtic and Teutonic beliefs. As Christianity struggled to gain followers, not only *daimones* were demonised, but whole religious and spiritual systems were denigrated, as the population was persuaded to believe that their old practices constituted reverence of demons. As Europe took shape in the middle ages, the religions of Greece and Rome, as well as their magical practices, were constructed as the work of the Devil, intended to lead humans down the wrong path. The stage was set for the persecution of witchcraft as devil-worship.

Chapter 2

By Bud and Stem, Medieval Menace

Saul, the first king of Israel, faced a confrontation with Israel's arch-enemy the Philistines. When he saw the extent of his opponent's army, he used various divination techniques, including dreams, prayers, and the Urim and Thummim (a means of revelation used by priests in ancient Israel[1]) to get advice. Although Saul had banished magicians and necromancers from Israel, he instructed his servants to find 'a woman that hath a familiar spirit' so that he could consult with her. The servants discovered a sorceress in the town of Endor. Saul disguised himself before approaching the woman, who would later become known as the witch of Endor. After reassuring her that she would not be reported to the authorities, Saul asked her to call up the spirit of the prophet Samuel. When alive Samuel had anointed Saul as king and had also prophesied his death. Samuel appeared like an old man covered with a cloak. Saul bowed down to the apparition and asked for advice on how to defeat his enemy. Samuel was not impressed about being called up from the underworld, especially since he favoured David over Saul as king of Israel. He bluntly told Saul that God had abandoned him; the Philistine forces would win the battle and Saul would die. Not exactly the advice Saul was looking for. He had fasted all day in preparation for this ritual, and after Samuel disappeared, he fell to the ground stricken with fear. The woman then proceeded to comfort and feed him. She had a calf killed and made bread to aid in his recovery.

***

This story, drawn from the Old Testament (*Samuel* 28:1–25), is obviously a case of necromancy, the raising of a spirit of the dead. Theologians and demonologists would debate whether or not Saul was guilty of necromancy and whether or not the apparition of Samuel was a trick of the Devil. However, they were usually in agreement that the woman was a witch. But note how she performed her magic at the request of the king and helped him recover from his fright afterwards. She was not performing *maleficium*, or witchcraft, to cause harm. Nonetheless, the church strengthened the condemnation of magic and witchcraft by drawing on biblical stories like the witch of Endor. Other scriptures, such as 'You shall not permit a sorceress to live' (*Exodus* 22:18), were used to defend the death penalty for the practice of magic.

As discussed in Chapter 1, there were many different ideas concerning magic and witchcraft floating around Europe by the time of the collapse of the Roman Empire. But the newly established Roman Catholic church would prove to have the biggest influence on the opinion of magic and witchcraft in Western Europe. Not only was the church determining its doctrines as an institution at the same time that Europe was forming and dividing into kingdoms, but the organisation of the institution served an important role in state development. The church's hierarchical system, from pope down to parish priest, acted as a means of administration for the emerging territories. In the early middle ages, the church had established a network of monasteries and bishoprics throughout Europe. The literate clergy acted as scribes for the (mostly) illiterate nobles and monarchs, making Latin the international language of learning and diplomacy. The opinion and support of the church was important to the developing states and the two worked closely together to rule the West. The religious influence on the development of Western civilisation would ensure that ideologies formulated by the church would get embedded in secular legislation. The importance of the Devil in Christian theology contributed to the emphasis placed on heresy, which also became a concern of the newly-formed states. Actual heretical groups, such as the Cathars and Waldensians, later served as templates for the imagined sect of witches. In heresy trials such as the one against the Templars (discussed below), devil-worship was one of the main accusations. All of this was taking place at the same time as medieval scholars were resurrecting the ideas of classical authors, particularly Aristotle. The Dominican friar, Thomas Aquinas, employed the ideas of Aristotle to support the concept of the Devil as an active force in the world, giving further weight to the importance of persecuting witches. The end result of all of these factors is that witchcraft shifted from a crime to a sin and became configured as an underground heretical sect. Just being labelled as a witch could garner the death penalty, even if no harm had been done.

At the height of the Roman Empire, most of Western Europe, the Mediterranean basin, and England was under its sway. But the many Germanic tribes inhabiting Europe at the time did not necessarily accept Roman rule. In the fifth century CE, various groups invaded and overwhelmed Rome, resulting in the collapse of the Empire in 476. Many of the groups who originated around the Rhine River in Germany subsequently united under one ruler. Clovis was the first king of the Franks in the territory that would eventually become France. Clovis converted to Christianity in 496 and encouraged conversion among his subjects. The medieval historian Gregory of Tours described Clovis's conversion in Book II of his *History of the Franks*. Clovis's wife Clotilda had encouraged the king to be baptised as a Christian, but he had refused. Then he found himself at war with other tribes.

> 'It came about that as the two armies were fighting fiercely, there was much slaughter, and Clovis's army began to be in danger of destruction. He saw it and raised his eyes to heaven, and with remorse in his heart he burst into tears and cried: 'Jesus Christ, whom Clotilda asserts to be the son of the living God, who art said to give aid to those in distress, and to bestow victory on those who hope in thee, I beseech the glory of thy aid, with the vow that if thou wilt grant me victory over these enemies, and I shall know that power which she says that people dedicated in thy name have had from thee, I will believe in thee and be baptized in thy name. For I have invoked my own gods but, as I find, they have withdrawn from aiding me.'[2]

Clovis implored Christ as a god of war, a god among many other gods. His invocation is reminiscent of how magicians called upon the spirit world for aid. Clovis won the battle and held true to his promise to be baptised. This was the beginning of European rulers' support of the church. With the support of the state, the church continued to establish monasteries throughout Europe, which were heavily engaged in teaching and missionary work. Of course, the general population was not instantly Christianised, but the parish church became the centre of village life, at least socially and culturally. With a firm foothold in the community, the church continued the battle to eliminate pagan beliefs and practices; it outlawed any magical practices, which it believed involved dealing with demons. Sorcery was redefined as heresy, thereby becoming a religious concern rather than a secular one. Due to the close relationship between church and state, these religious prohibitions were also incorporated into secular concerns.

The Christianisation of Europe continued slowly over the course of the following centuries. In the eighth century, Charlemagne inherited the flourishing Frankish kingdom. Much of Western Europe was united under

Charlemagne's rule, including modern day France, Germany, Austria, the Netherlands, and northern Italy. In return for his military protection of the papacy, Charlemagne was recognised by Pope Leo III as the emperor of this territory, which was named the Holy Roman Empire. He actively championed the church's mandates, sometimes implementing forced conversions as his Carolingian Empire expanded. Charlemagne supported the elimination of pagan practices, including any magic or dealing with demons, which the church had struggled to outlaw. In return, the clergy endorsed his secular legislation. This was just one of many marriages between church and state in Europe that would continue throughout the premodern period.

The church's ongoing concern with pagan beliefs is evident in various church regulations of the era. In the century following Charlemagne's rule, some of this material was compiled into books, to assist the bishops in their dioceses in fighting pagan influences and in Christianising the population. The *Canon Episcopi* was included in this matter and later incorporated into Gratian's collections of Canon Law, the *Decretum* (*c.* 1150), which continued to be very authoritative throughout the premodern period and into the twentieth century. The canon in question condemned the 'pernicious art of divination and magic', including love and weather magic. The more controversial part of the canon referred to women who believed that they rode out at night on beasts with the goddess Diana.

> 'some wicked women, who have given themselves back to Satan and been seduced by illusions and phantasms of demons, believe and profess that, in the hours of the night, they ride upon certain beasts with Diana, the goddess of the pagans, and an innumerable multitude of women, and in the silence of the night traverse great spaces of earth, and obey her commands as of their lady, and are summoned to her service on certain nights … For an innumerable multitude, deceived by this *false opinion* [italics added], believe this to be true, and so believing, wander from the right faith.'[3]

Perhaps surprisingly, the canon states that the idea of flying through the air was a false belief and should be condemned. The women were to be corrected and brought back to the right belief. The text provides evidence that belief in the 'Wild Ride' or 'Wild Hunt' existed in popular culture, to the extent that the church thought it needed to be controlled. There is no evidence that belief in the Wild Hunt was associated either directly or indirectly with the belief in witchcraft in popular culture. In other words, the general population did not think that the participants in the Wild Hunt were witches who were causing harm. The interpretation of the Wild Hunt as an element of witchcraft was added by the church. The text also indicates that the official church stance was that the phenomenon was not real but a pagan superstition. The Wild Hunt was a devilish illusion and believers needed to be corrected and to do penance, not be executed as witches. The fact that elements of the Wild Hunt later contributed to the construction of the witches' sabbat indicates both the influence of popular culture on elite beliefs and the power of the church to usurp popular culture beliefs for its own purposes. The integration of popular and elite beliefs was a two-way process. Elements of folklore were recorded in theological works by monks and other influential members of the church. They were preserved over the years in monastic libraries and would later be used by demonologists, who accepted flight to the sabbat as real. Also note that the text emphasises the exclusive participation of women in these activities, thereby contributing to the gendered nature of witchcraft accusations. We will revisit the Wild Ride in relation to the development of the witches' sabbat, which also drew on classical models such as the Bacchanalia (see Chapter 4).

Heretics: Cathars

The Catholic church's attack on pagan beliefs and practices emphasised the activities of the Devil in the earthly realm. The demonisation of pagan gods and spirits, which had started with Augustine, only served to strengthen the perceived power of Satan. The Greek *daimones* could do good or bad, but after they were condemned by Christianity, Satan, the leader of the demons, became God's archenemy. By constantly situating the Devil as God's adversary, the door was opened to the possibility of a dualistic theology. A dualist faith existed in Bulgaria at the time, which could have been introduced into Europe by missionaries. Dualistic influences could also have been strengthened when crusaders returned home from the East. By whatever influences, a religious sect with dualistic beliefs arose in northern Italy and spread to southern France and the Rhineland in the middle of the twelfth century. The members of the group were known as Cathars, which is derived from the Greek word *kathari*, meaning 'pure', which referred to the ordained members of the group. They were also called Albigensians, because there were many followers around the town of Albi in southern France. Their beliefs were based in Christianity, but with a few twists. They believed that Jesus was the god of good, who ruled over the spiritual realm; he had been sent to teach humans how to escape the physical realm, which could entrap the spirit. He was in opposition to the god of the Old Testament, whom they considered to be Satan. He was the god of evil, who had created and now ruled over the physical realm. According to this new religion, Satan existed before creation, thereby making him a rival (and coequal) of God rather than a creature (a fallen angel) made by God. They also embraced some ideas that appear to have come from Hinduism, such as reincarnation and vegetarianism, which supports the theory of Eastern origins or influence. Cathars rejected all earthly things, including all the rituals and sacraments of the Catholic church. They also criticised the wealth of the church, which they believed was the work of the Devil. Instead of individual wealth, they held property in common. Women were allowed to teach and preach the faith, which was another concern for the male-dominated church.

The Cathars' criticism of Catholicism, combined with their different interpretation of Christianity, was problematic for Rome. The Roman Catholic church held a monopoly on religion in Western Europe and did not appreciate sects with opposing views springing up. Anything outside its orthodoxy was interpreted as heresy and the work of the Devil. But the condemnation of the group did not stop at merely accusing it of heresy. Since the sect was forced to operate secretly, due to its unorthodox position, it was at risk of being accused of other nasty behaviours, such as ritual black magic, incest, cannibalism, infanticide, and sacrifice to the Devil. These were the same sort of accusations that had been flung at early Christians and Jews. Identical allegations would be made against the imagined sect of witches in the years to come. In 1209, Pope Innocent III authorised a crusade against them, which lasted for twenty years. With the help of the northern French nobility, who were promised the confiscated lands of the Cathars, the sect was virtually eliminated. The medieval Inquisition completed the extermination of the sect by the early-fourteenth century. What is important for our purposes is that the fear of heresy raised by the Cathars directly contributed to the fear of witchcraft. The Cathars were an actual sect that was accused of worshipping the Devil. This paved the way for belief in a sect of devil-worshipping witches.

More Heretics: Waldensians

At the same time as the Cathars were gaining ground in southern France, another heretical group was forming in northern France. Peter Waldo (also called Valdos) was a wealthy merchant of Lyons. In 1173, following the example of Jesus's apostles, he gave away his possessions in favour of a life of begging and preaching. A sect of mendicant preachers, similar to the later followers of Saint Francis of Assisi, formed around him. They became known as the 'poor men of Lyons' and were labelled Waldensians after their leader. A chosen life of poverty was not that unusual for the time, but they were excommunicated from the Catholic church, because they refused to restrict their preaching. They did not form an alliance with the church and answer to the pope in the manner of monastic groups. Waldensian women were also allowed to preach, which, of course, added to the bad reputation of the sect. In spite of persecution, including torture and burning at the stake, the group spread into southern France, northern Italy, and as far west as Austria. They studied the Scriptures in the vernacular, were anti-clerical, and were opposed to capital punishment. On account of being persecuted, they had to meet secretly, which contributed to suspicions about their behaviour. Accusations of incestuous orgies and devil-worship were once again brought into play.

The sect, composed mostly of artisans and peasants, survived underground in remote valleys of France and Italy well into the fifteenth century. The frontispiece of a fifteenth-century manuscript entitled *Traité du crisme de Vauderie*, or *Tractatus Contra Sectum Valdensium* in Latin, written by the theologian Johannes Tinctoris, depicted members of the heretical sect kissing the back side of a goat, while others rode through the air on animals and brooms. [See Image #4, Miniature illustrating Waldensians worshipping the Devil in the form of a goat and flying through the air in *Traité du crisme de Vauderie*] This corruption of the Wild Ride was applied to heretics before it was attributed to witches. The Devil is depicted as a goat. Kissing the Devil's posterior, or the *osculum infame*, was also mentioned in a medieval collection of anecdotes, *Errores Gazariorum,* in which the Waldensians worshipped the Devil in the form of a huge black cat. The 'infamous kiss' is another element that would become firmly linked with witchcraft in the years to come, as illustrated in Francesco Maria Guazzo's *Compendium Maleficarum* of 1608. [See Image #7, Woodcut of *osculum infame* in *Compendium Maleficarum*] In this instance, the Devil was depicted in a more human form, which added even more sexual connotations to the act. Although it is next to impossible to prove, the modern expression of 'kiss my ass!' is probably a derivative of the imagined practice of the *osculum infame*. The earliest record of it, according to the Oxford English Dictionary, was in 1705, when it was used as a term of derision.

The sect was also described in the mid-fifteenth century by Martin Le Franc, a secretary to two popes. *Le Champion des Dames* was a long poem in defence of virtuous women. The female members of the group referred to as *Vaudoises* or Waldensians were used as a foil to the ideal woman. An illustration in the margin of the manuscript portrays women flying on brooms, similar to the Tinctoris depiction. [See Image #8, Illustration in the margin of *Le Champion des Dames*] Although the broom would become the universal symbol of the witch, illustrations and confessions more often mentioned forked cooking sticks or animals as vehicles to the sabbat. Perhaps the broom emerged as the stereotypical means of transportation because it was a symbol of female domesticity, which was used for a deviant purpose. Straddling the riding implement also carried sexual connotations.

More than two centuries after the formation of Waldo's sect, a formal crusade exterminated the majority of the heretics from the valleys in southern France. Both the Cathars and the Waldensians were constructed as devil-worshippers by their persecutors. However, there is no evidence that any groups were actually worshipping the Devil in medieval Europe. The importance of these anti-social sects, for our purposes, is that the activities associated with these groups, as devil-worshippers, were later attributed to the imagined sect of witches. Once the heretical groups were suppressed, peasants and the judiciary turned their attention to sorcery more generally. Witches became the newest version of heretics. Individual practitioners of sorcery were transformed into an organised group of heretics.

Beguines

Both the Waldensians and the Cathars had wanted a return to the early Christian ideals of poverty and spirituality. Throughout the middle Ages, there was concern both within the church and among the lay population about the corruption in the church. But groups that appeared to compete with the Vatican were not welcomed into the fold. In 1215, the Fourth Lateran Council called for an increased vigilance against dissidence and heresy. The church strove to maintain its authority over the masses and was eager to control any religious expression, even if such expression was in line with monastic ideals.

Groups of women known as Beguines also wanted a life of spiritual poverty. These groups of lay women started to organise themselves at the beginning of the twelfth century in the Low Countries. The groups were mostly composed of single females and widows, who desired an unmarried, religious life outside of monastic rule. The women lived a spiritual life by rules similar to a monastery, but they did not take formal vows, which would have bound them for life. There was also no male supervision, as there would have been in a convent; however, they were supported spiritually by male confessors and priestly advisers. The Beguines were often from the merchant class and supported themselves with their own personal assets and through craft production. There was a higher level of urbanisation in the Low Countries than elsewhere in Europe, which meant a higher level of literacy. The women taught children, produced textiles, and established hospitals for poor and elderly women. They formed their own autonomous communities in urban centres by buying communal property. The living situation ranged from small houses with two or three occupants to large convent-like situations. These types of arrangements spread to France and Germany. But not everyone supported them. Some ecclesiastics viewed them as heretics, who subverted church authority.

One Beguine, the French mystic Marguerite Porete, was burned at the stake as a heretic. She had refused to recant the ideas of divine love put forward in her book, *The Mirror of Simple Souls* (early-fourteenth century). Women's access to knowledge, particularly theological knowledge, was a concern for the church, which closely guarded the interpretation of Scriptures and preaching. The only official version of the Bible was the Vulgate, which was in Latin. This meant that it was not accessible to the masses. When the Council of Vienne met in 1311 to officially withdraw support for the Knights Templar (see below), they ordered that the Beguines should also be disbanded. Some of the communities became official convents under various religious orders. Others managed to continue operating. There is no direct link between the Beguines and witches, but groups of females operating independently contributed to the fear of the imagined sect of witches. They served as evidence of the possibility of women acting as a group outside the hierarchy of the church.

Heresy Trials: The Templars

The period that came to be known as the 'witch-craze' did not happen until the middle of the sixteenth century. Before 1500, there were some trials for sorcery and witchcraft, but they were few and far between and the evidence is scant. Several of the cases in the fourteenth century that we do know about involved members of a royal family, an ecclesiastical member, or some other politically important figure. Sometimes they were the suspects, but more often they were the victims of alleged witchcraft. These well-known cases contributed to later configurations of witchcraft.

One case that drew a lot of attention at the time, and has continued to be the subject of discussion, is the trial of the Templars in the early-fourteenth century. Scholars have rigorously debated the truth of the allegations against the Knights. The Poor Fellow-Soldiers of Christ and of the Temple of Solomon were more commonly known as the Knights Templar or the Order of the Temple. The Templars were one of several religious organisations that were founded as monastic-military orders. In 1095, Pope Urban II agreed to send military aid to the Byzantine emperor in Constantinople because the Seljuk Turks were invading from the east. The objective of the crusade soon became the reconquest of the Holy Land. The First Crusade against the Muslims resulted in Jerusalem being taken from Islamic forces in 1099. After the Christian victory, many Europeans started making pilgrimages to the Holy Land. The Templars ensured the safety of the pilgrims and also fought in later crusades. During the next 200 years, the Templars accumulated vast amounts of wealth and lands in the Holy Land and across Europe, which also meant that they had considerable political influence. They built churches and castles along the route to the East and were heavily involved in trade. They were so wealthy that they acted as bankers or money-lenders to people of importance.

In 1244, the Muslims recaptured Jerusalem, slaughtering priests and pilgrims alike. The Templars, along with the other military orders, responded to this attack with devastating results. Only thirty-six of the 350 Templar knights survived the battle. In response, King Louis IX of France launched a crusade to retake the city via an attack on Egypt. The enterprise was funded by the Templars. Once again, the crusaders suffered devastating losses. King Louis was taken prisoner and held for a huge ransom. Not surprisingly, the crown turned to the Templars to help fund the ransom amount. Afterwards, Louis had little choice but to limp back to France in defeat. The ongoing troubles in the East meant that pilgrimages subsequently declined, along with the importance of the role of the Knights as defenders of the faith. Gradually, the fortunes of the Templars declined, as they lost their lands and castles in the Holy Lands. The Parisian branch of the Templars continued to have close connections to the French crown, which would ultimately lead to their downfall.

In 1285, Louis IX's grandson, Philip IV, inherited the French throne. The Capetian dynasty claimed descent from Charlemagne and Philip prided himself on his piety. History would label him a zealot. Along with the crown,

Philip had inherited several military campaigns in Aragón and Flanders, as well as a long, drawn out war with the English over land on the Continent. (This was the same conflict, known as the Hundred Years' War, which would see Joan of Arc accused of witchcraft in 1431.) As a result of these conflicts, France suffered from financial problems by the beginning of the fourteenth century. Philip's first money-raising attempt was to devalue the silver currency to a third of its original value, causing rampant inflation. When this failed to balance the budget, his next strategy was to target the Jewish population. Their role as moneylenders, and therefore their importance to the state, had declined with the rise of the Christian Italian banker families, such as the Peruzzis and Medicis. The age-old accusations of child murder and sexual impropriety were levelled against the Jews to raise popular support against them. They were driven out of France by a royal edict issued in 1306. Their goods, wealth, and property were expropriated by the Crown. But the total expulsion of the Jews still did not replenish Philip's coffers. With the Templars' vast wealth in mind, one of Philip's chief ministers started compiling a dossier of evidence against the order.

Rumours of misconduct by the Templars prompted the head of the order, James of Molay, to request aid from Pope Clement V. James asked the pope to conduct an official inquiry into the order, which, he felt, would prove their innocence. Any guilty individuals would be either discharged from the order or do penance. The pope agreed to James's request, but he was preoccupied with his own health at the time and did not initiate the investigation immediately. Instead, the chief papal inquisitor in France took action. He was a Dominican friar, who also served as confessor to the king. As an Inquisitor, he officially answered to the pope; but he was actually a creature of the king. In October 1307, warrants under the royal seal were delivered to all the Templar houses in France. The members of the order were charged with heresy and all their goods were seized.

By the time of these proceedings, the idea that heretics worshipped the Devil was well-developed. So it is not surprising that the charges against the Knights were similar to the accusations previously laid against the Cathars: denying Christ; spitting on the image of Christ; trampling or urinating on the cross; kissing initiates on the lower spine, the navel, and the mouth; kissing the Devil's posterior; worshipping the Devil, who sometimes appeared as a huge black cat called Baphomet; and making potions out of murdered babies. Since the Templars were monks, sexual misdemeanours focused on sodomy rather than incest. Sodomy was not only a sin but also a secular felony, punishable by death.

The men arrested were incarcerated pending investigation and interrogation. Medieval gaols were not particularly luxurious: cold, dark, damp, and rat-infested. Most of the men were chained inside their cells and fed on bread and water. Many of the brothers were held in solitary confinement. One Templar was kept in a pit that was so small he could only take one step forward or backward. Torture, including the strappado (see Chapter 7), was used for questioning. Some of the inmates died from the harsh treatment, others went mad. The knights were promised a pardon if they 'confessed' to the list of more than eighty formulaic charges against them. It should be noted that the Templars in France were not all war-hardened soldiers, who might have been more prepared for such ordeals. Most were older men who staffed and managed the order's property and acted as merchants and farmers. In response to the harsh conditions, confessions flowed freely, including that of the leader, James of Molay, who was coerced into writing a letter encouraging the other brothers to confess, as he had done.

The pope was not impressed with the methods or the mandate of the French crown. In an effort to regain control of the proceedings, he ordered secular rulers across Europe to arrest members in their territories. He did not want other state authorities to hinder the investigation of the order, which answered to him. The papacy also interfered directly with the inquisition of the French brothers. Given a chance to restate their case, many members recanted their previous confessions, including James of Molay. These men were absolved by the church, but they remained in prison until the investigation of the order could be completed. More than a year later, when James was interrogated about the general behaviour of the Templars, he appeared to be confused and rambled on about past deeds and battles. He was a broken man, not in any position to defend his order against the charges.

The pope's inquisition dragged on, and the king of France was impatient. In May 1310, Philip had fifty-four Templars judged as relapsed heretics. They were carted through the streets of Paris to a field and burned alive at the stake. [See Image #9, Illustration of Templars being Burned at the Stake] This sent a message to the remaining brothers, and anyone else who cared to come to their defence, that the king of France would not broker anymore resistance. Even Clement V had to submit to the will of King Philip. In March 1312, the pope issued a bull that officially dissolved the Order of the Temple. It included the accusations against them. Members of the order who had confessed to their alleged crimes and survived their ordeals were sent to other monastic houses; unrepentant brothers were sentenced to life imprisonment. King Philip took a good portion of their liquid assets in the form of silver, but the Templars landed estates were redistributed to the Knights Hospitallers. Two years after the pope's decision, James of Molay, who had lingered in gaol for six and half years, was paraded in front of a crowd outside Notre Dame cathedral. He was sentenced to 'hard, perpetual imprisonment'.[4] But James could not accept the judgement against him. He stood up on the platform and denied his previous statements and confession. This was more than King Philip could abide. The very same evening, James was taken to an island in the river Seine and burned alive as a relapsed heretic. His dying words were in the form of a curse against his persecutors. Perhaps coincidentally, both King Philip IV of France and Pope Clement V died within the year. The trial of the Templars contributed to the configuration of a sect of devil-worshipping witches. The trial also coincided with the end of the crusade period. The enthusiasm to spread and defend the Christian faith, which had supported the crusades for two centuries, was turned toward the emerging groups of heretics at home.

More Heresy Trials: the Kytelers

Another case in fourteenth-century Ireland contained similar accusations. Dame Alice Kyteler was an Anglo-Norman woman from Kilkenny. Her first husband had been a wealthy merchant and money lender, with influential friends and relatives. After his death, Dame Alice married three more times, which was not that unusual for the period. Marriage was considered the proper condition of women, and wealthy widows like Dame Alice were attractive matches. But Alice did not have very good luck in love. Her second and third spouses also passed away prematurely. Her fourth and last husband, Sir John le Poer, also fell sick: his fingernails dropped off and all the hair on his body disappeared, which are symptoms of arsenic poisoning. He suspected that his wife was responsible for his illness. His children from a previous marriage, as well as Alice's other step-children, became suspicious, and they subsequently accused her of sorcery. But this was no simple case of poisoning or *maleficium*. She was accused of denying the Christian faith, sacrificing animals at the crossroads, and making ointments from disgusting materials such as the bodies of unbaptised children, fingernails taken from corpses, rooster guts, and worms. She allegedly did these things in the company of eleven others, including her son from her first marriage, William Outlaw, and her maid-servant, Petronilla de Meath. The purpose of their activities was to incite love and hate and generally afflict people. The full-blown sabbat was not included, but the group was accused of engaging in sexual orgies at secret night meetings held in the local church. Alice was allegedly helped by a demon named Robin Artisson, with whom she had sex. The creature sometimes appeared as a cat or a dog, similar to the familiar spirits that would become common in English witchcraft allegations. This is the first recorded incidence of a witch having intercourse with an incubus.

The idea of a sect of heretical witches was probably introduced to Alice's case by Richard Ledrede, an English Franciscan friar, who was the Bishop of Ossory. The details of the episode were recorded by him. He had been educated in France at the time that the papacy was in Avignon. It is highly likely that Ledrede was familiar with an instruction booklet on how to catch a heretic written by Bernard Gui, a Dominican Inquisitor in Toulouse. Following the trouble with the Cathars, Gui had compiled a guide that instructed Inquisitors on how to question suspected heretics, including Waldensians, Beguines, Jews, and sorcerers. The manual was widely circulated at the time and would be echoed in later works of demonology. New ideas about witchcraft, which were introduced from the top down like this, were subsequently circulated in popular culture. It was common to have the witch confess publicly before execution and, starting in the sixteenth century, many pamphlets about witchcraft cases were printed.

The bishop had his work cut out for him in this case. A contest between ecclesiastical and secular authorities ensued. The king's chancellor was Roger Outlaw, a prior of the Order of Hospitallers and a relative of Alice's first husband, William Outlaw. Roger Outlaw refused to arrest Alice until she was excommunicated. Alice took refuge in Dublin while this was going on. Ledrede then summoned Alice's son William Outlaw to appear before him for harbouring a witch. But William had a very influential friend in the form of Arnold le Poer. As governor of Ireland, le Poer was chief judge. To put an end to Ledrede's proceedings, le Poer arrested and gaoled the bishop. In retaliation, Ledrede put an interdict on the diocese, which meant that no baptisms, marriages, or burials could be performed. Since unbaptised babies went to limbo if they died, this was a serious restriction. After his release from prison, Ledrede once again summoned Alice and her son. This time the bishop was served with a royal writ demanding to know why he had placed an interdict on his diocese. He was instructed to travel to Dublin to answer, but he refused. The contest between church and state continued, until Alice sued the bishop for defamation of character. Members of both sides met in a courtroom in Dublin, and Ledrede ultimately won the right to pursue his charges against Alice and her compatriots.

The maid Petronilla was tortured into confessing; she was subsequently flogged and burned alive at the stake. Alice's son William was charged with heresy and harbouring heretics, but due to his influential friends, he had his sentenced commuted to penance. Alice eventually fled, probably to England, and disappeared from the records. Alice's case is an example of how intellectual ideas trickled down to popular culture. This appears to be a straight-forward top down transmission.

Unfortunately, we do not have a great number of witchcraft trials from the middle ages from which to draw conclusions. Existing records indicate that toward the end of the fourteenth century and into the beginning of the fifteenth century, the number of witchcraft trials increased. Better record keeping, as well as record survival, from this period may have skewed the apparent increase. However, there is another reason that more accusations might have appeared. On the Continent, there was a widespread shift from accusatorial procedure to the practice of inquisitorial procedure in both ecclesiastical and secular courts. Under the accusatorial system, one individual could accuse another individual of a crime. The accuser was then responsible for proving the guilt of the accused in the resulting trial. If the accuser could not prove guilt to the satisfaction of the judge, he would be subject to *lex talionis*, or the law of talion, which meant that the accuser was punished for making a false accusation. The punishment was usually the same as would have been inflicted on the accused. Since the secret crime of witchcraft was very difficult to prove and the punishment was very harsh, the law of talion would have served as a major deterrent to making accusations against one's neighbour on account of some perceived harm or wrong done to the accuser. Inquisitorial procedure, on the other hand, gave the judicial system responsibility for proving the guilt of the accused. Inquiries and investigations were made by the prosecution. There were no repercussions for a false accusation. The result of this legal change was that a private citizen would feel more comfortable laying blame for misfortune on the village hag. He or she would not have to worry about the consequences if the accused went free. Unfortunately, the use of torture was often allowed as a method of inquiry, especially in the case of witchcraft.

Scholasticism

Another medieval influence on the construction of witchcraft was academic. The period known by historians as the high middle ages was an era of rich intellectual and artistic growth. The great cathedrals, such as Notre Dame in Paris, and the first universities in Bologna, Paris, Oxford, and Cambridge emerged in Europe during this period. Art, architecture, and philosophy thrived. The academics of the day were usually members of the clergy, because a university education was a path to a good position in the church. Medieval scholars admired the classic Greek and Roman philosophers, particularly Aristotle. The problem with Aristotle, along with the other classical writers, was that he was pagan. The medieval scholars did not want to throw the baby out with the bathwater; therefore, they attempted to reconcile the classical authors with medieval theology. As noted above, this was the same time that there was increasing concern over heretics. The discourse about heresy influenced the Christian intellectuals' growing fascination with the demonic world.

The method of inquiry commonly employed at that time was known as scholasticism, which took the form of questions and hypothetical answers. The Italian Dominican friar Thomas Aquinas is considered to be the most influential Aristotelian scholastic. He supported Aristotle's viewpoint concerning cause and effect. To put the theory into the simplest terms, Aristotle believed that everything in the world was subject to a 'prime mover', or an initiating cause. As a result of this cause, something came into being or initiated an effect. For Aquinas, it was a no-brainer that the prime mover was God. God, the cause of everything, was beyond human comprehension. But when God created the physical world, he made it subject to natural laws, which were comprehensible. By this definition, marvellous or unusual effects could not be produced through natural means. The repercussion of this idea was that any effect that was extraordinary was only considered possible with the aid of a superior agent, which was outside the physical realm. This left God and the angels or the Devil and demons, which explained the possibility of both miracles and magic, as in the story of Moses. The church sacraments, which could be viewed as magical, such as transubstantiation and baptism, were efficacious because they were the work of God. Likewise, magical rituals could only be effective with the Devil's assistance. It is only logical that scholastics would interpret magic in religious terms, as they were also members of the clergy. The theological faculty of the University of Paris was sometimes consulted for an opinion on whether acts of sorcery were heretical. According to the Aristotelian scholastics, magic and sorcery required the aid of demons. A pact with the Devil must have been made, whether explicitly or implicitly, which inevitably reinforced the connection of magic with heresy. Aquinas accepted the idea that the pact was sealed by sexual intercourse. Aquinas's opinions would be drawn on extensively in the sixteenth and seventeenth centuries by theologians looking for support for witchcraft persecutions.

Conclusion

In the period leading up to the 'witch-craze' of the early modern period, the idea of sorcery being an individual practice under secular jurisdiction was transformed into a conspiratorial group of witches guilty of heresy. By the end of the fifteenth century, the figure of the witch as a diabolical creature under the influence of Satan had taken shape in learned discourse. All of the key elements of witchcraft as a sect of devil-worshippers were in place. Although the Templars and the Kyteler group were not accused of flying to the sabbat, the idea of the sabbat was fully developed by the mid-fifteenth century. One group from southern Switzerland was accused of sacrificing black sheep to the Devil, engaging in orgies with bestial forms of demons, and flying to sabbats on chairs smeared with an ointment. (Perhaps more comfortable than broomsticks!) The stereotypical allegations against underground cults and heretical sects had made their way into witch trials. In the middle ages, suspected witches and heretics were punished and sometimes executed, but the church still saw the true enemy as Satan. The human agent was far less of a threat. A number of factors shifted the focus from Satan to sorcerer at the end of the fifteenth century. The next chapter examines how the figure of the witch became a diabolical creature in learned discourse.

Chapter 3

By Branch and Leaf, Demon Logic

In 1477, a man's cow got sick in Lausanne, Switzerland. The man struggled to understand why his livestock was ill and looked for someone to blame. Jordana de Baulmes became a likely suspect, perhaps based on her reputation or previous actions. The man denounced her as a witch to the ecclesiastical authorities to be investigated. Jordana denied the accusation of witchcraft, or heresy as it was called, but confessed that she had had an illicit affair some twenty years before, which had resulted in a pregnancy. She had killed the infant by leaving it to die of exposure in the mountains. Fornication and infanticide were sins, but there was nothing particularly magical about such activities. Nonetheless, such behaviour would be detrimental to a woman's reputation. Perhaps her inquisitors interpreted the criminal neglect of her baby as a sacrifice to the Devil. As part of their investigation, they questioned Jordana about heretical sects: what did they do? Jordana reported that she had heard that such groups flew on brooms, drank and feasted, ate babies, and had sex like animals. On a personal level, she reported seeing candles that burned with a blue flame in her prison cell. This offered enough probability of witchcraft for the inquisitors to put Jordana to the question in the torture chamber. Following a prepared script, her story eventually conformed to their expectations, and elements of devil-worship emerged. Under the duress of imprisonment, torture, and inquisition, she confessed to attending the sabbat, kissing the Devil on his posterior, and all the other aspects of the imagined witch cult. This additional material, which was not a concern in the initial accusation, helped the intellectuals make sense of the motives of the accused witch. This typical case illustrates how demonological ideas could transform a straightforward accusation of *maleficium* (in this case, causing a cow to become sick) into devil-worship and attendance at a sabbat. At the village level, the concept of a sect of devil-worshippers was mostly absent; diabolism was not rooted in popular culture.

Historians use the term 'demonology' to refer to the body of literature about magic, witchcraft, and demons that arose in the late medieval and early modern periods. Demonology also includes the discourse generated by these works. Some of these treatises were written as practical manuals for clergy and judges, with information concerning how to identify a witch, methods of interrogation, the use of torture, and techniques of punishment. Other volumes were more philosophical or theoretical, relating to how the actions of demons and witches meshed with theology. In a few cases, the books were personal accounts of torture and trial experiences by lawyers, judges, and, in one case, a priest-confessor. The men writing about the configuration of diabolical witchcraft are referred to as demonologists. Judges, bishops, theologians, scholars, and even King James VI of Scotland fancied themselves experts on the subject of demons. The majority of the texts were written in the international language of Latin; a few were written in the vernacular; and others were translated into the vernacular. Although they were not directly available to the largely illiterate population, the ideas expounded in the books were disseminated to the lower orders by means of sermons, confessions made at public executions, published pamphlets and images, and word of mouth.

The learned elites wanted to place all the blame for magic and witchcraft on demons. As we have seen with the medieval scholastics, the only conclusion they could come to was that the alleged witch had some relationship with the Devil. In addition, influenced by the battles against heretical groups in the middle ages, the concept of a sect of witches who worshipped the Devil had developed. This demonic sect could not only harm individuals, but could attack society as a whole, especially with the use of weather magic. The emergence of an alleged secret society happened against the backdrop of continuing outbreaks of the plague, severe economic crises, and the religious, political, and economic upheaval of the Reformation. From an anthropological point of view, the concept of an underground sect of devil-worshipping witches served the purpose of relieving stress in a crisis-filled world. The stressful conditions were not alleviated, but guilt and fear could be projected unto the alleged conspirators. The social consequences of granting Satan a primary role in magic and witchcraft were the mass witchcraft trials in the sixteenth and seventeenth centuries. Accused witches were tortured into naming other suspects, who had attended the diabolical meetings of the sect. Those named were subsequently subjected to the same treatment, causing a chain reaction that spiralled out of control.

For the theologians and judicial authorities discussing witchcraft, it was not enough to just blame the Devil. They were also concerned with how sorcery worked. What could a witch do on her own without the help of demons? What was possible for Satan and his colleagues to do? Why did the Devil need the witch to cause harm? Could witches really physically fly to the sabbat on their own power or did demons transport witches through the air? Or was it all a delusion? Were werewolves real or was shape-shifting only possible as an illusion produced by the Devil? Did witches eat babies or grind them up for ointments? Authors also discussed how witches interfered with fertility and male potency, as well as causing abortions. As surprising as it may seem, demonologists were anxious to prove the reality of witchcraft. The disbelief expressed by some writers was viewed as a threat to Christianity. After all, it was just a hop, skip, and a jump from discounting the power of Satan to discounting the power of God. The prominent demonologist Jean Bodin stated that 'it is hardly less of an impiety to call into doubt the possibility of witches than to call into doubt the existence of God.'[1] Belief in the spirit world was at the centre of the premodern world view. During the religious reformations initiated by Martin Luther, demonological treatises also engaged in intellectual warfare concerning differences between Catholics and Protestants, or even between different sects of Protestants, as the break-away group splintered. Discussions about demons and witches were also used as platforms to air political differences, which is largely outside of our concern.

The heretical aspect of witchcraft appears to be a top-down phenomenon. However, the demonological construction of the witch did not develop in a vacuum. The concepts developed by elites were connected to contemporary religious, political, and gender ideologies, as well as the understanding of natural philosophy. The men who wrote about witches drew on various sources for their opinions. Both the Old and New Testaments of the Bible as well as the Church Fathers were frequently cited as authorities to support the ideas put forward. Augustine of Hippo and Thomas Aquinas were considered particularly authoritative. But many of the underlying ideas were drawn from popular culture, not invented by elites from above. Theological precepts and ideas borrowed from the classical era were conflated with various folk ideas. For example, the Wild Ride appears to be a phenomenon drawn from popular culture, which got imbedded in the church document, the *Canon Episcopi*. This is not a defence of what the demonologists contributed to the persecutions. Rather, it is a caution to take a broad view of the construction of witchcraft. And in spite of the sources of their ideas, the demonologists' discourse was largely responsible for the triad that emerged of God, the Devil, and the witch. These ideas were then introduced by intellectual elites into the torture chambers and courtrooms.

For demonologists, there were three explanations of why something unusual happened. The first explanation was based on nature and natural philosophy, which was the forerunner of modern science. Natural events were based on the laws of nature, as established by God at the beginning of time. Even if humans could not understand how something worked scientifically (in the modern sense of the word), that did not mean that it was unnatural. For example, they did not understand why a magnet was attracted to iron, but they understood the phenomenon as natural rather than supernatural. It happened consistently, not as a rare occurrence needing explanation. One does not need to understand how a caterpillar metamorphoses into a butterfly in order to accept that it is part of the natural world. For some demonologists, even astrology was acceptable, because the heavens were made by God. The power of the planets was occult, literally meaning 'hidden' from human understanding, but not demonic. The term occult did not take on its present meaning of mystical or evil until the modern era. See Chapter 6 for a fuller discussion of natural philosophy in relation to ceremonial magic.

The second explanation for unusual occurrences centred on God. The lens for viewing the world was rooted in theology. Miracles, as opposed to magic, were orchestrated by divine power. Religious phenomena such as the Eucharist or baptism were supernatural, literally above the natural laws, because it was God's will.

The third explanation was that abnormal phenomenon were preternatural. Preternatural events were beyond ordinary nature, but they were not miracles perpetrated by God. Events such as shape-shifting from human to animal or flying through the air were deviant, not following the laws of nature. In order for these things to happen, if they were not considered miraculous, they needed the assistance of demons. Herein lies the rub. Who gets to decide what is supernatural and what is preternatural? For the demonologists, the Bible was the most reliable authority. People cannot fly, but the biblical verse *Matthew* 4:8 clearly states that Satan took Jesus to 'an exceedingly high mountain' to tempt him. If the Devil could transport Jesus through the air, then he could no doubt transport ordinary women. This verse was used to support the theory that the witch was physically transported to the sabbat by the Devil.

The power attributed to the Devil raised two issues. If the Devil was that powerful, why could he not wreak havoc on his own, without assistance from a witch? Why was she held accountable for his misdeeds? And if the Devil could cause harm on his own, anytime he wanted to, would he not be as powerful as God? This was a particularly dangerous thought, because it could lead to a dualistic theology similar to that of the medieval Cathars, who were considered heretics. In the first instance, the demonologist Henri Boguet said that, 'the witch has only the intent to harm, whilst Satan actually performs …'.[2] According to the demonologists, the demons needed the witches to provide the element of human malice. The Devil used his power to confirm the witch's soul to Hell, which was his real mandate. But the witch should still be held responsible, because she called upon the Devil to help her. Or, her faith was so weak that she was susceptible to his seduction. In relation to the second issue, the theologians theorised that demons could only cause harm with the permission of God. The theory concerning God's permission was drawn from the biblical *Book of Job*, in which Satan had to get God's consent to torment Job (see Chapter 1 for details). In Job's case, his faith was being tested. The other reason for God to give Satan permission to wreak havoc was when humans behaved badly, especially in relation to the seven deadly sins of pride, greed, lust, envy, gluttony, wrath, and sloth. God would then allow the Devil to play his tricks in order to corrupt and punish the wicked.

Another point of discussion was whether or not the Devil could take physical form. This was particularly relevant to demons having intercourse with humans, as incubi and succubi. Demons took the form of incubi to have sex with women and the form of succubi to have sex with men. For centuries, official theology had maintained that angels, and therefore fallen angels, were pure spirits that did not have any physical form; they were also considered asexual. But witches were confessing, usually under torture, that they were having sexual relations with demons and that, most of the time, intercourse was painful. Boguet offered a solution to the problem of how a spirit could seem to have intercourse with a human. The insubstantial demons could form bodies from the elements: air was made denser so that it felt like a real body. This conveniently explained why sex with the Devil was often reported as cold and painful. Apparently, the Devil could also take human form by entering into a real body, either an animal or the body of a hanged man.

The topic of sex with demons raised the question of whether a human and a demon could procreate or not. Generally, the demonologists agreed that a child could not be born from the union of demon and human. However, this did not mean that a woman could not get impregnated by a demon. In the middle ages, the Aristotelian scholastic Thomas Aquinas theorised that demons in the form of succubi took semen from a man and then changed into an incubi to inject the sperm into the body of a woman. The resulting child was human but without the woman having had intercourse with a man. Other writers thought that it was possible 'for issue to come of this coupling'.[3] In the Bible, the sons of God, that is, angels, produced a race of giants as a result of their intercourse with the daughters of men (*Genesis* 6:1–4). As an aside, this is just one example of the contradictions in the Bible. If 'the sons of God' were angels, then angels were not asexual in this instance. Boguet used this evidence to support the possibility that Martin Luther, the founder of the Protestant movement, was the Devil's spawn. And no one seemed to notice the implications that this discussion had for the virgin birth of Jesus.

Another interesting twist on the topic was the theory that sex with the Devil would result in the birth of a monster. During the civil wars in England, a member of the Ranter sect was accused of giving birth to a child of the Devil. The title of the anonymous pamphlet printed in London in 1652 says it all:

> 'The ranters monster: being a true relation of one Mary Adams, living at Tillingham in Essex, who named her self the Virgin Mary, blasphemously affirming, that she was conceived with child by the Holy Ghost; that from her should spring forth the savior of the world; and that all those that did not believe in him were damn'd: with the manner how she was deliver'd of the ugliest ill-shapen monster that ever eyes beheld, and afterwards rotted away in prison: to the great admiration of all those that shall read the ensuing subject; the like never before heard of.'

Practical Manuals of Demonology

Between 1435 and 1689, more than twenty-five major demonological works were written. This does not take into account the many pamphlets that touched on topics raised by the demonologists. The following discussion focuses on the most influential works. Most of them were somehow related to a particular outbreak of witchcraft, written either at the beginning of a hunt or after the fact. Each author built on the ideas and discussions of previous writers, thereby reinforcing the 'truth' of their theories. The one thing that these works held in common was the belief in a conspiracy of witches.

The most influential manual to be printed in the fifteenth century was Johannes Nider's *Formicarius* or *The Ant Hill* (1435). Nider had humble beginnings as the son of a cobbler in a small town in Swabia, in present-day Germany. Opportunity for advancement came in the form of entering a Dominican monastery as a young man. Following the path of many scholars of his day, he entered university and later gained a reputation as a theologian. At one point in his illustrious career, he lectured at the University of Vienna. This is a reminder of how academic studies were closely linked with theology. The popularity of his treatise is evident in the fact that it went through seven editions. Twenty-five manuscript copies have survived from the early modern period, indicating that it was also popular enough to be painstakingly copied. Nider's work was intended for priests, with stories that could be incorporated into their sermons. This was one of the ways that the ideas of the intellectuals were disseminated to a wider lay audience. Book Five of Nider's treatise deals specifically with witchcraft, although he did not have first-hand experience in dealing with witchcraft. He drew most of his stories from cases that had been investigated by an Inquisitor who operated in France and in the area around Bern, Switzerland. He collapsed the differences between necromancers, cunning folk, and practitioners of harmful sorcery, lumping them all together as equal. This trend would continue. He was one of several demonologists who thought that the 'white witch' or cunning person was just as bad as the witch who harmed, because the power came from the same devilish source. Some authors also condemned the people who consulted a cunning person for a cure or to find lost goods, because the person was indirectly consulting with Satan.

First and foremost, Nider was concerned with spiritual reform within the only European Christian organisation at the time, the Roman Catholic church. As we have seen in the previous chapter, a concern over heresy had been growing throughout the thirteenth and fourteenth centuries. According to Nider, the Devil was the basis for a witch's power, clearly making witchcraft heretical. Of course, this was not an original concept; the idea that any type of magic employed demons had existed since Augustine. What was new in Nider's configuration of witchcraft was the portrayal of witches as part of a sect, similar to the heretical sects in the middle ages. According to Nider, witches gathered in groups and denied the Christian faith in favour of submission to Satan. To join the sect, a person had to deny his or her Christian faith (the sin of apostasy) and then pay homage to the Devil. This strengthened the concept of a pact with the Devil. The promotion of the concept of a sect of witches, who entered into a covenant with the Devil, meant that crimes committed through sorcery were no longer the only issue. Now, just becoming a member of the wicked sect of witches was enough to warrant the death sentence.

Although Nider fully developed the idea of a Satanic cult, flight to the sabbat was still not an element of his descriptions. He seemed to support the view put forward in the *Canon Episcopi* that women's belief in flying with the goddess Diana was just an illusion. In the second book of *Formicarius*, he recounted a story of a woman who thought she flew with a group of women by smearing an ointment on her body and reciting magic words. A friar who observed the procedure reported that she never left the cauldron on which she was seated. Nider still considered night flight only a dream or an illusion.

Modern scholars have argued that Nider was not promoting the persecution of witches as much as he was concerned about reform in the Catholic church. Involvement with demons was more of a cautionary tale to keep the congregation on the straight and narrow. Regardless of his intent, his work was built on by subsequent authors and contributed to the terror of witchcraft that would result in many thousands of deaths. Nider was also the first demonologist to state that women were more prone to witchcraft than men. Although he gave many examples of male witches, he argued that the moral and mental inferiority of women made them more susceptible to evil.

Nider's discussion of women's weaknesses were taken up and elaborated in the *Malleus Maleficarum* or *The Hammer of Witches* (1486). The authors of this infamous, although not the most influential, manual were Jacob Sprenger and Henry Kramer (also called by the Latin rendition of Institoris), preaching friars from the Dominican order. Scholars have determined that the treatise was largely written by Kramer; Sprenger's name was just used to add authority. For the sake of simplicity, I will just refer to the author as Kramer. The Dominican order was at the forefront of Aristotelian scholasticism, and Dominican friars were more often Inquisitors than members of other monastic orders. Kramer had started an Inquisition in 1484 in Ravensburg, a free Imperial city in what is now southern Germany. At first he was successful in discovering and executing witches with help from the city council, but eventually he ran into a lot of opposition from secular authorities. To support his activities, he obtained a bull from Pope Innocent VIII, which gave him authority to prosecute witches who were causing harm. The *Summis desiderantes* (1484) stated that many people had given 'themselves over to devils male and female' to cause *maleficium*. The bull did not mention the sabbat as an aspect of witchcraft. Even with the backing of the pope, Kramer did not get the support he wanted and needed to pursue his witch hunt. After limited success in Ravensburg, Kramer initiated an Inquisition in Tyrol, in the Alps of northern Italy. Seven women, of the fifty persons denounced, were arrested. But the local bishop stepped in and shut down Kramer's operation. In the hierarchical organisation of the Roman Catholic church, Inquisitors answered directly to the pope rather than to the local bishops or archbishops. They were often considered unwelcome outsiders in a diocese, as they undermined the bishops' and archbishops' authority.

Kramer retreated to a cloister to lick his wounds, and there he wrote the *Malleus* to justify his actions. Kramer's zealousness about the reality of witchcraft and the need to attack it was partly born from the opposition he was getting from his work as an Inquisitor. At the time of publication, the papal bull was inserted as a preface to his treatise, which made it seem that the pope approved the contents of the book, but this is questionable. Kramer hoped it would serve as a handbook for would-be witch hunters and Inquisitors. Much of the material was borrowed from Nider and other authors. Written in the scholastic style of questions and answers, the *Malleus* was printed fifteen times between 1486 and 1520, and another nineteen times during the height of the persecutions. It was also translated from Latin into German, French, and Italian. The first English edition was not published until the twentieth century, but that does not mean it was not available to an English audience, as Latin was the language of the learned. The impact on immediate trials was not that great. There was no instant increase in persecutions following the publication. In fact, the German authorities ignored it. But it was available as a manual for future judges and was frequently referred to in other handbooks on witch hunting.

Rather than being a cautionary tale about the power of the Devil, as Nider's work was, the *Malleus* emphasised how destructive witches were and how they must be eradicated to keep the world safe. The book was divided into three parts. In the first part, theological questions about witches were addressed.

> 'And the words of S. Augustine in his book on *The City of God* are very much to the point, for he tells us who magicians and witches really are. Magicians, who are commonly called witches, are thus termed on account of the magnitude of their evil deeds. These are they who by the permission of God disturb the elements, who drive to distraction the minds of men, such as have lost their trust in God, and by the terrible power of their evil spells, without

> any actual draught or poison, kill human beings … For having summoned devils to their aid they actually dare to heap harms upon mankind, and even to destroy their enemies by their evil spells. And it is certain that in operations of this kind the witch works in close conjunction with the devil.'[4]

Kramer used the classical Church Father, Augustine of Hippo, to defend his view concerning the alliance between witches and demons. The reader was encouraged to accept the reality of witchcraft.

One of the more difficult issues that demonologists faced was whether or not witches actually flew physically to the sabbat. As we discussed in Chapter 2, the *Canon Episcopi* had denounced the flight of women with the goddess Diana as superstition and devilish illusion. The *Malleus* argued that while some women flew in their imaginations, as suggested by the *Canon*, others flew in body, as confessed by women examined by Kramer. One wonders why the testimony of witches was taken as fact, given their deceptive nature and allegiance with the Devil. But the demonological literature is full of such paradoxes, including taking the word of witches as valid testimony against other witches. Although not all writers agreed with the theory of actual flight, it gained enough support to become more or less mainstream and contributed to the next step, which was belief in the sabbat. Flying to the sabbat would become a favourite subject in illustrations of witchcraft. [See Image #10, Chiaroscuro woodcut of 'The Witches', Hans Baldung Grien] However, the sabbat was still not a part of the discussion in the *Malleus*. The meetings of the diabolical sect were more in line with church gatherings than wild parties.

Kramer was a big promoter of women as witches. Even the Latin title refers to female witches rather than male (*maleficarum* not *maleficorum*). Much of the modern feminist commentary on the witch persecutions has been drawn from the opinions put forward in the *Malleus*, without consideration of how the persecutions played out. For example, Barbara Ehrenreich and Deirdre English, who wrote *Witches, Midwives, and Nurses* (1973), used only the *Malleus* as a primary source to argue that men used accusations of witchcraft to take over female-dominated health care from midwives. The historical evidence does not support their thesis. It is true that the *Malleus* was extremely misogynistic. However, Kramer was using the gender ideologies of the time for theological purposes rather than using theology to promote misogyny. In other words, the *Malleus* was not written as a woman-hunting manual. It was a witch-hunting manual, but the medical, theological, and philosophical beliefs about women caused Kramer to come to the conclusion that women were more likely to be witches than men. He was also reflecting what he was seeing: more women than men were being accused.

Not only did Kramer think that all women were potential witches, but he was obsessed with sexuality, including the sexual activity of incubi and succubi. He reinforced the connection between sexual immorality and witchcraft every chance he got. The sorceress as temptress had been established in the classical era, with figures such as Circe. The late medieval witch became increasingly sexual, in more ways than one. As we saw in the case of the Templars and Alice Kyteler, both male and female witches allegedly engaged in orgies and ritual copulation with demons. Although the Devil could take male or female form, as an incubus or succubus, intercourse with the Devil was mostly attributed to female witches. This can be partially attributed to the gender ideologies of the premodern period. A woman's reputation at that time was inextricably tied up with her sexual behaviour. Giving birth to illegitimate children or even being a bastard child oneself tainted one's credibility. Women accused of witchcraft were often painted as being sexually promiscuous in real life. Women were considered to be lustier than men, although weaker and more passive. Therefore, it was easier for demons to seduce women than men. After all, if a woman could be seduced by a human male, how much easier would it be for her to be seduced by Satan? Therefore, sex with the Devil was construed as consensual, because the woman was seduced by him rather than raped. More importantly, sexual intercourse became a symbol of a binding agreement or pact with the Devil. This was based on the tradition of intercourse being the consummation of the marriage contract. A marriage without intercourse was not binding and could be annulled. So intercourse with Satan was part of a contract or pact.

Kramer's obsession with sexuality extended to how a witch could affect a man's performance. He was dearly in need of a Freudian therapist! The most humorous part of the text is a passage concerning how a witch could steal penises.

> 'And what, then, is to be thought of those witches who in this way sometimes collect male organs in great numbers, as many as twenty or thirty members together, and put them in a bird's nest, or shut them up in a box, where they move themselves like living members, and eat oats and corn … for a certain man tells that, when he had lost his member, he approached a known witch to ask her to restore

> it to him. She told the afflicted man to climb a certain tree, and that he might take which he liked out of a nest in which there were several members. And when he tried to take a big one, the witch said: You must not take that one; adding, because it belonged to a parish priest.'[5]

This passage was included in the second part of the *Malleus,* which contained descriptions of witches' actions and methods of counteracting them. Much of the material was drawn from the Inquisitor's own experiences. Kramer supported Nider's idea of a sect and included initiation rites. At a predetermined time and place, the Devil appeared as a man. Satan asked the novice if she would forsake the Christian faith and, once she agreed, she swore with her hand raised to uphold the covenant. She then had to swear an oath of homage to the Devil, along with the willingness to give him body and soul.

As an Inquisitor, Kramer was also concerned about quelling any fears about questioning witches. The third part of the treatise instructed inquisitors and judges in how to prosecute a witch. The *Malleus* states that judges and inquisitors were immune from attack by witches, because they were doing God's work. Nevertheless, he cautioned authorities to be careful about having physical contact with the suspects. He advised them to carry consecrated salt and blessed herbs for protection, practices which reflect the ubiquitous superstition of the era.

Almost a century after the publication of the *Malleus Maleficarum*, Jean Bodin wrote *De la Démonomanie des Sorciers* or *On the Demon-Mania of Witches* (1580). His book went through twenty-six editions, was translated into four languages, and was widely read. Before the publication of *Demon-Mania*, Bodin had written a treatise on political theory, which had been very well-accepted. He was also a big promoter of the French monarchy, which was under attack at the time. Religion was a major element of politics, and Bodin was extremely hostile to both the French Protestants, called Calvinists or Huguenots, and radical Catholics. But as a French lawyer and member of the *parlement* of Paris, his main concern was how to establish proof of a crime. He argued that witchcraft should be considered a *crimen exceptum*, or an exceptional crime, because it was carried out in secret, and there were seldom any witnesses. He allowed for evidence not normally accepted, such as the testimony of a family member, the testimony of children, and only one witness to the crime rather than the customary two. The use of torture was also condoned to extract the 'truth'. Torture was referred to as being 'put to the question'.

By the time Bodin was writing, the concept of witches as a sect of devil-worshippers was widely accepted in the intellectual discourse. For Bodin, the sabbat, where large groups of men and women gathered to worship Satan, was the main activity of the sect. The belief in the sabbat, in combination with the use of torture, contributed to more deaths than any other aspect of witchcraft belief. Accused witches were encouraged to name others whom they had seen at the gathering. Their testimony was considered legal evidence. The people named in this manner were subsequently arrested, interrogated, and tortured, in a vicious chain of allegations. This scenario facilitated mass trials and huge witch hunts.

Rather ironically, *Démonomanie* was put on the Vatican's Index of Prohibited Books in 1596, because Bodin supported the belief in lycanthropy or werewolves. He argued that if the Devil could transport women through the air, he was powerful enough to transform people into animals. The church maintained that it was not possible for a human to metamorphose into another animal, because man was made in God's image. Shape-shifting was generally considered to be an illusion of the Devil rather than an actual transformation. Despite the official church stance on animal metamorphosis, a number of people, both men and women, were executed as werewolf-witches. The hatred of werewolves came from the village level. When official justice was not meted out, a suspect was liable to being lynched or stoned to death.

Another author who allowed for testimony given under extreme torture was the suffragan bishop Peter Binsfeld. Binsfeld was the son of a humble craftsman, but he was given the opportunity to study in Rome by a local abbot. He became a priest and a theologian, working against the Protestant movement in the archbishopric of Trier. He took an active part in a huge outbreak of witchcraft accusations in Trier where there were over 6,000 accusations, mostly stemming from the accused witches, who were tortured until they named others whom they had seen at the sabbat. There were between 500 and 1,000 executions. In two villages, only one woman from the adult population was left alive. Based on his personal experience with these trials, Binsfeld wrote *Tractatus de Confessionibus Maleficorum et Sagarum* or *Confessions of Male and Female Witches* (1589). It was reprinted four times and translated into German. [See Image #11, Frontispiece, *Tractatus de Confessionibus Maleficorum et Sagarum*] Binsfeld was less concerned with sexual fantasies than the *Malleus*, but he supported the idea that women were more prone to seduction by the Devil due to their strong desire for revenge and general melancholy in the face of troubles. As a member of the clergy, he was not concerned with legal niceties. He did not think the accused should have any legal defence and abdicated for unlimited torture to get to the truth. In general, he encouraged judges to break the law when it came to trying witches. However, he did denounce the use of swimming, pricking, and the witch's mark as valid evidence, perhaps on the grounds that these were superstitions drawn from popular culture. His treatise was influential in the persecutions in the Holy Roman Empire, particularly the Catholic regions.

Another contribution from the legal perspective was *Daemonolatreiae libri tres* or *Three Books of Demonolatry* (1595) by the French magistrate Nicolas Remy. There were eight editions and a German translation. Remy's work was based on hundreds of cases that he oversaw in the duchy of Lorraine. According to his own admission, he sentenced 800 people to death for witchcraft. There are no other sources to support his claim; he may have been exaggerating. His approach to witchcraft was extreme in that he believed that almost everything was possible, including weather magic, flying to the sabbat, the pact with the Devil, and the Black Mass. He even believed that witches could transform into wolves, because their nature was so closely related to the wolf. As a lawyer, he condemned any form of judicial leniency towards those accused. His work was even more influential than the *Malleus*.

At the very end of the sixteenth century, Martin Antoine del Rio wrote *Disquisitionum magicarum libri sex* or *Six Books of Disquisitions on Magic* (1599). The Spanish-Dutch del Rio began his career in politics and was a colleague of Nicolas Rémy, but he left a position as attorney-general of the Spanish Netherlands to become a Jesuit theologian and a scholar. He viewed the world as a battlefield between good and evil, not an uncommon view at the time following Martin Luther's reform movement. The Jesuits were a Catholic order of priests who were at the forefront of the Counter-Reformation, as teachers and missionaries. Del Rio's book was reprinted at least twenty times, and was one of the most authoritative texts in the seventeenth century. It was aimed at theologians, legal experts, physicians, and scholars. He offered advice on arresting, trying, sentencing, and executing witches. He was an advocate for a hard-line approach to treating witchcraft. Del Rio took elements of the sabbat from a variety of sources and presented a detailed description. Particulars included flying to the sabbat on brooms or animals, the Devil in the form of a goat presiding over the assembly on a throne, the *osculum infame*, and the ritual of the Black Mass. Sacrificing children, feasting, and dancing back to back were all part of the celebration. Under torture, these stories would come out of the mouths of the accused, which would, in turn, confirm their validity in the minds of their persecutors.

Another legal point of view was presented by Henri Boguet. In *Discours des sorciers* or *An Examen of Witches* (1602), he discussed his personal prosecution of witches as Chief Justice of St Claude in the Compté of Burgundy in the French Alps. His manual was highly praised by lawyers and clergy and was adopted by most of the local courts of France as authoritative. There were at least a dozen editions in the original French. His work incorporated many of the previous ideas of Kramer, Bodin, Remy, and others, as well as classical authors such as Ovid and Pliny, and, of course, the Bible. He believed that anyone who dared to doubt the existence of witches must be a witch himself.

The idea of the sabbat was fully developed in *Discours*. Boguet argued that a witch could not go to the sabbat in spirit only, because 'when the soul is separated from the body, death must necessarily follow'. But what about husbands who testified that their wives were in bed beside them all night when the wives, or other witnesses, said they were at the sabbat? Boguet countered that 'Satan then places a fantom in their likeness' so that the husband is fooled into thinking his wife is in bed. As to the women who professed that they went to the sabbat in spirit, he argued that Satan revealed 'to them in their sleep what happens at the Sabbat so vividly that they think they have been there'.[6] Boguet went on to say that the Devil had sex with women 'because he knows that women love carnal pleasures' and 'there is nothing which makes a woman more subject and loyal to a man than that he should abuse her body [a euphemism for sexual intercourse].'[7] A modern reader is hard-pressed not to think that there was a lot of sexual projection in play by these authors.

Another lawyer personally involved with witchcraft prosecutions was Pierre de Lancre, a member of the *parlement* of Bordeaux. In 1609, he was sent to the Basque region of southwest France. Pays de Labourd, in northern Navarre, was in the Pyrenees mountain range on the border with Spain. Navarre had been independent during the middle ages, but part of it had been annexed to Spain in 1515. The northern territory was eventually merged with France following marriage alliances, which resulted in the king of Navarre eventually becoming King Henry IV of France. The king had ordered de Lancre to investigate an outbreak of witchcraft in the area, following reports that witches were more numerous than caterpillars. It was de Lancre's job to bring French law to an area of France that was not culturally French. The men of the Pays de Labourd were mostly deep-sea fishermen, leaving the women alone for months at a time to manage everyday affairs. De Lancre found the Basque culture exotic and believed that the beautiful women, who loved dancing, were especially vulnerable to seduction by the Devil. He supported the reality of the sabbat and added acts of sodomy to the list of undesirable behaviours. As a result of his investigation, de Lancre wrote *Tableau de l'Inconstance des Mauvais Anges et Demons* or *A Display of the Inconstancy of Evil Angels and Devils* (1612). A second edition in 1613 included the engraving by the Polish engraver Jan Ziarnko, which illustrated de Lancre's main focus of the book: the sabbat. [See Image #12, Illustration of sabbat by Jan Ziarnko, in *Tableau de l'Inconstance des Mauvais Anges et Demons*] The treatise was a defence of his actions. In four months, 80 to 100 people were executed for witchcraft under his direction, including several priests. More than 1,000 of the suspects were children, who were allegedly going to the sabbat every day and reporting back to de Lancre. Many of the witnesses were teenagers and children. In the end, he was recalled to Paris because the local authorities resented his interference.

The Italian opinion of witchcraft was represented by Francesco Maria Guazzo's *Compendium Maleficarum* or *Book of Witches* (1608). Guazzo was a Catholic monk from Milan, whose experience with witchcraft was limited to the exorcism of members of elite families in Europe. His examples of witchcraft were drawn from Remy's and del Rio's work. The pact with the Devil was particularly important to him. According to him, the Devil placed a brand on the witch's body to mark the pact. [See Image #13, Witch receiving the Devil's Mark, in *Compendium Maleficarum*] The brand could be painful or painless. The marks differed from person to person. They could resemble the footprint of a hare, a toad, a spider, a dog, or a dormouse. Men were commonly marked on the eyelids, armpit, shoulder, or posterior; women were marked on the breasts or private parts, another gendering of witchcraft. He supported the idea that if the mark was pricked deeply with a pin, the person would feel no pain and the spot would not bleed. This idea led to professional witch prickers being hired to identify witches by poking and prodding. Not everyone in Satan's service received a mark, only those whom the Devil thought might be inconstant, which really undermines the importance of the mark as evidence of being a witch. If you have a mark, you are a witch; if you do not have a mark, you still might be a witch. There was no escaping the logic of demonology. Guazzo's book was extensively illustrated with woodcuts depicting the various acts of heresy.

Catholics were not the only ones writing demonological treatises. The Protestant King James VI of Scotland (later James I of England) wrote

Daemonologie (1597) after a series of trials in Edinburgh in the 1590s, in which he was personally involved. James had negotiated a marriage with Princess Anne of Denmark. The young bride had attempted to sail to Scotland for the nuptials, but had been forced to return to Denmark on account of bad weather. The admiral of the Danish fleet, who was escorting her, blamed the bad weather on witches. To demonstrate his anticipation of the wedding, James decided to go personally to Denmark in August 1589 to fetch home his new wife. Inclement weather kept James at the court in Denmark with his in-laws for six months. During this time, James engaged in philosophical debates with the theologian Nils Hemmingsen concerning witchcraft trials. As a result of these discussions, Continental ideas, including the belief in the sabbat, were introduced into Scotland. Once again, there were strong winds and rough seas on the couple's voyage home in May 1590. One of the king's fleet sank. Three months after their return, witches in Copenhagen were charged with causing the tempest.

When James arrived back in Scotland, he got involved in an outbreak of witchcraft accusations, which started in East Lothian in 1590 and extended until 1597. Geillis Duncan, a maidservant, had suddenly acquired healing powers, which brought her to the attention of the local bailiff. Upon examination, a witch's mark was discovered on her neck. Torture with thumbscrews led to a confession that she and others were involved with the Devil. Thirty women and men were arrested. The usual charges of *maleficium,* included causing sickness and making charms emerged. Further examinations revealed a plot against the king. Eventually, the alleged leader of the witches, Agnes Sampson, confessed in front of the king and the Privy Council that she had attended a sabbat on Halloween and pledged to hurt the monarch. James took her testimony very seriously after she reportedly described the exchange of words between himself and his bride on their wedding night. One of the accused male witches, Richard Graham, implicated Francis Stewart Hepburn, the fifth earl of Bothwell, saying he had commissioned the group to do weather magic and also to make wax poppets against the king's life. Bothwell was James's cousin. His uncle, the fourth earl, had been married to James's mother, Mary Queen of Scots, which meant that if anything should happen to the king, Bothwell had a tenuous claim to the throne. In this case, charges of witchcraft were obviously used for political purposes. Bothwell was arrested and imprisoned, but was powerful enough to avoid a trial. He was eventually banished from Scotland. His reputation as a sorcerer followed him in his travels throughout Europe; he was known as the 'Wizard Earl' to his contemporaries.

Because of Bothwell, witchcraft ranked in importance with treason for the king. The North Berwick trials prompted James to educate the masses concerning the need to persecute witchcraft. His treatise, *Daemonologie,* introduced Continental ideas about witchcraft to Scotland. He approved the swimming of witches to determine guilt, even though swimming was not legal. He also approved the use of torture. In the Third Book, James explained how fairies were the same as what the *Canon Episcopi* 'called Diana, and her wandering court'.[9] He considered the fairies as evil spirits, who deluded people into thinking they visited the fairy kingdom. This is an example of how folklore became demonised by elites.

Sceptics

Not all men who wrote about demons and witchcraft were in favour of the level of prosecutions taking place. This group can also be called demonologists, because they were discussing what was possible for demons to do. They accepted the reality of witchcraft, but not the ability of the poor women who were usually accused.

One of the earliest voices to speak out against the prosecutions was Johann Wier or Weyer. Wier was a Dutch physician with a strong interest in the occult. He had studied with the well-known magus and humanist scholar Cornelius Agrippa. *De Praestigiis Daemonum* or *On the Tricks of the Devil* (1563) was published in six Latin editions, as well as one French and two German versions. Wier was a Lutheran, the original Protestant denomination. He argued that the Devil was powerful enough in his own right to wreak whatever havoc he wanted. He did not need the assistance of a weak, inferior woman. Although his work was defending women against attack, he was no feminist. Wier claimed that women who confessed to fantastic acts, such as causing hailstorms, were more likely insane, senile, or melancholy. He felt they should have been offered medical attention or spiritual counselling rather than prosecution, torture, and death. Freud would later considered him the founder of modern psychology. His argument that witchcraft was an impossible crime went against the idea that the Devil worked through witches. His book was condemned by both of the main Protestant sects, the Lutherans and the Calvinists, and was put on the Index of Prohibited Books by the Catholic church. Jean Bodin denounced him as a witch, but he was not formally accused of witchcraft. Wier was harsher toward the learned magicians, who knowingly invoked demons during ceremonial magic. These educated men were not usually caught up in witchcraft accusations, and not even Wier thought they deserved the death sentence. Wier's main contribution to the demonological discussion was that it raised opposition to his views. Rather than reducing the persecution, he gave his opponents something to attack, which just gave them fuel for their fires, literally.

Some of Wier's ideas were adapted by the Englishman Reginald Scot in *The Discoverie of Witchcraft* (1584), written in English. Scot was skeptical about the actual existence of witchcraft, which makes his work rather unique in the field of demonology. As an Anglican Protestant, he ridiculed witchcraft belief as a Catholic superstition. He denied the possibility that demons could take physical form and have interactions with humans. Scot could be considered an early advocate of the new science. He insisted on empirical evidence to support the far-fetched notions connected with witchcraft. He carefully explained how most of what passed for magic was merely tricks and sleight of hand. He reinforced the gullible nature of women, and felt that people were too willing to blame an old, melancholic woman for their problems when it was God who was responsible for providence. He did understand how a woman might earn a reputation as a witch, and how a woman might come to believe that she was one. He laid out the following scenario. A poor woman, reduced to begging for a living, is refused charity and curses her neighbours. Eventually, something bad is bound to happen. Based on her bad behaviour, the community suspects the old woman of witchcraft. When she sees that her curses have apparently worked, she buys into the delusion as well. This is one possible explanation for why accused women confessed. Scot considered all this to be superstition, which he was more than happy to lay at the feet of the papists. Scot points out that fear and torture were the other reasons for false confessions, and that it was a no-win situation for the suspect. If she withstood the torments, her inquisitors would assume the Devil was protecting her. If she confessed, it was because the Devil had abandoned her. The other variety of witch was the fraud. Scot gave several examples of how so-called magicians could fool a gullible public. In Scot's opinion, witches were not servants of the Devil; they were either deluded old women or cozening rogues. *Discoverie* was condemned by James VI of Scotland. Somehow a story was circulated that James had all the copies of *Discoverie* burnt when he came to the English throne as James I, but there is no evidence to support this tale.

A second edition of *Discoverie* was published in the middle of the seventeenth century, when skepticism about witchcraft was growing after the largest English episode in the 1640s. The trials that were initiated by Matthew Hopkins in East Anglia resulted in more than 100 executions, sparking the publication of several pamphlets on witchcraft, some of them overtly skeptical. However, the real reason for a second edition may have been the popularity of the text as a conjuring manual for would-be magicians. Scot had hoped to illustrate how ridiculous the practices of magicians were by including a lot of information from ceremonial magic texts, such as the *Key of Solomon*. He provided a wealth of information on how to cast circles, conjure demons, make magical tools, construct charms and talismans, and communicate with angels and spirits of the dead. He presented magicians and conjurers as 'Juglers and their tricks', but he inadvertently instructed his readers in the practice of ritual magic. His work was widely used by cunning folk, as well as being a source for magic and witchcraft material in dramatic literature. In 1687, Ann Watts was arrested for several misdemeanours, including pretending to be a fortune teller. She had in her possession Agrippa's *Occult Philosophy* and Scot's *Discoverie*. Ironically, Scot's treatise had become a source for the practice of witchcraft and magic rather than a statement against them. The popularity of *Discoverie* has continued into the twenty-first century.

Neither Wier nor Scot had first-hand experience in dealing with witchcraft and torture. Friedrich Spee, on the other hand, was a Jesuit who had witnessed prosecutions at Wurzburg. He taught moral theology in several German cities and was active in the Counter-Reformation. *Cautio Criminalis* or *A Warning on Criminal Justice* (1631) was published anonymously, probably because Spee was worried about the reaction from his ecclesiastical superiors. As the confessor of condemned witches, he was not convinced of the guilt of those who were executed. In fact, he maintained that he had never met a witch, thereby saying that all the condemned people who confessed to him were innocent. Nevertheless, he believed in witchcraft and the power of Satan. But he disagreed with the legal procedures by which accused people were being interrogated and tried. Spee was particularly concerned with women as victims of witchcraft accusations, because they were weak, irrational, and vulnerable.

Spee was outspoken concerning the use of torture to establish the 'truth'. The legal confessions necessary to convict a witch were extracted under torture, but the confessions given to the priest were for the purpose of receiving absolution before death. The person could not escape the death sentence already handed down by the judge, but she could hope to shorten her time in purgatory by telling God that she had lied and by asking forgiveness. The condemned routinely denied what they had said as a result of interrogation. Spee doubted that any of the condemned were guilty of the acts they confessed to under torture. He argued that anyone would confess to stop the pain. He made note of how the tortured suspect was forced to denounce others, who would suffer the same fate. He maintained that these denunciations were meaningless, because either the person being tortured was not a witch or the person was a witch, in which case her words should not be taken as truth since she was in league with the Devil. The Devil was more likely to accuse innocent people than his own servants. Spee debunked the idea of the sabbat and flying through the air to get there as delusions, if not outright lies. He accused the judicial authorities of profiting from the witch trials by confiscating the property of the victims. His intended audience was the sovereign princes and rulers of the many principalities in the Holy Roman Empire. Each leader had the responsibility for godly rule in his own territory and, therefore, had the power and the duty to stop the persecutions. Sixteen editions of *Cautio* appeared in several translations. But the big hunts were coming to an end before his work was published. Spee's treatise stands as a testimony to the increasing scepticism of the men in authority.

Conclusion

Ever since the institutionalisation of the church at the end of the Roman Empire, the presence of the Devil in the world had been promoted by theologians. During the middle ages, the concept of a sect of devil-worshippers became more prevalent in relation to heresy. By the end of the fifteenth century, the emergence of actual heretical groups set the stage for imagining the solitary witch, accused of performing harmful magic or *maleficium,* as a member of a diabolical sect. Heresy and sorcery became inextricably combined. The source of the witches' power shifted from the technical charms and potions of the lone practitioner to the demons that were acting behind the scenes. The witch's actions were merely signs sent to the demons to act. Witchcraft was impossible without the power of the Devil. God had designed humans to have free will (as evidenced in the Adam and Eve story), which meant that witches agreed to work with the spirit world, either explicitly or implicitly, which led to the idea of the pact. This new sect engaged in extremely destructive magic aimed at both individuals and the broader population.

At this time, secular rulers were responsible for the spiritual welfare of their subjects, as well as their physical welfare. The views of the demonologists gave theological backing to rulers to support the persecution of witchcraft. The emphasis on witches as part of an underground heretical organisation shifted the focus from punishing a person who committed a crime by means of sorcery to exterminating a person believed to be a member of such a group. Ironically, in their efforts to eradicate individual witches, demonologists created the concept of an abominable sect. As we shall see in the following chapter, the concept of the sabbat, as elaborated in the demonological literature, was a key element in the persecution of thousands of innocent people suspected of belonging to this imagined group.

Chapter 4

By Life and Love, Sexual Sabbats

On 4 June 1598, Françoise Secretain begged lodging at a house belonging to the parents of an 8-year-old girl. The woman allegedly gave the child 'a crust of bread resembling dung and made her eat it' under threat that if she did not, she would 'kill her and eat her'.[1] The next day, the girl 'was struck helpless in all her limbs so that she had to go on all-fours'. An exorcism at the local church revealed that the girl was possessed of five demons, called 'Wolf, Cat, Dog, Jolly and Griffon'. The girl accused Françoise of casting a spell on her. The next day, the girl 'was thrown to the ground and the devils came out of her mouth in the shape of balls as big as the fist and red as fire, except the Cat, which was black'. Françoise was arrested and put into gaol. For three days, Françoise sat in prison, fingered her rosary, and protested her innocence. During this time, she did not shed any tears, which was a sign that she was a witch. The authorities decided to threaten her to tell the truth, probably by showing her the instruments of torture. They then proceeded to strip her naked, shave off all the hair on her head and body, and search her for the Devil's mark. No mark was found, but after her hair was cut, she 'trembled all over her body, and at once confessed'. First, she confessed to sending the demons into the little girl. Second, she said that she had given herself to the Devil, 'who at that time had the likeness of a big, black man'. Third, she had sex with the Devil in the form of a dog, a cat, and a fowl and 'his semen was very cold'. Fourth, she had flown to the sabbat in a nearby village by placing a white staff between her legs. Fifth, she had danced at the sabbat and performed weather magic to cause hail. Sixth, the Devil had given her a powder that could kill people. Seventh, she had made cattle die by touching them with a wand.

***

Françoise's accusation of witchcraft started out in a familiar pattern. A child was ill and someone with a dubious reputation was accused of causing the illness. The child's family did not accuse Françoise of attending a sabbat or worshipping the Devil. Their only concern was the bewitchment of their daughter. Françoise's confession was fairly mild, given the elaborate activities that took place at a sabbat according to the judge and demonologist Boguet, who recorded her case in his treatise. She admitted to flying to the party, dancing, and performing weather magic. But the full-blown sabbat with feasts, orgies, and metamorphosis into animal shapes was not part of her story. The sabbat had not been part of the demonological discourse in the fifteenth century, even in highly imaginative works such as the *Malleus*. But it gradually became part of the standard fare of confessions in the sixteenth century. Perhaps Françoise only knew a few of the required details in order to satisfy her tormentors.

The addition of the sabbat to the concept of heretical witchcraft was mostly a top down phenomenon imposed by the dominant literate culture via inquisitors and judges. The demonological discourse that we examined in the last chapter happened after the development of printing with moveable type (*c.* 1450), which allowed for the faster circulation of ideas and published reports of trials. Such treatises on witchcraft were not available to poor, illiterate women like Françoise, but she may have heard about the activities of the sabbat through rumours and gossip. Pamphlet literature had started to report aspects of the sabbat in relation to witchcraft cases. Even illiterate members of the community had access to this level of information. Pamphlets were sometimes read aloud in public by the more educated members of a community, and the many woodcuts and engravings in the literature of the time illustrated the ideas propounded by the demonologists.

The term sabbat or sabbath was used by French and German demonologists to refer to a gathering of witches. The term was probably borrowed from the Jews, who were widely persecuted in the middle ages when the idea of the witches' sabbat started to take shape. Both classical and folkloric elements were included in the concept of the diabolical sabbat as developed by the demonologists. Alleged activities at the sabbat were also comparable to activities at other festivities that were extremely common to the era. According to the demonologists, the sabbat served a purpose for the Devil. It served a different purpose for the intellectuals who engineered it. An anthropological analysis demonstrates a broader interpretation of the inversions of the sabbat. Unfortunately, the consequences of the concept caused more deaths than the imagined sect of witches ever could have.

Classical Influences

Elements of the sabbat can be seen in mystery cults of the ancient world. The cult of Dionysus was widespread in the Graeco-Roman world and was the biggest rival to the cult of Christianity in the early days of the church. The god Dionysus (called Bacchus in Rome) was a part of Greek culture as early as the thirteenth century BCE. The god of wine and nature travelled with male followers called satyrs or fauns, who were usually depicted as half man and half goat, or half man and half horse. Sometimes they had horns. The satyrs loved sex, wine, and frenzied dancing (who doesn't?). In the ancient Greek literature, Dionysus and his followers were associated with many animals, and sometimes he was transformed into a bull or a goat in myths.

Dionysus's female human followers were called maenads. They performed secret rituals, including sacrifice, an oath, and sexual union with the god, strikingly familiar to the activities of the sabbat if one considers Dionysus equal to Satan, which the theologians did. Other sources mention celebrations that included feasting, singing hymns, and dancing. In one version, the maenads suckled animals, another aspect that resonates with accusations of witches nursing familiars. Plato said that 'many are fennel-carriers' referring to a stalk from the aromatic fennel plant that was carried by participants.[2] This is particularly interesting given the activities of the *benandanti* discussed below, who also carried stalks of the edible and medicinal fennel to do battle with witches. Fennel was also hung over doorways to repel evil spirits, and is still considered magical by modern witches and herbalists. The cult of Dionysus was a mystery cult, as opposed to one of the many public religions common to Greece and Rome. Followers had to undergo a rite of passage or initiation. Given that the cult was veiled in secrecy, we only know fragments of the rites. The initiation ritual, which took place at night, contained symbolism concerning death and rebirth. A sarcophagus or coffin was associated with the cult, which obviously represented death. Sarcophagi were frequently sculpted with images of figures engaged in ecstatic dancing, drinking, and sex, representing the happiness of the afterlife for the initiated. Augustine berated the Bacchanalia for its frenzy, which he attributed to the 'power unclean spirits, when held to be gods, [can] exercise over the minds of men'.[3] Of course, this was part of Augustine's and the other Church Fathers' efforts to reduce the Greek and Roman gods to demons.

Modern historians are not the only ones to see connections between the cult of Dionysus and the depiction of the witches' sabbat. In a publication dated 1615, a French collector of 'tragic histories' declared that Bacchus or Dionysus was the Devil, not surprising given Augustine's demonisation. According to the author, the satyrs were demons and the maenads were witches. The author believed that the tradition of the sabbat had been transmitted over the centuries by its demonic participants. It is impossible to trace the transmission of these ideas; there is no evidence to support the unbroken continuation of the practices. I am not suggesting that any of these rituals or celebrations were direct forerunners of the witches' sabbat. Rather, they are evidence of similar scenarios that were drawn on for the formulation of, and the belief in, such events. The men who composed the demonological treatises were schooled in classical literature and would have drawn on these examples for precedents to the sabbat. The woodcut on the English pamphlet *Robin Good-Fellow, His Mad Prankes, and Merry Iests* (1638) clearly illustrates that this configuration of the Devil as a satyr made its way into witchcraft accounts. [See Image #5, Woodcut on title page of *Robin Good-Fellow*] In the illustration, witches are dancing in a circle while a piper plays on the sidelines. The Devil holds a broom overhead just in case there is any doubt about the figure's association with witchcraft.

Folkloric Influences

The human desire for reckless abandon, as associated with the cult of Dionysus, whether in actuality or fantasy, has a long history. Another common theme is the human desire to go beyond the earthly realm, whether to the heavenly realm, the underworld, or the land of the fairies. There are many tales from various places in the Western world of hosts of beings, both spirit and human, that could have been drawn on for the construction of the sabbat. Each myth may have had its own origin stemming from different cultures, or there could have been diffusion from some central point. But some caution is advised in the interpretation of this material. Because most of our evidence of folk belief comes from written accounts recorded after the advent of Christianity, it is impossible to know whether the stories were drawn from ancient popular traditions that predated Christianity or were stories that illustrated theological concerns about the fate of the soul during the development of Christian theology.

As we have already seen in the *Canon Episcopi*, folk culture got combined with the theology of the demonologists. According to the *Canon*, women claimed to travel with female spirits led by the Roman goddess Diana. Chroniclers often substituted the names of Roman goddesses, such as Diana or Hecate, for the original pagan goddesses such as Holda, Abundia, Satia, or Perchta. In this manner, both Roman and pagan deities were transformed into devils. The procession described in the *Canon Episcopi* is one version of a folktale variously called the Wild Hunt, the Wild Ride, or the Furious Horde.

Different versions appear in Teutonic or Germanic folklore. A procession of demonic spirits, or ghosts of people who had died prematurely, flew across the night sky wreaking havoc, sometimes breaking into cellars and drinking alcohol. Fairies, demons, spirits of the dead, and living humans were often combined in ways that make it very hard to present just one model of the beliefs. The most common time for these devastating rides was the Ember Days, special days set aside for prayer and fasting, at which time people put out food to appease the spirits. The Christian holy days called Ember Days also have their roots in pre-Christian rituals. They are roughly equal to the two solstices and two equinoxes that mark the changing of the seasons. This is one example of the difficulty in sorting out the relationship between folk legends and Christian rituals.

By the twelfth century, the idea of spirits wandering the earth until they atoned for their sins had also been established in literature. Aspects of the beliefs made their way into other tales, including a procession of ghostly knights as part of the King Arthur legend. We know of several of these beliefs through the accounts of monks and clergy, who reported similar myths and legends throughout the middle ages: the Norns, the Valkyries, and the Celtic Sidh Army, to name a few of the better known. Theologians worried that the travelling souls were either accompanied by demons or were demons themselves. One version of the tale said the demons could cause weather damage, another link to the sabbat where groups of witches caused hail by beating water. Another account, recorded by a Byzantine historian in the sixth century, described a group of Frankish men who were called up in the night to go down to the sea and row special boats to the opposite shore. The boats appeared empty, but they sat low in the water as if they were full, implying that they were occupied by spirits. This was yet another version of the journey into the world of the dead. In at least one instance, a priest told his congregation that soldiers killed in battle, unbaptised children, and souls separated from their bodies wandered at night during the Ember Days. This was obviously a cautionary tale and suggests how these legends could have been re-introduced to the peasantry from the top down and demonised at the same time. As discussed in Chapter 1, the Wild Hunt was declared a delusion in the eleventh century, but the passage would later be used to support the idea of women flying to the sabbat.

Other sources from the middle ages supported the belief in women travelling at night with the souls of dead females. These supernatural females were referred to as the 'good ladies' or 'good society', and a privileged few living humans were allowed to join them. The group was considered benevolent and visited houses to eat and drink offerings left for them, a similarity they shared with participants of the Wild Hunt. If they were happy with the provisions, they would bless the household for the coming year. A similar rite had been performed by the Romans as part of the practice of ancestor worship. They set out food for their ancestors, who were believed to be in control of fertility and prosperity.

During the witchcraft trials of the early modern period, people sometimes confessed to travelling with similar hordes of spirits, mostly in the Alps and northern Italy, where the idea of the sabbat first developed. For example, in fourteenth-century Milan, two women, interrogated separately, confessed to attending the 'game of Diana', although they called the leader 'Signora or Madonna Oriente'. This society of women, which included both living and dead, roamed through wealthy houses where they ate and drank. They killed animals to eat during their nocturnal journeys, but afterwards they put the bones back into the skins and Oriente brought them back to life with a magic wand. As a reward for their participation, the members of the society were given remedies to cure illnesses and the knowledge of how to find lost or stolen goods, services commonly offered by cunning folk. The society of women was linked to the sabbat by the demonologist Martin del Rio in the sixteenth century. In his description of the sabbat, he reported that the witches arrived at the games of the 'Good Society' as it was called in Italy.

A similar belief existed in Sicily. There were women well-known for their ability to cure and their abilities of divination, known in Sicilian as *donni di fuora* or 'ladies from outside'. In Sicily, the term was also used to describe a male or female fairy, who went out on nocturnal excursions. The queen of the fairies led the group. She was usually described as a beautiful woman but with the feet of a cat or a horse. The Sicilian women travelled with the fairies and entered people's houses. They would dress up in rich people's clothes and play with children in their beds. A tidy house garnered a blessing. During the process of interrogating these women, the Spanish Inquisitors attempted to turn these accounts into demonic sabbats, but there was no tradition of the wicked witch in Sicily. Some of the women told the Inquisitors that such stories were only told to impress their clients. Others said that the fairies and their human companions were organised in companies according to district.

In 1587, Lauria de Pavia, a fisherman's wife in Palermo, confessed to the Spanish Inquisition, whose jurisdiction she was under, that she and her companions rode goats through the air to an alternate kingdom in Naples, ruled by a beautiful king and queen. There she was instructed to kneel to the monarchs and to stop worshipping God. She promised her body and soul to them. After she did this, the company ate, drank, danced, and had sex. She said that these agreeable experiences seemed to take place in a dream; afterwards she woke up in her own bed. In Sicilian tradition, the women were intermediaries between humans and the fairy realm. Fairies sometimes caused illnesses, often because of some accidental action of a human, such as sitting on a fairy in the garden. The 'fairy doctors', as they were called, were consulted by the general population as healers or wise women. The women who accompanied the fairies were given remedies to cure the sick by the king and queen of the fairies. The *donni di fuora* would offer to attend the next nighttime meeting and persuade the fairy to make the person well again. An offering of a ritual meal was needed to appease the fairy. In one case, a table was outfitted with jugs of water and wine, sweetmeats, bread, and honey cakes.

Similar ideas appeared elsewhere. The practices of the *donni di fuora* is very reminiscent of the actions of an English fortune teller, Judith Phillips. She told a wealthy widow that in order to get the aid of the queen of the fairies in locating hidden treasure, the woman had to provide a turkey and a couple of capons. When Isobel Gowdie was accused of witchcraft in Scotland in 1662, she told about her adventures with the fairy folk. Are these stories evidence of an overactive imagination, the vestiges of folk tales, or mental illness? Regardless of the reason behind the tales, trying to rationalise the belief in night flight does not undo the execution of the men and women who were punished for their beliefs in benevolent societies.

The agrarian fertility cult of the *benandanti* is a good example of how folklore was integrated into ideas about witchcraft from the top down. In the duchy of Friuli, a group believed that they were defenders of the harvest and the fertility of the fields. Friuli was in the north-western part of Italy, north of Rome and south of the Alps. The area is mountainous and was isolated from the mainstream culture, therefore slower to change. The *benandanti* were mostly men and a few women who were born with the caul, that is, still wrapped in the amniotic sac. Mothers kept the caul, preserved it, and had it blessed by priests, then gave it to their boys to wear around their necks. There was widespread belief in Europe that the caul had magical properties and would bring good fortune as a charm. The men believed that they were called to join the ranks of the *benandanti*. The entire community would have accepted that the man was special from a very early age. On Thursday nights of the Ember Days, these chosen ones went into a trance state to join their leader. They flew in spirit to fight the witches with bundles of fennel stalks. A similar group of mostly women claimed that they went out at night in procession with the dead.

When this sect first came to the attention of the Roman Inquisition in 1575, they were ignored as too fantastical to be taken seriously. The men told the Inquisitors that they were fighting witches in the service of Christ. In return for their service, the *benandanti* were granted the power to identify witches and to heal victims of witchcraft, similar to the skills of the Sicilian women. Little by little, the Inquisitors made these accounts fit their ideas about witchcraft; as a result, the stories offered by the *benandanti* were gradually altered. By 1634, the Holy Office had transformed the *benandanti* into witches who met at the sabbat. The men were seen as harming people rather than curing them, and they were denounced by the peasantry as well as the Inquisition.

Later authors and artists would link the Wild Ride to sexual immorality. Lucas Cranach the Elder was the leading German artist in the first half of the sixteenth century. He promoted the new theology of Martin Luther. As an apothecary, he was also interested in the subject of melancholy. According to the medical theories of the time, melancholy was caused by an excess of black bile, one of the four humours of the body. Melancholy had a physical cause combined with what modern readers would call psychological effects. As mentioned in the last chapter, two of the authors who had spoken out against the witchcraft persecutions, Wier and Scot, attributed the delusion of witchcraft to melancholic old women. In a series of four paintings entitled *Melancholia* (1528–1533), Cranach depicted the quality of melancholy as an opportunity for Satan. [See Image #14, One in a series of paintings titled *Melancholia,* Lucas Cranach the Elder]. In the background of one of the 1532 paintings, a cavalcade of wild riders gallops across the night sky. Except for the male, the figures are naked and female. Nudity, in this case, portrays sexual immorality. The participants ride a wild boar, a cow, and a dragon. One is carrying a forked cooking stick, which was a common method of transportation to the sabbat and a visual clue that the women were witches. Some scholars interpret the sole male rider as the leader of the horde; others think he might be a captive of the witches, on account of his passive demeanour and the position of the cooking stick directed toward him. By including the wild ride in the painting, Cranach was linking the melancholic state of women with witchcraft. The sexual, night-flying witch would become one of the most powerful representations of witchcraft.

Flying

This brings us to the topic of flying. Meeting in a secret place to engage in dancing, feasting, and sex is one thing, getting there by flying through the air is another. The idea of flying to the sabbat is the most obvious borrowing from folktales like the Wild Hunt. Witches' confessions often specified the implement used for flight: forked oven sticks, broomsticks, pieces of gallows, and animals of various sorts, especially goats and rams. Françoise Secretain confessed that 'she placed a white staff between her legs and uttered certain words, and that she was then conveyed through the air to the witches' assembly.'[4] Sometimes the demons carried the witches on their backs. Another woman described the demon as 'a gigantic man, black-bearded and clothed in black' who took her on his back and 'carried her like a cold wind' to the sabbat.[5] The witch might also transform into an animal herself to fly. They often left their houses through the chimney. Any connection here to Santa??

There were several theories about witches flying, which were discussed by theologians, demonologists, and Inquisitors. Some believed that a witch could actually fly with the help of the Devil. Others believed that the witches only flew in their imaginations. The last theory was that the soul left the body to travel to the sabbat, in what one might call an out of body experience. This theory had been rejected by Bodin on the basis that a person dies when the soul leaves the body, and the Devil does not have the power to resurrect the dead. That would have been giving him too much power in relation to God. Remy suggested that the soul just appeared to leave the body, because the person fell into a very deep sleep. In this condition, the Devil filled the soul with visions.

Whether travelling in actuality or in the imagination, flight could be augmented with the use of special ointments smeared on the body or the travelling implement. The Basque witches had a peculiar method of making the flying salve. The witch fed her familiar toad on maize, bread, and wine, which the toad ate like a pig. Then the witch whipped the toad with a little switch until the toad swelled up. With her left food the witch stepped on the toad until a greenish-black liquid exploded out both ends, which she collected. I really worry about how many toads have been subjected to such cruel experiments. Drugs such as hemlock, nightshade, bella donna, mandrake, and henbane were also cited as ingredients in the witch's ointment, along with the requisite fat of unbaptised babies. Several of these plants are from the nightshade family and contain a psychoactive alkaloid that can produce hallucinations similar to LSD. However, they are very toxic and can cause death. Historians who were writing in the era of the drug culture of the 1960s and 1970s suggested that the reports of flying to the sabbat were a result of this type of drug use. However, later historians argued that the use of the magical ointments was a fabrication of the demonologists, who believed that the power of the unguents came from the Devil rather than any medicinal properties. Occasionally, these mixtures were tested. Several of the demonologists claimed to have observed people who used a salve and appeared to fall into a deep and prolonged sleep or trance. When the person awoke, she reported fantastical experiences including flying. In Edward Bever's recent book, *The Realities of Witchcraft and Popular Magic in Early Modern Europe*, he suggests that psychotropic drugs were part of the popular culture's pharmacopoeia and could have played a role in the construction of the witches' sabbat. He points out that some of the accused mentioned specific herbs in the concoctions, which had psychoactive properties that could cause hallucinations and dreams. Testing done in the early modern era does not support this theory. The Spanish Inquisitor Salazar conducted experiments with ointments that were allegedly used for flying. Twenty-two jars were tested on animals and even on one old woman. All of the contents were declared false and fake.

Sabbats: Where and When

Mountains and wooded areas were popular locations for a sabbat, but Boguet reported that witches told him they sometimes met in meadows and courtyards. He also thought water was necessary, so that the witches could beat the water with their wands to cause hail. Other authors mentioned cross-roads, churches, and town squares. Often the location would be specifically named by an accused witch.

Of course, night was the most common time to meet, considering that secrecy was necessary. There was also a long association between night and darkness with fear, evil, and death. The sabbat usually started at midnight in some secluded location. The gathering only lasted until the cock crowed, at which point every evidence vanished. Not only is the crowing of the rooster a sign of sunrise and daylight, but the crowing cock is related to a biblical story. In the Garden of Gethsemane, Jesus told his disciple Peter that 'before the cock crow twice, thou shalt deny me thrice' (*Mark* 14:30). This connected the call of the rooster with apostasy or the renunciation of faith. There was no fixed day for the sabbat, just whenever Satan commanded it, but there were often associations with the Ember Days.

Sabbat Activities

The illustration by the Polish engraver Jan Ziarnko, which appeared in the second edition of Pierre de Lancre's *Tableau de l'Inconstance des Mauvais Anges et Demons* or *A Display of the Inconstancy of Evil Angels and Devils* in 1613, sums up what witches did at sabbats. [See Image #12, Illustration of sabbat by Jan Ziarnko, in *Tableau de l'Inconstance*] Dancing was an activity engaged in by all levels of society in all areas of Europe. It was a common activity at village celebrations such as church ales and festivals, as well as a popular entertainment in royal courts. Nonetheless, the demonologists managed to make dancing at the sabbat evil. Some writers believed that dancing opened a window to other vices. The English Puritans were particularly adamant about the evils of dancing. Remy pointed out that the Israelites danced in a ring around the golden calf on their journey out of Egypt, thereby linking dancing with idolatry. At the sabbat, sometimes participants danced in a ring back to back and to the left, which Remy compared to the Druids, yet another inference to pagan (and therefore demonic) practice. In addition to being an inversion, dancing back to back, as well as wearing masks, was for the purpose of concealing the identity of the dancers so that they could not identify each other if caught. Obviously, this did not work very well, since giving the names of others seen at the sabbat was what led to the large witch hunts. Occasionally, witches danced in couples or singly. Remy compared the frenzy of the dance to the maenads, the female followers of Dionysus. Interesting that he had the means of comparison, having witnessed neither event. Sometimes the dancers were naked, which was another sexual perversion. Music with pipes, violins, lyres, and drums was provided by other participants. Satan sometimes played the flute, which would appear to be another reference back to the cult of Dionysus or perhaps even the Greek god Pan. Pan had given his name to the pan flute, made from hollow reeds. An unusual testimony from a young boy said that the witches went to the sabbat dressed as gypsies and danced to the sound of a tambourine that was 'tuneless'. Gypsies lived on the periphery of society and were considered exotic (among other things). This just goes to show how people drew from their own experiences and cultures when pressed to make confessions.

Feasting, another common element of any village festival, was also a feature of the sabbat. The food was often described as either tasteless or so foul in smell and appearance that a person was 'compelled to spit it out at once'.[6] Bread was seldom offered because of its significance in Christianity as a symbol of Christ's body. When it was present, it was made from black flour ground from the bones of unbaptised babies. Repulsive items on the menu included the bodies of hanged men, the hearts of unbaptised children, and dead cats. The Basque witches allegedly dug up the corpses of their fellow witches, which they took to the next sabbat to be served roasted, boiled, or raw. The heart was reserved for the Devil. No salt was allowed because of its importance in biblical texts and Christian ceremonies. Salt had a long history as a symbol of immortality and purity, based on its preservative properties. In the Catholic church, salt was mixed with the water used in baptisms and exorcisms. Most of those accused of being at the sabbat said they went away as hungry and thirsty as they came; the food did not satisfy the appetite. This sounds like a metaphor for devil-worship not satisfying the soul. Cannibalism was sometimes an element of the banquets. Remy attributes this to the customs of the Bacchi, who were called flesh-eaters by ancient authors, which demonstrates that the demonologists were making mental comparisons with the ancient cult of Dionysus. One demonologist said instead of wine the celebrants drank 'clots of black blood',[7] but alcohol was not a prominent aspect. The celebrants were never described as drunk. Did the demonologists not want to give them an excuse for their bad behaviour?

Sexual orgies, including incest, were an integral aspect of the sabbat. Occasionally, sodomy and homosexuality were specifically mentioned. In addition to sex with other humans, witches had intercourse with demons. Demons took the form of women for the men (succubi) and the form of men for the women (incubi). Since the demons also took the form of animals, bestiality was also included in the 'monstrous crimes against God and nature'.[8] Sex with the Devil himself was understood as part of the pact or covenant made between the witch and Satan. Satan sometimes appeared 'in the form of a black man, sometimes in that of some animal, as a dog or a cat or a ram'.[9] One woman reported that the demon's penis was 'as cold as ice and a good finger's length, but not so thick as that of a man'.[10] Others said that the Devil's member was allegedly 'so huge and so excessively rigid' that it caused a great deal of pain.[11] Many women described the experience as rape rather than an encounter with a lover. However, a French witch, Jeanne Harvillier, confessed that she started having sex with the Devil at the age of twelve and continued until the time she was accused of witchcraft at the age of fifty. She said the Devil appeared to her whenever she wished, rather than at his desire. He appeared as a gentleman, with spurs, boots, a sword, and a horse waiting at the door.

In England, where the sabbat was not a prominent aspect of witchcraft, the sexual encounters with the Devil were not as frequent nor as traumatic as reported on the Continent. In 1645, Elizabeth Clarke told the self-styled witch-finder general Matthew Hopkins that 'shee had had carnall copulation with the Devill six or seven yeares; and that he would appeare to her three or foure times in a weeke at her bed side, and goe to bed to her, and lye with her halfe a night together in the shape of a proper Gentleman, with a laced band, having the whole proportion of a man, and would say to her, Besse I must lye with you, and shee did never deny him.'[12] This account makes it sound as if she had the option of refusing him. The fact that he stayed with her for half the night makes it sound more like a romance than a rape. And maybe just for the fun of it, she told Hopkins that the Devil appeared 'like a tall, proper, black haired gentleman, a properer man then [*sic*] your selfe'.[13]

Animal sacrifice was another common element of the sabbat. Sacrifice had been part of classical religion and Judaism, as well as pagan practices. After the crucifixion of Jesus, sacrifice was no longer necessary according to Christian theology. The continuation of sacrifice was viewed as a rejection of Christianity and was linked to pre-Christian pagan beliefs. The sacrificed animal, usually a sheep or a cock, was usually black, following the custom of the ancient Greeks and Romans. The colour black, like night, had been associated with evil at least since the classical era. The sacrifice was viewed as both a gift to the Devil, therefore a form of worship or adoration, and also a payment, similar to the obligation of a vassal to his manorial or feudal lord. This added a level of treason to the heresy. The aspect of feudal fealty was also demonstrated in the kiss of homage. In imitation of a royal court, the chief demon sat in a high throne as the witches fell prone at his feet with their hands behind their backs. The *osculum infame* was also part of the adoration of the Devil. The supplicants kissed the posterior of the Devil when he was in the form of a very smelly goat.

Another form of offering was that of giving candles to the Devil, which burned with a blue flame. Del Rio stated that the tapers were made from pitch and umbilical cords. Remy described a similar light made from the right arm and shoulder of the disinterred corpse of an infant. When the witch wanted to poison someone at night, the fingers of the 'candle' burned 'with a blue sulphurous flame' without burning up the flesh.[14] This appears to be a version of the 'Hand of Glory', which was made from the hand of a hanged criminal. Either the left or the right hand was supposed to be wrapped in a piece of the man's winding sheet, then pickled in a jar for fifteen days with salt, pepper, and saltpetre. All the fat was extracted from the hand in a furnace, or by the heat of the sun, and then combined with virgin wax and sesame from Lapland. In the Pappenheimer case, discussed in Chapter 7, the candles were made from the right hands of foetuses, whose mothers the family had allegedly murdered and disemboweled. Apparently, the spirits of the unborn babies floated around and could tell the thieves if anyone came close. Thieves' candles could also make a person invisible or open locks.

Harming children was one of the most common accusations against a witch at the village level, but the demonologists took killing babies to a whole new level. Since the most logical way to obtain aborted foetuses and dead babies would be from a midwife or wise woman who assisted at birthing, midwives were frequently accused in demonological treatises. Boguet stated that midwives — who were witches — offered newborn babies to the Devil before killing them 'by thrusting a large pin into their brains' through the crown of the head.[15] The dead infants were then offered as a sacrifice to the Devil. In the *Malleus*, Kramer told the story of a child taken from its cradle to be murdered by witches, so they could drink its blood and eat it. When not murdering and eating babies, witches offered them up to Lucifer by the kitchen fire in a sort of mock baptism. The other reason for infanticide was for producing ointments. Aborted foetuses were boiled up in cauldrons to make unguents. The witches anointed themselves with this brew when they flew to the sabbat. Baby bones were ground up for flour. In a pinch, a witch could dig up a recently dead infant and melt the body and reduce the bone to ashes, which was especially good for damaging fruit trees. Decoctions made out of toads would also ruin fruit crops. The ointments made at the sabbat were also used to harm cattle and people.

Groups of witches had more power to do weather magic than individual witches. To raise hailstorms, they beat water with black wands 'until there arose a dense vapour and smoke'.[16] In some cases, they threw a particular powder that Satan had given them into the air or the water. Remy reported that many witches confessed that they were enveloped by the cloud raised by their actions and 'borne up on high' to steer the cloud where they wanted it to go.[17] Boguet thought that Satan also used women's hair to cause hail. The witches gave their hair to him as part of their pledge of loyalty. He cut it up and mixed it with 'exhalations from which he forms hail'.[18]

The North Berwick witches, who were investigated by James VI of Scotland, also did weather magic, among other things. On Halloween of 1590, more than 100 witches sailed into North Berwick in sieves. Tricky. They were trumpeted into the church where they were met by the Devil in the form of a small, black monster in gown and hat. He had a nose like the beak of an eagle, burning eyes, hairy hands and legs, claws on his fingers, and feet like a griffon. The witches gave him the obligatory *osculum infame* and then proceeded to feast and drink. The highlight of the evening was the desecration of some graves in the churchyard. The witches removed fingers, toes, and noses from the decaying bodies. Satan instructed them to take the joints home, dry them, and grind them into powder to do evil.

At a subsequent meeting, they were given instructions on how to make a poison out of roasted toads, stale urine, and snake skin, with which they were going to poison King James's bed linens. They had also made a wax poppet of the king that was going to be melted in the fire. Now comes the weather magic. They 'tooke a Cat and christened it, and afterward bound to each parte of that Cat, the cheefest partes of a dead man', and threw them into the sea.[19] The intent was to raise a storm to destroy James's fleet on the way back from Denmark. And, indeed, he did have trouble on the high seas.

In general, the witches' sabbat was the ultimate inversion of Christianity, particularly Catholicism. Every form of perversion and deviance imaginable were included. Boguet and de Lancre believed that an inverted Catholic Mass was celebrated at the sabbat. The elements of the 'Black Mass' were symbolic. The altar was covered with a black cloth and decorated with pictures of Satan. The host was a black-coloured slice of turnip or something that looked like the sole of a shoe with the Devil's portrait on it. On other occasions, the host and the sacramental wine were desecrated and the cross was trampled on. Holy water was imitated by using Satan's urine, which was sprinkled on the participants. (It seems that sometimes the demonologists forgot that the Devil did not have a physical body.) The liquid in the chalice was bitter and left a freezing sensation around the heart. Elaborate descriptions of the Mass included hymns sung in tuneless voices, sermons about enduring poverty and suffering, and prayers to the Devil.

A relatively late report of several private Black Masses was part of the so-called 'Affair of the Poisons'. During the reign of King Louis XIV, an investigation of some poisoning cases between 1677 and 1682 led to many accusations of witchcraft and murder. A midwife, nicknamed La Voisin, was among the fortune-tellers, apothecaries, and alchemists accused of selling poisons to members of the royal court. During her confession, she charged one of the king's mistresses, Madame de Montespan, of participating in Black Masses with her and a priest, Étienne Guibourg, in order to influence the king's affections. La Voisin's daughter Marie supplied a wealth of detail concerning the masses. The priest performed the rite on the stomach of a naked woman, who lay on a mattress between two stools with her head hanging backward and her legs hanging down. The cross and the chalice were balanced on the woman's belly. Holy water was mixed with salt and sulphur. Yellow candles made from the fat of a hanged man were used on the altar. Instead of wine, the participants used the blood of a white pigeon. On one occasion, Marie claimed that she saw the priest cut the throat of a newly-born premature baby with a penknife and drain the blood into a chalice, which he proceeded to consecrate. The guts were ripped out so that they could be distilled for some other evil purpose. In his confession, the priest supplemented the information. He said he sacrificed to the demons Astaroth and Amodeus. Instead of kissing the altar, he kissed the woman's private parts. The priest consecrated the host on her vagina and then inserted a fragment of it inside her. Afterwards the priest had sex with the woman. On another occasion, the priest confessed that he celebrated mass on the afterbirth of an aborted infant. La Voisin was burned at the stake for witchcraft along with more than thirty other people.

This is a rare example of an alleged Black Mass, which happened after the height of the witchcraft persecutions. It was not part of a full-blown sabbat, but was a private affair. It is possible that the participants were actually trying to perform magic and borrowed ideas liberally from the accounts of the demonologists. There are also elements of ceremonial magic in the proceedings. The description of the ritual was horrific, but there were no supernatural elements included, such as shape-shifting or flying. The aspect of using a naked woman as an altar would be taken up later by Aleister Crowley, as part of worshipping the spirit of creation. The twentieth-century founder of the American Church of Satan, Anton LaVey, certainly modelled his Black Masses on similar patterns, especially the aspect of performing Mass on a naked woman. [See Image #15, Photograph of Altar for a Black Mass performed by Anton LaVey] The practices of the Church of Satan are neither Satan worship nor pagan witchcraft, so are outside the boundaries of our discussion.

The Carnivalesque

The demonologists discussing the sabbat drew on classical models and folkloric elements borrowed from popular culture. Under the pressure of interrogation and torture, the accused witch might also draw on elements of folklore such as the Wild Hunt and the realm of fairies. However, there were other more mundane events from which to borrow. Festivals and carnivals provided easily accessible examples of excess for the accused to draw on during a confession. Perhaps they also served as models for the demonologists to shape the demonic sabbat. De Lancre's description of the sabbat, gleaned from over 500 witnesses in the Basque region, painted the image of an extravagant celebration comparable to a wedding or a court festivity. He said the sabbat was like a merchant's fair of a hundred thousand people.

One of the reasons that the activities at the sabbat appeared so wrong to the men who were recording the alleged proceedings was that they were based on what was familiar. The sabbat was not an exotic and strange ritual, like Muslim or Jewish practices. It was, quite simply, an inversion of the ordinary. Village festivals, such as weddings and church ales, as well as annual events such as carnival were drawn on to construct the sabbat. Some critics of popular culture painted public festivities with the same brush as the sabbat: the Devil's playground. Proponents of the Protestant Reformation frequently criticised drinking, dancing, singing, music, gambling, masquerading, and anything else that might be fun as opportunities for the Devil to take hold of one's soul. The activities engaged in on these common occasions were then further denigrated when transferred to the sabbat.

The underlying theme in descriptions of the sabbat was inversion: discordant music, nasty food, backward dancing, and taboo sex. Ritual inversion was very familiar to the premodern population. The world turned upside down was a common theme in early modern art and literature. From the traditional 'lord of misrule' manorial celebrations to pre-Lent carnival to the local charivari or skimmington, a period of temporary disorder and upheaval of social status and values was allowed. The lowly peasant was elevated to the place of the lord, the foolish were consulted by the wise, and men dressed like women. These popular festivals were first and foremost a form of entertainment and release for the masses.

Throughout Europe, carnival was a period of excess prior to the abstinence of Lent, which led up to Easter. It stood in contrast to the hard life of the peasantry and the hardships of the coming winter. It began in late December or early January. Dancing and singing in the street was part of the excitement. Over-consumption of food, drink, and festivities continued throughout the carnival period. There was more than the usual amount of meat available at that time, because livestock that could not be kept over the winter due to lack of food were traditionally slaughtered. In fact, the term carnival comes from the Spanish word for meat or flesh, *carne*. In parody of carnival, the sabbat banquet frequently consisted of 'the flesh of animals which have died … a cat, a black kid, a dunghill-cock'.[20] Given the excessive drinking of alcohol and the general air of revelry during carnival, it is not surprising that this was also a period of intense sexual activity. Historians measure this by the number of births that occurred nine months later. Sexuality was also a theme of carnival. In at least one instance, a wooden phallus the size of a horse's was paraded down the street. Unmarried young women pulled ploughs; 'ploughing' was a euphemism for sexual intercourse.

Masquerading was another element of carnival festivities. The Devil was one of the most popular figures for this purpose. Other popular masques were wild animals, sometimes complete with horns. People not only dressed up in disguise, but sometimes acted like the character they were portraying. The mask or costume allowed the person to pretend to be someone else, an inversion of the everyday self. Under the cover of anonymity, repressed aggression was allowed to surface. Physical and verbal violence were normal parts of the festivities. Innocent animals, such as cocks, cats, and dogs, were sometimes beaten or stoned to death. When violence got out of hand, even murder became a part of the proceedings. The memories of a carnival would have provided plenty of material for a tortured witchcraft suspect to draw on for a confession concerning the chaos of the sabbat. Under the duress of interrogation, perhaps the accused's masked neighbours transformed into demons. In one case, a 15-year-old young man in Augsburg confessed that the Devil appeared to him as a man in black, and gave him nuts, pears, and coins. However, the friends that were with him at the time said the man was a carnival character not Satan. This demonstrates the fine line between imagination and reality. The charged atmosphere of carnival is evident in Pieter Bruegel the Elder's painting *The Fight between Carnival and Lent* (1559), which also depicts the more formal procession of floats that took place during the last few days of the festivities. [See Image #16, *The Fight between Carnival and Lent*] Both witchcraft suspects and the demonologists discussing them could have borrowed elements of carnival to be inserted into descriptions of sabbats. The literature of demonology was not so much a new imaginative world as it was a borrowing of pre-existing themes.

In addition to carnival, there were several other festivals that employed the theme of inversion and could have been drawn on for material for the sabbat. The festival of Corpus Christi honoured the Eucharist. Processions through the streets included floats with fantastical figures such as dragons, which represented the Beast of the Apocalypse. People dressed in costumes and performed mystery plays. Demons engaged in mock battles with angels. The Devil was of particular importance in a St John's Eve festival in Chaumont, France. Men portraying demons terrorised the countryside, and were interpreted as Satan's active power in the world. The purpose of the activities appears to be the same as it was for the sabbat: beware the power of Satan!

The clergy themselves had parodied the Devil in the late middle ages. The historian Stuart Clark sums up the proceedings:

> 'they intoned meaningless liturgy, sang in dissonances, rang bells to symbolize folly, brayed and howled like asses, made indecent gestures and contortions, wore hideous animal masks, repeated prayers in gibberish, cursed rather than blessed their 'congregations', mocked the sermon with fatuous imitations, parodied high office with inversions of place, title, role, and costume, and negated the sacredness of holy places with dicing, running, feasts, and even nudity.'[21]

As Clark points out, there was little to choose from between the burlesque follies of the clergy and the demonic profanities of the sabbat.

Inversion was also used as ridicule during a charivari or skimmington, also known as rough music. [See Image #17, Print titled 'Hudibras encounters the Skimmington'] Communities used loud exhibitions to publicly disapprove of a person's moral behaviour, usually in relation to marriage. Wife beating, living together without the benefit of matrimony, an older man marrying a much younger wife, or child abuse could draw out the neighbours, who banged pots and pans, sang bawdy songs, and cross-dressed to indicate their dislike of the situation. The subject of the demonstration, or his effigy, was sometimes made to ride backwards on a horse or donkey. The symbolic inversion of riding backward found its way into images of witchcraft as well. The German artist Albrecht Dürer and his student Hans Baldung Grien both depicted witches riding backward to the sabbat on goats. [See Image #10, Chiaroscuro woodcut of 'The Witches', Hans Baldung Grien]

During periods of temporary inversion, the community came together, eliding the divisions of status and wealth. These controlled periods of social disorder demonstrated the danger to society when gender roles and social roles were flouted. In anthropological terms, festivals of misrule and inversion served to reinforce the hierarchy of the premodern world. Temporary licence was followed by a return to the status quo. The inversion or mocking of the conventional world actually reinforced the values of that world. Of course, festivals of misrule could erupt into riot or rebellion, but under normal circumstances traditional values were reaffirmed not undermined. However, when the social order was already in question, in times of extreme unrest, the carnivalesque was not condoned. If hostility to authorities was already rampant due to bad harvests, increased taxes, or religious strife, the excitement of celebration was at risk of turning into a riot. In an era characterised by social disorder, the sabbat represented the extreme of the carnival. The danger of civil and religious disorder was frightening in an already topsy-turvy world.

The inversions of carnival and other festivals were readily adaptable to the perversions of the sabbat. The difference between carnival and the sabbat was that the carnival was allowed by authorities and had a definite beginning and end. Order was restored at the end of the frenzy, which was public and visible. The sabbat, on the other hand, was an independent and secretive rejection of the normal social order. The sabbat was not under any controls, ecclesiastical or secular. Witches were like rebels or rioters, who were trying to overthrow both church and state. The imagined witches' sabbat did not serve the purposes of the ruling elite by reinforcing social values; it frightened them. Both religious and state authorities were threatened by a sect of witches capable of wreaking havoc on crops as well as individuals. Secular festivals of misrule pointed out what might be changed in society, thereby questioning the culture or norms. But the sabbat was supposedly questioning the sacred. To those who were the guardians of the sacred, there was no room for interrogation. The attention to detail in the depictions of the sabbat reflects the creators' concerns with the importance of those details, especially against the background noise of the Reformation when the particulars of ritual, costumes, and format of religion were under question.

To demonologists, attendance at the sabbat was a sign that the person had made a covenant with the Devil. They believed that Satan attempted to entice and bind the participants. According to Remy, the sabbat was a party that the Devil threw 'in order to attract to himself more numerous and more devoted followers'.[22] Once the base passions of people were satisfied, Satan could lure them into more wrong-doing. At the sabbat, the witches renewed their vows to the Devil, thereby damning their souls to perdition. The witches had to render an account of all their wrongdoings since the last meeting, which appears to be a parody of Catholic confession. The Devil encouraged his followers to avenge themselves against their neighbours, and he gave them powders or ointments to cause harm. For Satan, the sabbat was an opportunity to plot against the rest of the human race. It did not matter whether or not the person had performed any sorcery or *maleficium*. The homage to the Devil and the intimacy with demons was proof enough that the person was a witch and should be punished with death.

Consequences

There is absolutely no proof that a celebration of Satanists took place in the premodern period. There is also no evidence that a pre-Christian pagan

1. Lead Curse Tablet (*c.* 1–399 CE), currently housed in the British Museum

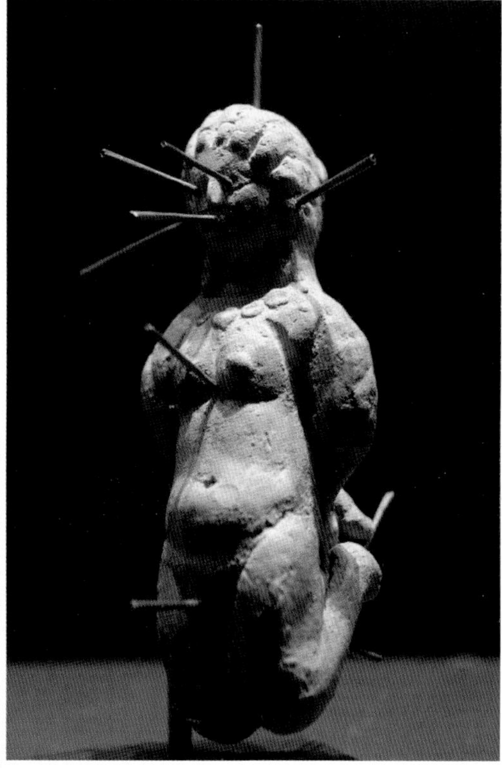

2. Clay and bronze 'Voodoo' Doll discovered in Egypt (4th century CE), currently housed in the Louvre Museum

3. Copper engraving of the 'Temptation of St Anthony', Martin Schöngauer (*c.* 1480–90), currently housed in The Metropolitan Museum of Art, New York

4. Miniature illustrating Waldensians worshipping the Devil in the form of a goat and flying through the air in *Traité du crisme de Vauderie,* Johannes Tinctoris (*c*. 1460), currently housed in the Bibliothèque Nationale Paris

ROBIN
Good-Fellovv,
His Mad Prankes,and merry
Iests,
Full of honest Mirth, and is a fit
Medicine for Melancholy.

LONDON,
Printed for F. *Groue* dwelling on Snow-hill
ouer against the Sarasens head. 1628.

5. Woodcut on title page of Anon., *Robin Good-Fellow, His Mad Prankes, and Merry Iests* (London, 1628)

6. Detail of silver Gundestrup Cauldron (*c.* 150–0 BCE), currently housed in the National Museum of Denmark, Copenhagen

7. Woodcut of *osculum infame* in *Compendium Maleficarum*, Francesco Maria Guazzo (1608)

8. Illustration in the margin of *Le Champion des Dames*, Martin Le Franc (1451)

9. Illustration of Templars being Burned at the Stake, from an anonymous chronicle, *From the Creation of the World until 1384* (1384)

10. Chiaroscuro woodcut of 'The Witches', Hans Baldung Grien (1510)

TRACTAT
Von Bekanntnuß der Zauberer vnd Hexen. Ob vnd wie viel denselben zu glauben.
Anfänglich durch den Hochwürdigen Herrn Petrum Binsfeldium, Trierischen Suffraganien/vnd der H. Schrifft Doctorn/kurtz vnd summarischer Weiß in Latein beschrieben.
Jetzt aber der Warheit zu stewr in vnser Teutsche Sprach vertiret/durch den Wolgelerten M. Bernhart Vogel/deß löblichen Stattgerichts in München/Assessorn.
EXOD. XXII. CAP.
Die Zauberer solt du nicht leben lassen.

Gedruckt zu München bey Adam Berg.
ANNO DOMINI M. D. XCII.
Mit Röm: Kay: May: Freyheit/nit nachzudrucken.

11. Frontispiece, *Tractatus de Confessionibus Maleficorum et Sagarum* or *Confessions of Male and Female Witches*, Peter Binsfeld (1589)

12. Illustration of sabbat by Jan Ziarnko, in *Tableau de l'Inconstance des Mauvais Anges et Demons* or *A Display of the Inconstancy of Evil Angels and Devils*, Pierre de Lancre (1613)

13. Witch receiving the Devil's Mark, in *Compendium Maleficarum*, Francesco Maria Guazzo (1608)

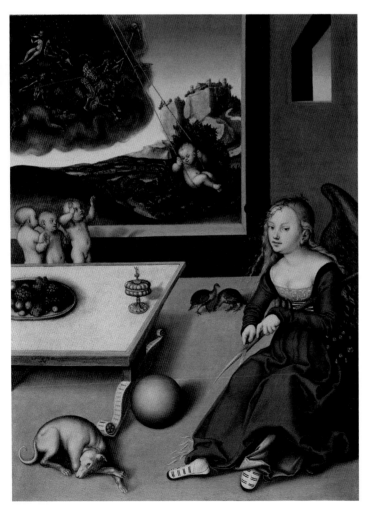

14. One in a series of paintings titled *Melancholia*, Lucas Cranach the Elder (1532), currently housed in the Unterlinden Museum, Colmar, France

15. Photograph of Altar for a Black Mass performed by Anton la Vey (1966)

16. *The Fight between Carnival and Lent,* Pieter Bruegel the Elder (1559), currently housed in Kunsthistorisches Museum, Vienna

17. Print titled 'Hudibras encounters the Skimmington', William Hogarth (1726)

18. Engraving by Jan Luyken of the burning of a Dutch Anabaptist, Anneken Hendriks in Amsterdam in 1571, *Martyrs Mirror* (second edition,1685)

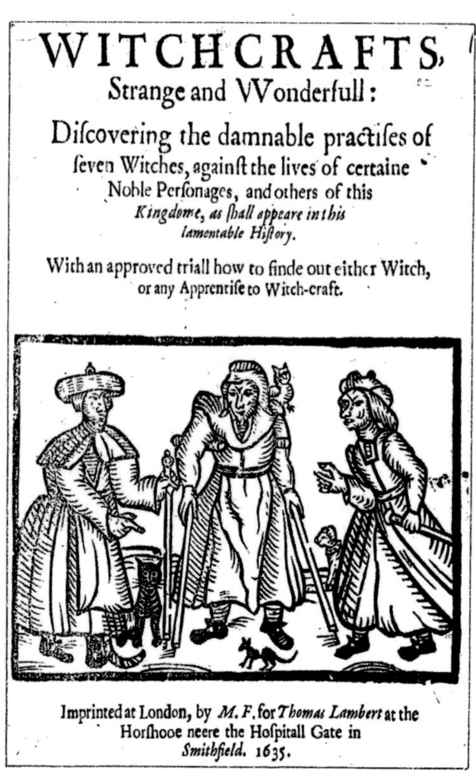

WITCHCRAFTS,
Strange and VVonderfull:
Diſcovering the damnable practiſes of
ſeven Witches, againſt the lives of certaine
Noble Perſonages, and others of this
*Kingdome, as ſhall appeare in this
lamentable Hiſtory.*

With an approved triall how to finde out either Witch,
or any Apprentiſe to Witch-craft.

Imprinted at London, by *M. F.* for *Thomas Lambert* at the
Horſhooe neere the Hoſpitall Gate in
Smithfield. 1635.

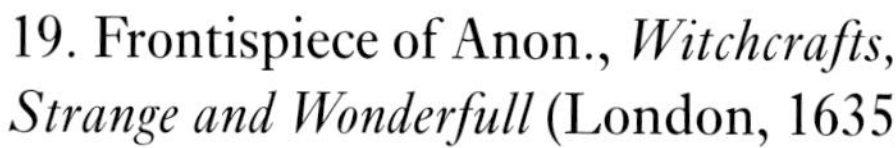

19. Frontispiece of Anon., *Witchcrafts, Strange and Wonderfull* (London, 1635)

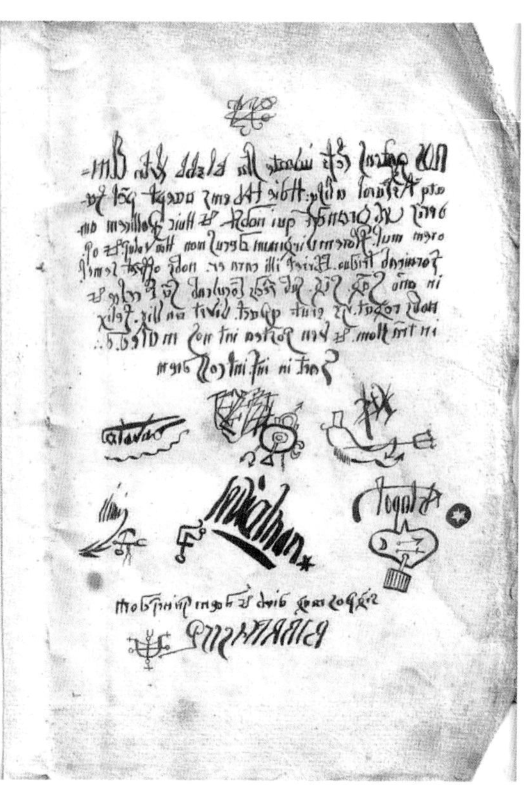

20. Pact allegedly signed by Urbain Grandier and several demons (*c.* 1634), currently housed in the Bibiotheque Nationale, Paris

21. Joan Prentice's familiar in Anon., *The Apprehension and confession of three notorious Witches* (London, 1589)

22. Woodcut of swimming a witch from Anon., *Witches Apprehended, Examined and Executed, for notable villanies by them committed both by Land and Water* (London, 1613)

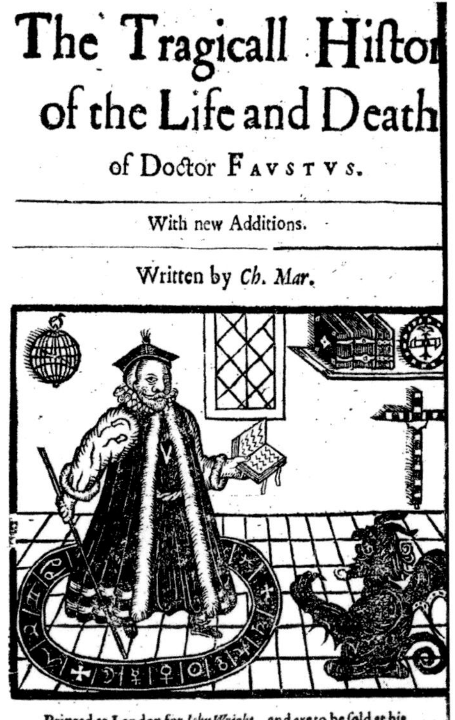

The Tragicall Hiſto
of the Life and Death
of Doctor FAVSTVS.

With new Additions.

Written by *Ch. Mar.*

Printed at London for *Iohn Wright*, and are to be ſold at his ſhop without Newgate, 1624.

23. Frontispiece, *The Tragicall History of the Life and Death of Doctor Faustus*, Christopher Marlowe (London, 1624)

24. 'How to inclose a spirit in a crystal', in *Discoverie of Witchcraft*, Reginald Scot (1584)

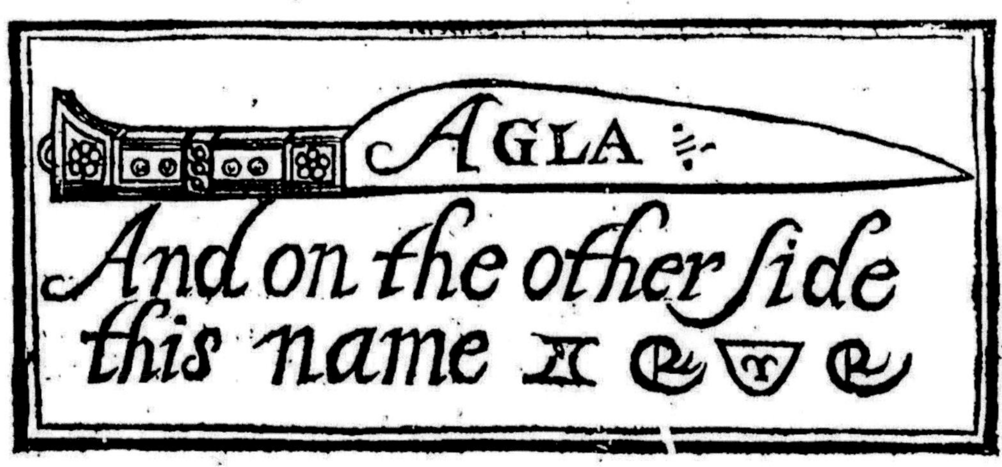

25. Conjuring Knife, in *Discoverie of Witchcraft*, Reginald Scot (1584)

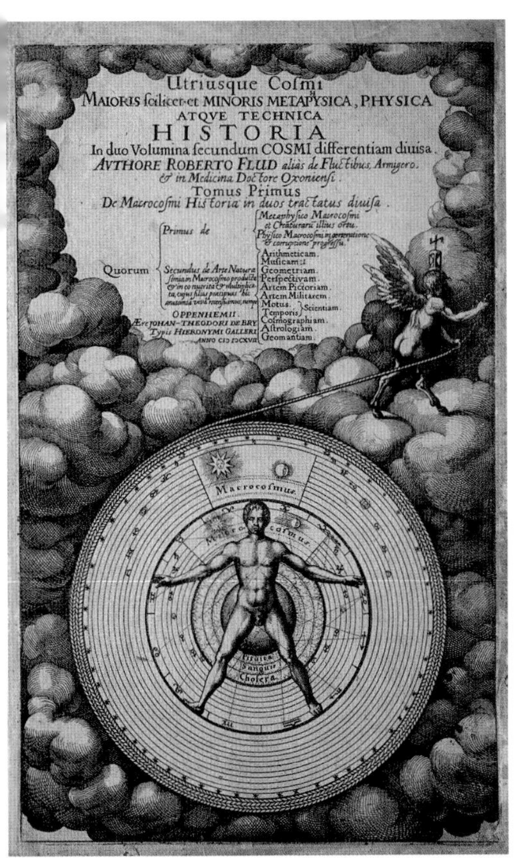

26. Illustration of macrocosm and microcosm on the title page of *Utriusque cosmi maioris scilicet et minoris metaphysica, physica atqve technica historia*, Robert Fludd (1617–19)

27. Woodcut of 'Matthew Hopkins Witch-finder General', in *The Discovery of Witches*, Matthew Hopkins (1647)

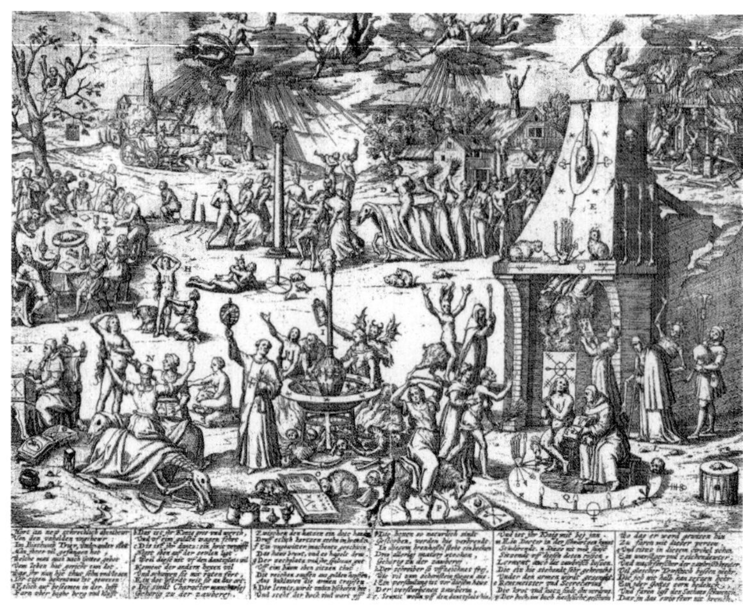

28. Image of sabbat from leaflet titled *Trier Hexentanzplatz* (1594)

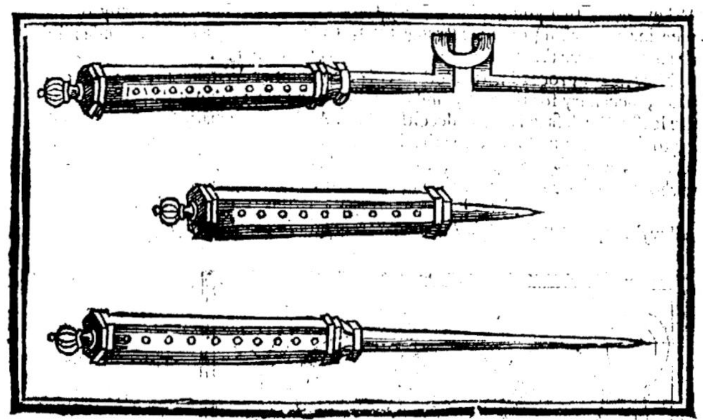

29. Trick Bodkin from *Discoverie of Witchcraft*, Reginald Scot (1584)

30. Sketch of a heretic wearing a *sanbenito*, Francisco de Goya (*c.* 1810), currently housed in Museo del Prado, Madrid

31. Painting of an *auto de fé* held in Plaza Mayor, Madrid, in 1680, Francisco Rizi (1683), currently housed in Museo del Prado, Madrid

32. 'The Love Spell', Unknown Flemish Artist (*c.* 1470), currently housed in Museum der bildenden Künste, Leipzig

33. Depiction of Satirical Witch in *Credulity, Superstition, and Fanaticism*, William Hogarth (1762)

34. Illustration of the idol Baphomet, in *Dogme et Rituel de la Haute Magie*, Eliphas Lévi (1854)

35. The 'Devil card' from the Arthur Waite's Tarot deck (1910)

36. A female Paleolithic figurine known as the Venus of Willendorf, found in Willendorf, Austria (24,000 BCE–22,000 BCE), currently housed in the Naturhistorisches Museum, Vienna

group continued to practise its beliefs and was simply misunderstood and labelled as witches. Testimony from the *benandanti* of Friuli and the Sicilian fairy ladies indicates that some people believed that they travelled at night in spirit, but by their own testimony, they were not devil-worshippers. They were either fighting witches for the fertility of the crops or helping people by obtaining cures for illness. The fear of heresy raised by real Christian sects in the middle ages, such as the Cathars and the Waldensians, caused both ecclesiastical and secular authorities to become hyper-vigilant in the hunt for the newly-revealed cult of Satanists. Witches were being burned at the stake at the same time that both Protestants and Catholics were burning Anabaptists, a break-away Christian group that had been forced into becoming an underground sect. [See Image #18, Engraving by Jan Luyken of the burning of a Dutch Anabaptist] The imagined sabbat, where congregations of sorcerers came together, added another layer of fear to witchcraft beliefs. A diabolical underground sect was much more threatening than the solitary village witch. Belief in the sabbat and the fear that it raised contributed to a more serious effort to find and exterminate the devil-worshippers.

In conjunction with the concept of the sabbat was the condoning of the use of torture to interrogate suspected witches. The accused were pressured into naming others whom they had seen at the sabbat, which led to the torture and interrogation of new suspects, who were, in turn, tortured and interrogated, *ad infinitum*. In an outbreak in Ellwangen, Germany, one woman named twenty-four others whom she had seen at the sabbat. Another denounced twenty-nine. Some of the accusations did not result in death for witchcraft at the time, but surfaced more than twenty years later. Besides intensifying a panic in one area, sometimes alleged witches named people from other areas, thereby spreading the witch hunt like the plague. The large trials that occurred because of the belief in the sabbat resulted in unlikely subjects getting accused. The authorities started to doubt their ability to correctly identify witches. What historians refer to as a 'crisis of confidence' brought the judicial aspect of witchcraft accusations to a halt. The belief in the reality of witchcraft did not end, but a particular panic would come to a conclusion. This would eventually contribute to the end of the persecution era.

The concept of the full-blown sabbat was largely the product of demonologists. But the intellectual elites cannot be held responsible for all of the witch trials in Europe. Once a person was accused of witchcraft, the concepts formulated by the judges and inquisitors had an impact on the trial.

The average person was not concerned with heresy but with more practical matters. Most charges against suspected witches came from neighbours, who were concerned about personal, community conflict rather than any diabolical activities. In the next chapter, we turn our attention to witchcraft beliefs and practitioners in popular culture.

Chapter 5

By Flower and Fruit, Popular Culture

In 1582, Elizabeth Bennett of Essex was accused of having two familiar spirits: Suckin, which looked like a black dog, and Lierd, which appeared as a red lion. At first, she denied that the two spirits slept in a pot of wool under the stairs of her house. But eventually, without torture, she confessed to sending the spirits to kill her neighbour's wife and cattle. Elizabeth explained to the magistrate why she was so angry with William Byet and his wife. In the three years that they had been next door neighbours, they had 'fell out sundry and oftentimes'.[1] Mr Byet called her 'old whore, and other lewde speaches' as well as 'olde trot and olde witche, and did banne and curse [her] and her Cattell'. On one occasion, she told him that his curses would 'light upon' him. Shortly thereafter, three of his cows died. But Elizabeth claimed that he 'beat the saide Cowe in such sorte' that she believed he was responsible for its death. She also said that Mrs Byet beat Elizabeth's swine, and killed one by thrusting a pitchfork in its side. One can easily see why Elizabeth would have reason for revenge. But why was she accused of witchcraft in the death of Mrs Byet and the cattle? Why did she not accuse Mr Byet of trying to curse her? And Mrs Byet of killing her pig? Although the role of the familiars was explored in great detail in the deposition, there was no mention of attending sabbats or devil-worship. Neither was Elizabeth accused of casting spells or brewing potions to do *maleficium*. Unfortunately, Elizabeth's story is not uncommon. A poor, old woman, with few resources to defend herself, was an easy target to blame in the face of misfortune.

***

Between 1450 and 1750, there were approximately 110,000 witchcraft trials throughout Europe. Roughly half of those cases ended with the execution of the accused. The peak of the persecutions was between 1560 and 1660 when Europe was sorting out its religious reformations and associated conflicts. There is no evidence to suggest that accusations of witchcraft were used to play out religious squabbles between Catholics and Protestants during the

Reformation. Nonetheless, religious disputes were the background noise of the period, which involved a lot of discourse about the power of the Devil. During this period, a few genuine 'witch-crazes' with mass trials took place. For example, in the small town of Ellwangen, Germany, approximately 400 people were executed as witches between 1611 and 1618.

Without a doubt, demonologists and clergy intensified the fear of witchcraft and shaped the concept of the devil-worshipping witch, who flew to the sabbat, had sex with the Devil, and roasted babies. As accusations increased in the early modern era, these concepts were increasingly reinforced by judicial and ecclesiastical players, and subsequently reiterated by the accused themselves under the duress of torture and the inquisitorial practice of leading questions. But the largest number of witch trials were a result of accusations from within a community, as opposed to charges instigated from above. In other words, we cannot hold the church and state responsible for the full extent of witchcraft prosecutions.

All levels of premodern society believed in the supernatural. The early modern world was populated with many beings, including angels, demons, ghosts, goblins, and fairies. Even those who spoke out against the witchcraft trials still believed in the existence and the power of the Devil. Medieval Christianity had not lessened pagan 'superstitions' but had replaced them with Christian 'superstitions', such as the Eucharist, baptism, and saints' relics, to name just a few. There was also a huge body of folklore, including fairy tales and legends, which supported belief in magic. The ubiquitous belief in the supernatural allowed for belief in a witch's power. We have a great deal of evidence that people in the premodern era employed various techniques, recipes, and charms that would fall short of scientific or medical approval today. Sometimes these methods were considered witchcraft, but not always. Folk magic was not inherently evil. The intent of the procedure was more important.

Outside of a few witch hunts that were instigated by the state, the majority of witchcraft accusations arose from the village level. The common people who initiated accusations were more concerned with the results of the alleged witch's actions or intentions than with her methods. *Maleficium*, the ability to cause harm by supernatural means, was not associated with devil-worship. Women, men, and children were not accused of witchcraft because they held heretical opinions. The accusers did not need theological explanations or diabolical influence to suspect a witch. In popular culture, the underlying reasons for witchcraft accusations were quite different from the demonological ideas of a witch. Suspects were accused of causing illness or individual misfortune. Once an accusation was made, the rest of the community came forward to testify against the accused. Analyses of these testimonies support the theory that accusations of witchcraft were often rooted in personal conflict or were used as a means of resolving a village quarrel. Witches filled an anthropological purpose as scapegoats, to allay human fear and grief in an age of constant crisis. Ideas about community, charity, and gender played a role in the stereotype of a witch that developed at the village level.

Who: The Usual Suspects

The majority of people executed as witches were women. On average, eighty per cent were female. In some areas, such as England, the number was as high as ninety per cent. In other places, such as Iceland where shamanism played a role, men were the primary targets. Local studies suggest that the average female witch was over 50-years-old; that is, she was postmenopausal. The contemporary writer Reginald Scot suggested that old women were more often accused because menopause caused women to suffer from delusions. One wonders what caused the delusions suffered by their accusers. Women were more likely to be accused for several reasons, including poverty and social position, physical disfiguration, reputation, and the gender ideologies of the time. The accused often fit the stereotype of the poor, old woman.

Alleged witches were often the poorest and most marginal members of society. One factor that contributed to their socio-economic status was not having the support of a male. Not only were women ideally supposed to be under the protection and guidance of a man — father, husband, son, or some other male relative or guardian — but the household was the social and economic building block of premodern society. The head of the production unit, the man, was a craftsperson or peasant farmer. A woman became an important part of the economic process when she married and became mistress of the household, managing servants and apprentices, or working side by side with her husband in the workshop or on the land. At the mid to lower ends of society, a woman usually found it harder to succeed financially on her own. Not only did her household lack the income of another adult, but her education and employment options limited her own revenue. In general, a poor widow or a never-married single woman was marginalised by the patriarchal system. This put independent women at risk. In order to survive, they sometimes acted in aggressive ways that presented them as unwilling to accept their place in the social and gender hierarchy. But do not think that these women were early feminists. They were simply struggling to make the best of a bad situation.

A woman's poverty and social status could also have been exacerbated by her physical condition. Disability would have made it even harder for the woman to make a living, and disfigurement or an unpleasant appearance were attributes that were linked to the Devil. The physical characteristics might have been the result of a birth defect, disease, or accident. Women with physical deformities were not necessarily targeted as witches on account of their appearance. However, a link between physical and moral deformity was often made after the fact. Being crippled, disfigured, or ugly were sometimes emphasised in accounts of witchcraft cases. [See Image #19, Frontispiece of *Witchcrafts, Strange and Wonderful*] This contributed to the stereotype that has survived until today of the witch as an ugly, old hag. But accusations of witchcraft were not used just to get rid of undesirable members of the community. Ordinary crimes such as theft were not usually an aspect of the accusation. There had to be real suspicion that the accused had some supernatural power.

Elizabeth Sawyer of Buckinghamshire was a stereotypical suspect. She was described as pale and ghost-like, with a crooked and deformed body. She was also poor, with limited resources. In 1621, she was accused of bewitching her neighbour to death, because the woman had hit Sawyer's sow after the pig had eaten some soap belonging to the neighbour. Sawyer threatened the woman by saying 'that it should be a deare blow vnto her'.[2] When the neighbour subsequently fell sick, Sawyer's words were remembered and interpreted as a curse. Apparently, she had a reputation for having a tongue that cursed, swore, and blasphemed. This could have been a function of the frustrations resulting from the hardships of her life or a defensive position. Perhaps she felt it was better to stand up for herself and be aggressive than just to be a passive victim. Similarly, Elizabeth Clarke of Manningtree, Essex, was a poor, single woman with only one leg. She was the first woman to be accused in the Matthew Hopkins trials of 1645. In her testimony, she made reference to 'picking up a few sticks' in a field near her house, perhaps for her own use or perhaps to sell. Her friend, Anne West, apparently had offered to send her a familiar in the form of a kitten that could 'fetch home some victualls' for her so that she could 'live much better' than she did.[3] The witchcraft narrative, in this case concerning a familiar, was often integrated into actual circumstances of the accused, such as her socio-economic situation.

Older, crippled women like Sawyer and Clarke, who were economically vulnerable, were more likely to need the charity of the community. A poor, older woman, especially a widow, would consider herself part of the 'deserving poor', who merited community assistance. The deserving poor were widows, orphans, cripples, the insane, maimed soldiers, the sick, and the elderly. The 'undeserving poor' were members of society who were able to work, regardless of whether or not they were in need or had experienced bad luck. According to the Catholic church, charity was a way to shorten one's time in purgatory, so giving to the needy had religious as well as social significance. During the Reformation, charity gradually became more of a state responsibility and less of a personal obligation, even in Catholic countries. However, the old women being refused charity may not have viewed it that way. The early modern world was based on community. A network of women interacted on a daily basis: in the streets, in the fields, in the marketplace, and in the lying-in chambers. A woman's gossips — her female friends and neighbours — assisted in childbirth and childcare, shared resources, and offered advice on household management. Survival was largely dependent on neighbourly cooperation. But when a woman constantly needed assistance and was unable to reciprocate, she was more likely to come under suspicion as a witch when something went wrong. On the other side, constant refusals for help could result in the needy woman getting angry: grumbling or scolding the uncharitable members of her community could be interpreted as a curse. As discussed below, revenge was considered to be the chief reason a witch wanted to cause harm, and vengeance was configured as a female vice.

Elizabeth Sawyer's situation was typical of witchcraft suspects. Due to her economic and social position in a community, she was somewhat antisocial, or at least considered as such. Accused women were often portrayed as bad neighbours, persistent beggars, or persons who were just generally a nuisance. However, a single incident of unneighbourly behaviour was unlikely to result in witchcraft accusations. The suspect's poor reputation was built up over a long period of time. Gender ideologies dictated that silence, subservience, and submission were the appropriate behaviour of the ideal woman. This meant that women had limited options of how to obtain fair treatment. Men could settle disputes with legal recourse or violence. But poor women did not have the resources necessary for legal justice, and they were considered deviant if they used physical violence. Verbal violence was more commonly a woman's weapon. But verbal attacks contributed to a woman's reputation as a shrew or a scold, and could be interpreted as witchcraft in the form of a curse or a spell. In 1570, Anne Vicars' behaviour appeared to be more overtly a curse. She publicly called another woman a whore and a thief, then proceeded to 'cast her apron upon the side of the woman's face' while she made crosses and recited prayers. The object of Vicars' actions subsequently fell sick and lost the sight in one of her eyes. Was this simply a verbal attack or an actual attempt at casting a spell? In either case, constant grumbling or mumbling under one's breath was detrimental to a woman's general reputation.

In the case of Elizabeth Sawyer, the local justice of the peace had 'A Great, and long suspition [*sic*]' that she was a witch.[4] Suspected witches often had vicious tongues, brawled, quarrelled, and were generally disorderly. Or, at least, these were qualities that the community attributed to them. It was not uncommon for a woman to be suspected of being a witch for a long time before she was legally prosecuted. This is evident in the fact that after an initial accusation was made, witnesses came forward with stories about the accused that sometimes dated back more than twenty years. Sometimes the accused woman had a mother or grandmother who had been called a witch in the past. It took years to build a reputation, and the community had a long memory. In some cases, counter-magic techniques (see below) were used by a community to manage a witch for long periods before it had recourse to legal prosecution.

A woman's sexual behaviour was a huge part of her overall reputation. Lewd behaviour or playing the bawd contributed to a woman's chances of coming under suspicion of witchcraft. An unattached woman who gave birth to illegitimate children, or was a bastard herself, was at risk. Slander suits indicate that a woman sometimes went to court to defend against being defamed as a whore, just as she sometimes defended her name when called a witch. It was not just morality that was the issue. Female sexual behaviour was also a major concern for the state. Illegitimate children were a drain on community resources, in the form of charity and taxes. But again, this circumstance must be treated with caution. In 1589, Joan Cunny was accused of witchcraft. Apparently, she lived a lewd life along with her two lewd daughters, each of whom had a bastard son. At the time of the accusation, Joan was an 80-year-old widow. Many years had passed since her children had been a drain on the community. But her past behaviour was still held against her. Inappropriate sexual behaviour was just one of the conditions that contributed to a woman being accused of witchcraft. Burning women as witches was not part of some misogynistic plot to eradicate women who acted outside of patriarchal ideals.

Certainly, gender ideologies about women during this period contributed to women being accused more often than men, but witch-hunting was not woman-hunting. Women were generally believed to be physically, morally, and intellectually inferior. This philosophy had been in place since at least the classical era. Both the influential philosopher Aristotle and the second-century physician Galen viewed women as imperfect, undeveloped versions of the ideal human — a man. The reason for a woman's imperfection was that she was not as 'hot' as a man. Men produced more heat, which transformed the food they ingested into bodily fluids, including semen, which was considered to be the most refined version of blood. Women, on the other hand, shed excess blood every month, because the food they ate did not all convert into useful bodily fluids. The only time that all the nutrients were used was when the woman was pregnant or nursing a child, in which case the blood was transformed into a baby or milk. So menstrual blood was biological evidence of a woman's lower social status. Ancient scholars believed that a menstruating woman could wither crops in the field and dull knives. Menstrual blood was often included as an ingredient in magical potions, both real and imagined. On the other hand, women who had ceased menstruating were even more dangerous. Because the woman had dried up, so to speak, she fed on the fluids of others. Several accounts reported that an infant's breasts or other teat-like sores had been sucked by the witch in question. In turn, the witch was sucked by her imp. The older woman's loss of fertility and the ability to nurture a baby was transformed into fostering demons.

Christianity had reinforced these philosophical and medical ideas in the *Genesis* myth of Adam and Eve. Women were believed to be the lustier sex and, therefore, more prone to seduction by the Devil. Eve's weakness was evident in the fact that she had been tricked by the Devil in the form of a serpent, resulting in her and Adam being expelled from the Garden of Eden. Eve's punishment for her disobedience was that women would suffer pain in childbirth. Both the cause of her weakness and her punishment were associated with her sexuality. The aspect of a woman's physical body that differentiated her from a man — her sexual parts — became aligned with the diabolical realm. The polluting potential of women's bodies was linked with original sin.

There is a modern misconception that the women targeted as witches were all healers, wise women, or midwives, who were being attacked by the male-dominated medical profession. Actually, midwives were under-represented as a group. Midwives were usually well respected members of the community rather than the marginal women who were accused of witchcraft. The practice of male midwifery did not emerge until the eighteenth century, long after witchcraft prosecutions had waned. It is true that some demonologists suggested that midwives were witches, because the women were in a position to secure unbaptised babies to make potions. And, of course, they were well situated to play a role in abortion and infertility. However, in actuality, a midwife was more often employed to help identify a woman as a witch than she was to be accused as one. Midwives were called upon to search a suspect for the Devil's mark or witch's teat (see below). In one investigation by the Spanish Inquisition, midwives examined young women who had claimed they had sex with demons; they were found to be virgins and, therefore, innocent.

A wet nurse or a lying-in maid, in charge of looking after a new mother and her baby, was more likely to be accused of causing harm than the midwife who supervised the birth. In 1669, the lying-in maid Anna Ebeler was accused of causing the death of a new mother by giving her a bowl of soup fortified with brandy. After the initial accusation, other mothers reported that they also suspected Ebeler of harming their offspring. One baby had grown thin and died, another had been unable to nurse from its mother, a third had died after blisters appeared on its body. After being threatened with torture, the 67-year-old Ebeler confessed. She was 'mercifully' executed and her body was burned. Ebeler's case reflects the primary concerns of early modern women: maternity and child care. It is not hard to understand the grief and guilt felt by the mothers, which drove them to look for a reason for their infants' deaths.

Occasionally, a wise woman was accused of witchcraft, especially if her cure did not work. For example, a female healer got in trouble with the Venetian Inquisition because she failed to relieve a client of the symptoms of syphilis, the so-called French disease. But we should keep in mind that the knowledge of herbal remedies and simple charms was extensive. When reference is made in a witchcraft accusation to a woman employing such means, it does not necessarily mean that she was practising as a wise woman or cunning person. More on this topic to follow.

Men as Witches

Although not as common, men were also accused of performing magic and witchcraft. There was no single model of a male witch. Male suspects were often related to accused females, as husbands, brothers, or sons. Occasionally, cunning men were caught up in accusations (see below). In Italy, priests sometimes got in trouble for using the host and other holy items for magical purposes. In areas with a shamanistic tradition, such as Finland and Iceland, magic was conceived of as a male activity, resulting in a very high percentage of men accused. As we shall see in Chapter 6, men were more often actually practising ritual magic than they were suspected of practising *maleficium*. But those men were not usually charged with common witchcraft and were rarely executed.

When elite men were accused of witchcraft, it was usually part of a larger occurrence of persecution, such as took place in parts of the Holy Roman Empire, which included present-day Germany and Austria. During one of these outbreaks in the prince-archbishopric of Trier, more than 6,000 people were accused of witchcraft between the mid-1580s and the early 1590s. In this episode, which can truly be called a 'witch-craze', many people outside of the stereotype were affected, including men, aristocrats, clergy, and children. The suffragan bishop Peter Binsfeld fuelled the witch hunt and wrote a treatise to justify his persecutions including the use of repeated and unlimited torture. Dr Dietrich Flade, a wealthy lawyer, was included in the victims. He had been the former chancellor of the university and a councillor to the prince. Jesuits of a newly-established college, who were heavily involved in this hunt, employed young boys as spirit-mediums, who could allegedly recognise witches who had attended the sabbat, because they had been there as drummers. Flade was denounced by one of these boys. He was tortured into making a confession and burned at the stake. Mayors, parish priests, and a count were also caught up in that particular frenzy.

Child Witches

During the witchcraft prosecution era, there were a disturbing number of children accused of witchcraft. In the town of Wertheim in southern Germany, the citizens petitioned the rulers to investigate the problem of witchcraft, particularly to protect the children, who 'prefer evil over good', from seduction.[5] Two brothers were arrested, ages ten and five, who named others whom they had seen at the sabbat. The denunciations continued until eighty-six people were accused, including more children. Ten of the adults were executed. Downstream from Wertheim, in the archbishopric of Mainz, the phenomenon of children as witches was severe enough that a guide was written titled, 'New Treatise on the Seduced Child-Witches', which encouraged children to be treated as adults in the case of witchcraft. In the

Basque case, discussed in Chapter 7, hundreds of children under the age of fourteen confessed that they had been forcibly taken to the sabbat and made to participate in the activities. The same children were used as witnesses against the adults accused of transporting them. As late as 1723, well beyond the height of the witchcraft persecution era, parents in Augsburg requested the town council to arrest their children on account of their evil acts. They were accused of attending sabbats, putting diabolical powder in the beds of their parents, and behaving indecently with one another. The parents wanted them removed from their homes, because they were worried that the accused children would corrupt their peers and siblings. Twenty children, aged six to sixteen, were kept in small, dark cells for a year before they were transferred to a hospital. The investigation into allegations lasted six years.

Parents in Sweden had been similarly concerned about their children's involvement with witches in the summer of 1668. The local court of northern Dalarna investigated accounts by children and young women who claimed they had been taken by witches to Blåkulla or Blue Hill, a mythical location of the witches' sabbat. Parents were hysterical about rumours that children were flying with witches on goats or sticks. Sometimes parents kept the children awake all night to prevent their abduction. At other times the parents sat by their beds and watched their sleeping bodies. As a result of the children's testimonies, seven people were executed as witches in May 1669 by beheading and then burning, the common method in Sweden. The outbreak spread to nearby Mora. Commissioners were appointed by the king to investigate hundreds of children who were allegedly seduced. The testimony of the children alone was enough to sentence twenty-three women to death. The children were often kept in a separate building for their protection, which allowed them to coordinate their testimonies and accusations. Sometimes as many as forty children testified against the same witch. There was a lot of peer pressure on the children who gave testimony. If a child did not agree with the majority of the witnesses, he or she was at risk of being accused of being a witch who abducted others. Parents and other adults encouraged or bribed the children to tell their tall tales. Clergy and parish administrators paid a special group referred to as 'wise boys' to identify witches. The craze continued to spread from district to district until 1678. In total, 719 people were accused; 250 to 300 persons were executed. The craze came suddenly to an end in Stockholm when some of the children admitted that they had made the whole thing up. The ringleaders were investigated and four of the witnesses, including a 13-year-old boy, were executed. According to the English clergyman Joseph Glanvill, who wrote an account of the panic, thirty-six children between the ages of nine and sixteen were made 'to run the gantlet [gauntlet]' and twenty others were sentenced 'to be lash'd with Rods upon their hands, for three Sundays together at the Church-door' because 'they were very young'.[6] In other words, they were shown mercy on account of their age.

Others

One would think that vagrants and gypsies would have been easy targets for witchcraft accusations, since they were bothersome to communities. But strangers passing through a village were seldom accused, because they did not have time to develop the sort of reputation that contributed to accusations. There is one case in the Holy Roman Empire that involved four 'gypsies', but given the difficulty in accurately identifying the gypsy population, there is room for doubt as to the label used. In one area of present-day Austria, both old and young vagrants were targeted. The beggars were often physically and/or mentally disabled as well. Weather magic was the main accusation against them at a time of economic crisis. In Chapter 7, we will examine an unusual case of an entire family of vagrants who were accused, brutally tortured, and executed.

What: Types of Accusations

Given the level of disaster and resulting stress in the early modern era, it is a marvel that accusations of witchcraft were not thrown about on a daily basis. Epidemics of plague ravished Europe well into the eighteenth century, and war was a constant event. Some extremely bad weather also occurred during this period, with resulting damage to crops by wind, hail, rain, and frost, which contributed to famine and disease. Occasionally, in coastal areas, weather magic was suspected in the sinking of vessels. The accusation could be against a witch attacking another individual in a small boat or against a group of witches attacking a fleet of ships, thereby causing many deaths. Individuals were also sometimes accused of raising strong winds that caused damage to buildings. But environmental catastrophes that affected a whole community or region did not usually result in accusations of witchcraft, because they were not personal misfortunes. The belief in weather magic was more often discussed as part of the sabbat activities, rather than being a part of an accusation against an individual. Nevertheless, disasters that affected an entire region, such as bad weather, famine, and plague, were part of the background noise that contributed to social disorder and raised the level of anxiety and the resulting fear of the Devil. Misfortune on a grand scale supported the concept that God was punishing mankind for his sins. This was linked to the general belief that witches were active in the world. If the evil elements of society were removed, God might treat mankind more kindly.

At the village level, the most common reason for a charge of witchcraft was a personal misfortune that could not easily be explained in natural terms. But not every mishap in a community led to an accusation of magic. If a disease or an accident was straightforward, the victim would not immediately resort to allegations of supernatural interference. Testimony frequently reveals that the accuser looked for several other solutions or reasons for her problems before resorting to accusations of witchcraft.

What appears to the modern reader as relatively minor problems could lead to suspected witchcraft. Many people's livelihoods depended on cows producing milk, butter churning, and cheese and cream staying fresh. In the face of failure, an individual might look for magical interference. Other domestic problems laid at the feet of a witch concerned the production of honey, the laying of eggs, and the brewing of beer. Production in the dairy and the husbandry of livestock were predominantly female occupations at this time. Women milked cows, and made cream, cheese, and butter from the milk. Women and children took cows, pigs, goats, and geese to and from common areas to graze. When animals broke loose and caused damage to a neighbour's garden, witchcraft accusations could result. In some cases, it was not the person who owned the destructive animal who was accused, but it was the woman whose garden or goods were damaged. If she uttered harsh words on account of the damages, they could be interpreted as a curse when harm came to the animal or its owner later. Suspected witches were accused of decreasing the milk production of cows or stealing milk from cows in some magical manner. The demonologist Francesco Maria Guazzo reported how a woman inserted a pipe into the wall of her house and charmed all the milk from her neighbours' cows. He explained that it was possible because a demon actually milked the cows and carried the milk to her house.[7] Linked to the production of the dairy was infertility or miscarriage in cattle, or the illness and death of livestock. Both accusers and accused were overwhelming concerned with food, home, and neighbourliness. They were anxious about the survival of the household in a largely subsistence economy. The accusations also reflect the gendered nature of witchcraft allegations.

The most common reason for witchcraft accusations was the illness and death of people, especially children. If the illness appeared to be unnatural or was unresolvable by the medical profession, it was more likely to result in someone having to take the blame. An obvious accident, such as drowning, was not usually the cause of an accusation. However, even being thrown from a horse could be attributed to the malice of a witch. This, no doubt, relieved the (male) rider from the embarrassment of having poor equestrian skills. But a lingering illness was a more probable cause of suspicion, such as fever, loss of the use of limbs, or loss of sight.

Although epilepsy was a known medical condition, seizures and convulsions were still often blamed on a witch. In 1604, 21-year-old Anne Gunter started to have fits and sometimes fell into a coma-like trance. She vomited up pins and other foreign objects. Doctors were unable to diagnose her condition and suspected witchcraft. Anne, in her lucid moments, accused three local women of bewitching her. One of the women ran away, but the other two were subsequently tried. Anne's father, Brian Gunter, was gentry and had more influence than the accused women. Nevertheless, to his dismay, the women were acquitted. In the hopes of overturning this decision, Gunter arranged a meeting between King James I and his daughter, when James passed through Oxford. James had just recently come to the throne of England from Scotland, with a reputation as a witch-hunter based on his involvement with the North Berwick witches. James took the matter into his own hands, but not with the result Gunter had hoped for. In the custody of the king's chaplain, Samuel Harsnett, Anne confessed that her father had put her up to the simulated possession as part of a feud between him and the families of the accused women. Anne and her father were charged with making false accusations. The case was heard in the Court of Star Chamber, one of the royal courts at Westminster. Unfortunately, the decrees from the Star Chamber for this period have been lost. Anne was probably released without repercussions. Her father may have been fined. We know that he was released from prison, because he was still the wealthiest man in the parish of North Moreton in 1624. This case underscores the importance of social status in the transmission of justice.

A more extensive case of possession by witchcraft happened in 1634 in France. The Jesuit priest Urbain Grandier was burned alive for causing the demonic possession of several Ursuline nuns in a Loudun convent. Years of public exorcisms, including enemas with holy water, had not relieved the symptoms of the nuns. Even though they had never seen the handsome priest, the women named him as an evil spirit based on his character. Grandier had a reputation as a womaniser and had impregnated the daughter of one of the most powerful men in the town. He had also made enemies with very important members of the clergy, including Louis XIII's chief minister, Cardinal Richelieu. Although this case had obvious political overtones, it demonstrates the credibility of charges of sorcery in connection with demonic possession. Part of the evidence against Grandier was a pact signed by him, the Devil, and several other demons, which was allegedly found in his quarters. [See Image #20, Pact allegedly signed by Urbain Grandier] A similar incident had happened in 1611. The Ursuline nuns in Aix-en-Provence accused their confessor, Louis Gauffridy, of seducing them into witchcraft, for which he was executed.

How: Methods of Sorcery

The simplest way to harm a neighbour was a verbal curse. Verbal cursing was usually a tool of the poor and weak members of society, who did not have access to legal or economic solutions against the more powerful. In a mostly illiterate society, the power of the spoken word was important. A couple could be betrothed by the simple question of 'will you marry me' and the response 'I will'. Verbal contracts were considered legally binding. The church had strengthened belief in the power of words with such rituals as baptism and the Eucharist. The priest's words magically transformed the bread and wine into the body and blood of Jesus. Cursing has a long history, which was entangled with praying when Europe became Christianised. Prayers and curses were considered equally effective. If a person had been the victim of some injustice, he or she was justified in calling down God's anger on the enemy. At the village level, a person was suspect if the curses appeared to be successful. This was even more likely if the curse was intentional or delivered publicly and ritually as in the case of Anne Vicars. Another woman cursed a man while kneeling on her knees with a crowd of people around her. This does not mean she acted intentionally as a witch, but perhaps she was invoking God's wrath. Grumbling or mumbling something incoherent could also be understood as a hex. If an old woman said 'you'll be sorry' when she was denied charity, her words could be interpreted as threatening, especially if the person felt guilty about refusing the requested item. When accident or illness occurred, the formal or informal curse was recalled and taken as proof of witchcraft. The demonologists' beliefs concerning the role of the Devil in witchcraft strengthened the fear of curses.

Ordinary food could be a means of causing harm, depending on who offered it. Common things such as bread, soup, and the infamous apple were considered dangerous, if they came from the hands of the village hag who was already under suspicion. In 1664, a Somerset butcher's wife had a falling out with Elizabeth Style. She subsequently ate a 'very fair red apple' from her. The woman became sick and died a few months later with her 'hip having rotted'.[8] Style died in prison before she could be executed as a witch.

Potions and ointments have a long history of being tools of witchcraft. Many disgusting ingredients were suggested: bird bones and feathers, especially from black fowl; bones or clothes from hanged men; ashes; menstrual blood and other bodily fluids; fingernails; pubic hair; and the stereotypical bats, toads, and snakes. Boiling up babies in a cauldron was a favourite trope of artists, an idea that was borrowed from the demonologists. Unbaptised babies or infant bodies exhumed from the grave were especially prized. [See Image#11, Frontispiece, *Tractatus de Confessionibus Maleficorum et Sagarum*] As the ideas of the sabbat and devil-worship were integrated with witchcraft accusations, there was also mention of a white powder that the Devil gave the witch. The nastier the better, so it was often described as being made from the pulverised bones of children. The Basque witches flayed toads 'by biting a hole in the skin of the toad's head and pulling the head free. Then, closing their teeth on the skin, they would get hold of the head with their fingers and with a sharp tug they stripped the skin off the toad, which was still alive and kicking them in the face.'[9] The meat of the toad was mixed with the bones and brains of disinterred corpses and boiled in a cauldron. The substance was dried out and ground to a green, yellow, or black powder in a mortar and pestle. Investigation sometimes revealed some suspicious powders or ointments in an accused's home, but there was seldom any empirical evidence that the person was actually practising any form of sorcery or even cunning craft. The Spanish Inquisitor, Alonso de Salazar, conducted experiments on animals and people using powders and alleged flying ointments. His tests revealed that the materials were harmless. Unfortunately, his empirical approach to witchcraft was not widespread.

The use of image magic also survived, or was revived, from the classical era. The use of props of this sort was more often a tool of cunning folk or Italian prostitutes than the village witch. In the sixteenth and seventeenth centuries, these images were commonly sculpted of clay or wax. Some hair of the intended victim made the likeness more effective. An image of unbaked clay could be gradually crumbled away to cause the victim to languish and die. John Walsh, an English cunning man, confessed to using images of wax and clay. The wax images were effective for a couple of years, because it took that long for the wax to degrade. He said his images of clay were made with dirt from a grave, ashes of rib bones, a black spider, and water used to wash toads. The victim was injured wherever Walsh pricked the image with pins or thorns.[10] In Venice, a wax statue of Jesus, meant for devotional purposes, was used to stand in for the intended object of love magic. The statue was skewered and roasted over a slow fire so that heat or passion would arise in the lover. The image could also be punctured or bound to produce impotence. One can see how this would be viewed as heresy by the church. In Venice, fragments of glass were used in a similar fashion. Image magic falls in the realm of sympathetic magic. The practitioner did not need to employ demons to achieve her or his ends. It is hard to sort out when this sort of magical technique was actually employed and when it was merely an accusation to strengthen the case against a suspect. For instance, Elizabeth Style confessed to making a picture in wax to harm her victims, but the story loses credibility when she reports how she and her companions presented the image to the Devil, who baptised it with oil and stuck thorns into the neck, wrists, and fingers. At this point, the tale sounds like something that has been suggested to her by her interrogators.

Images for the purpose of *maleficium* could also take the form of a drawing on parchment. In one suspect's home, a parchment approximately fifteen inches long and fifteen inches wide was discovered with the life-size image of a red heart drawn in the centre. Around the perimeter were illustrations of the other anatomical parts of a man. The accused witch confessed that she could harm a person by pricking the corresponding part on the picture. This case has come to our attention because one of the woman's alleged victims had scratched her face to relieve his illness (see counter-magic below). The woman, in turn, sued him for battery. He had to pay a five shilling fine plus the cost of the legal proceedings. As soon as he paid the fine, he suffered a relapse and died. So in at least some cases, the accused woman got the last word! If the witch could acquire hair or a garment from the victim, similar effects could be obtained. Margaret Flower confessed that she obtained a glove from Lord Roos. Her mother stroked her familiar cat with the glove, dipped it in hot water, and pricked it many times to cause Lord Roos to become ill.

Another common magical technique, which was definitely employed, was the making of love charms. Love magic was either practised more in Italy or has come to our attention more due to the Roman Inquisition's concern about it. Another factor that could contribute to a higher incident of love charms in Italy is that Italian men married at a later age than northern European men, which resulted in a higher number of unmarried women who might have been competing for a mate. Love magic was used to arouse affection in the desired person or to cause impotence in a wayward lover. The Inquisition's concern was that the magician was trying to interfere with man's free will. No doubt the exclusively male officials of church and state were not impressed with the possibility that a female could cause male impotence. The specialists in love magic were urban prostitutes, who were attempting to attract and keep clients. One woman in Venice used the heart of a rooster, wine, water, and menstrual blood mixed with flour to ensure the affection of her paramour. Be on guard if your lover serves you coq au vin!! Sage, a common herb for flavouring poultry, was used in the same manner. Love spells were also activated with words, which could take the form of a sort of conjuration, calling up the sun, moon, and stars. Practitioners called on souls of the damned to help, so that the recalcitrant lover would fall to the ground for his intended and 'his member shall be bound' for her.[11] The recitation was accompanied with the tying of three knots in a rope, which was a common binding spell, especially when trying to cause impotence. [See Image #32, 'The Love Spell', Unknown Flemish Artist]

In the parts of Europe that had remained Catholic after the Reformation, ecclesiastical authorities were concerned about the use of holy objects for unholy purposes. The average layperson viewed any sacramental item as magical. Even the ground from the church graveyard was considered supernatural. Instead of swallowing the host during mass, a woman could hold it in her mouth or handkerchief so she could take it home to be used in spells and charms. The demonologists suspected that the Eucharist was taken to be defiled at sabbats, as part of the pact with the Devil. Other items intended for use in magic were hidden in the altar cloths or the garments of a baby being baptised, so they could be consecrated or have masses said over them. In Italy, priests were often accused of misusing religious elements or providing them for others, including the host, holy water, holy oil, and consecrated candles.

The Christian emphasis on the miraculous qualities of the sacraments provided a wealth of materials for magical purposes in popular culture. In both Protestant and Catholic areas, Christian prayers and bits of scripture were often used in charms and spells. If written, virgin parchment was considered the most effective medium. The charms were worn around the neck or carried in a pocket for protection against injury or death in battle, for easy childbirth, or for safe travels. There was no limit to how these charms could be employed. Prayers to saints served similar purposes, for love magic, restoration of lost goods, and protection from disease. These practices, which were offences according to the church, bring to mind the modern practice of wearing a medal of the patron saint of travellers, St Christopher. Whether this is witchcraft, superstition, or religion appears to be in the eye of the beholder. According to the Venetian Inquisition, which discovered the prolific use of these charms, the intent of the user was the main concern. These sorts of charges were more likely to show up in the ecclesiastical courts rather than secular ones, and more often resulted in penance than punishment. The Italian Inquisition was more concerned with sacrilege than witchcraft.

The Witch's Familiar

In England, the concept of the witch's familiar as a demon helper was very popular. In 1566, Elizabeth Frauncis of Essex confessed to receiving a white, spotted cat named Sathan from her grandmother. She kept the creature in a basket and fed it milk and bread. In 'a straunge holowe voice', the animal promised her goods, sheep, and a wealthy husband.[12] Upon the advice of the cat, Elizabeth allowed her potential husband to 'abuse' her body, after which the man refused to marry her. In retaliation, Elizabeth requested Sathan to kill the man, which he did. Elizabeth, and other witchcraft suspects, could have drawn on stories from folklore to construct their tales of familiars. Stories about the animal as trickster or animal helper had a long oral history. A similar cat-cum-fairy story, called *Puss in Boots* in English, was widely known in Europe, and was published by an Italian author in the mid-sixteenth century.

In the accounts of witchcraft cases, the familiar or imp was considered to be a demon in disguise, which the witch employed as a helper. Since it was demonic, demonologists argued that it was the witch who was the servant to the familiar rather than the animal being subservient to the witch. Suspects often reported that they had no control over the imp. They tried to shift as much blame as possible unto the Devil. The demon helper could take the form of a domestic pet, such as a cat or dog, or other common animals, such as a rabbit, a rat, a mole, a ferret, or a toad. [See Image #19, Frontispiece, *Witchcrafts, Strange and Wonderful*] In the Basque area of Spain, toad familiars were allegedly dressed in clothes and given to the novice witch by a senior witch. The witch fed the little beast on corn, bread, and wine. At the sabbat, children guarded the herd of toads. [See lower left corner of

Image #12, Illustration of sabbat by Jan Ziarnko] Even butterflies, bees, and grasshoppers could serve in a pinch. In other instances, the familiar was described as a bizarre, unnatural creature. One of the familiars belonging to the accused witch Elizabeth Clarke was called Vinegar Tom. The self-styled 'witch-finder' Matthew Hopkins described him as 'a long-legg'd greyhound, with a head like an Oxe'.[13] [See Image #27, Woodcut of 'Matthew Hopkins Witch-finder General'] A 12-year-old victim described another witch's familiar as a black dog with a face like an ape, horns on its head, and a silver whistle around its neck. One of Joan Cunny's nine spirits was a black dog with a face like a toad.

The witch could inherit her familiar from her mother, or it could be a gift from another witch or from the Devil himself. The familiar aided the witch in doing harm, either directly or indirectly. In return, the imp was fed bowls of milk or beer, or was rewarded with a chicken, a cat, or a dog to eat. The demonologists interpreted the witch's relationship with the familiar as a pact with the Devil. To seal the contract, the witch fed the familiar on either blood or milk from her body. This constituted a sort of illiterate signing of a pact, just as sex with the Devil did. In 1589, Joan Prentice confessed that the Devil in the shape of a ferret with fiery eyes sucked blood from the forefinger of her left hand to seal the pact between them. Joan then instructed the animal to spoil a batch of beer being brewed by a neighbour. One woman apparently fed her companion cat by making her nose bleed. Some witches kept their familiars in a cozy box or a basket lined with wool.

In 1612, Alizon Device, one of the accused Lancaster witches, had 'a thing like vnto a Blacke Dogge'.[14] The creature had appeared to her after a pedlar had refused to sell her some pins. It generously offered to lame the man on her behalf. She rewarded it by allowing it to suckle her chest a little below her breasts. Perhaps Alizon had supernumerary nipples. In England, the idea of feeding a familiar with a drop of blood grew into the concept of the witch's teat. Any protuberance on the body, such as a wart, a haemorrhoid, or an extra nipple became a place where the witch suckled her familiar. Midwives or other respectable matrons were employed to search the suspect for such marks, which served as empirical evidence of a pact with Satan. Early accounts located the teat on the face, the nose, the chin, and the finger, but later accounts discovered such growths in the genitals on women, another gendered aspect of the witchcraft trials. [See Image #21, Joan Prentice's familiar] On the vicar John Lowes, the teats were on the crown of his head and under his tongue.

Animal familiars appear to be born from a collision of folk tales about 'grateful' animals that acted as mediators between humans and the supernatural, such as *Puss and Boots*, and the ideas drawn from Augustine concerning the Greek *daimones*. There is also a collapse between fairies and familiars in England. Both alleged witches and cunning folk were accused of, and sometimes confessed to, conversations with and assistance from fairies. In popular culture, fairies were understood as elemental spirits or supernatural creatures, sometimes with an underground society similar to humans. Brownies were household spirits that could help with the housework, in exchange for a bowl of milk or cream. A bad housekeeper or lazy servant might be chastised by the brownie wreaking havoc or playing tricks. Outside of witchcraft accusations, the fairies of folklore could be either benign or malicious. But fairies were unanimously considered malignant spirits by the demonologists. Henri Boguet said the witches danced at the sabbat like fairies, 'which are truly devils in bodily form'.[15]

The fairy of folklore was transfigured into a demon after witchcraft accusations were made. In 1607, Susan Swapper of Sussex was visited by several fairies, who came to give her medical advice. She later met the fairy queen in a green field. Her trouble started when the fairies suggested that she dig for hidden treasure in the neighbour's yard. Once word spread of their activities, Swapper and her neighbour were charged with dealing with wicked spirits, under the same clause of the witchcraft act that allowed for punishment for having a familiar. Susan was sentenced to be hanged, but her neighbour's trial dragged on and, as a result, she was kept in prison until 1611 when she received a pardon.

Why: The Witch's Motive

Charges of witchcraft were often used to resolve family issues, village feuds, or political rivalry, as noted in the Anne Gunter case discussed above. Historians have done a lot of work on how interpersonal conflicts at the village level related to witchcraft accusations, using social-anthropological models. Historian Keith Thomas led the way by developing the guilt-refusal theory. The consensus of historians is that the quarrel over resources or some unresolved personal conflict was the basis for most accusations. The following scenario was a common pattern. The person who was eventually accused first requested a small gift of food or drink, or she wanted to sell or borrow some object. Or perhaps the accuser owed money to the accused for a service rendered and had refused to pay. Disputes could also arise over the use of common land, grazing, or an animal that trespassed into someone's garden. The person who did the accusing refused the woman who was accused. Then the person who had refused charity or payment suffered a misfortune. The refuser felt guilty, because charity was an important part of both social and Christian duty. The refuser also thought that the accused had a right to feel angry and seek revenge. As a result, the refuser projected his or her guilt unto the refused and accused the person of witchcraft in relation to the misfortune experienced. Accusations then might spread to other relatives or friends of the alleged witch. It was at that point, after the initial accusation, that the person's reputation came into play. Often members of the community would come forward with stories about how the alleged witch had caused harm many years ago.

Of course, the concept of blaming someone else for one's troubles was not new. The use of a scapegoat is based on the Old Testament verse of *Leviticus* 16:8. On the Day of Atonement, a goat was sent out into the desert to symbolically take away the sins from the community. In modern terms, scapegoating is the process whereby one person is blamed unfairly for another individual's problems or for the emotional cleansing of the community. The need to scapegoat is born out of the frustration over inexplicable events or extreme bad luck, accompanied with the desire to either stop the difficulties or avenge them. In the case of early modern witchcraft accusations, the targets for scapegoating were usually marginalised members of the community, such as the stereotypical poor, old widow. In addition to being vulnerable to attack, the scapegoat had to be a credible suspect, with a bad reputation and a low probability of retaliation. This did not mean that the person was completely powerless. The person being scapegoated usually had a history of community conflict, which meant that she had enough agency to cause trouble. Unfortunately, she did not have enough power to avoid an accusation. She was also usually the object of previous prejudice.

Feminist historians have taken this guilt-refusal theory one step further. They suggest that women projected their guilt and anxiety about being a bad mother or house-keeper unto motherly or grandmotherly figures. In a society with a high rate of childhood mortality, women looked for reasons for their losses to mitigate any self-blame. An old woman's curse, criticism, or even advice could be interpreted as evidence of the mother's poor maternal skills. The lying-in maid was the perfect candidate for blame, as the woman became a substitute mother who cared for the newborn baby, while the actual mother lay passively in her bed. In the case of Ursley Kempe, a woman testified that she refused to allow Ursley to nurse her newborn daughter. Shortly after the falling out between Ursley and the woman, the baby's cradle broke, and the child fell out and broke her neck. The witch was constructed as the inverse of the ideal woman — a good wife and mother. The good mother suckled babies; the bad mother suckled demon familiars. This theory is supported by the many cases where children were sick or died and a care-giver was blamed. According to this psychoanalytical theory, the accused care-giver was more likely to accept the charge of doing harm, because she felt emotions of envy for the new mother. Envy not only provided a motive for the woman to do harm, but was one of the seven deadly sins. Emotions such as envy, jealousy, and vengeance were believed to have material force, that is, the ability to actively manifest physical harm. They were also emotions that the Devil took advantage of to seduce women to witchcraft.

Counter-Magic

Several contemporary writers believed that suspected witches were handled with kid gloves in their community. In other words, an accusation of witchcraft was sometimes the last step in a long process of managing a witch in a community. The initial accusation of witchcraft was often informal rather than a complaint to a justice of the peace or other authority. Instead of legal justice, the accuser hoped that the accused would take responsibility for the misfortune and undo the bewitchment or curse. In the investigation process of a trial, the witch's neighbours often came forward with stories of previous episodes of witchcraft, indicating that the person had been suspected of being a witch for many years. The community had previously managed the suspect, by either placating her or counteracting her magic. Reconciliation was preferable to confrontation, especially if the community believed that the power of the witch was strong. In 1593, Alice Samuel was accused of afflicting the children of the Throckmorton family. The woman agreed to stay in the family's home to see for herself if her company affected them. When the children acted possessed in her presence, she confessed to being responsible for bewitching them. She asked for the parents' and the children's forgiveness, and her penitence was acknowledged in the parish church. This would have been the end of the situation except Mother Samuel's husband did not think she was responsible; he encouraged her to deny her confession. After she recanted, formal charges of witchcraft were made, and eventually she, her husband, and her daughter were all hanged as witches.

Even before a person suffered a supposed attack of witchcraft, he or she could use magical means of protection. Cunning folk made amulets and talismans for people worried about being bewitched. Magical charms could be as simple as a Bible verse hung about the neck. The astrologer-physician Simon Forman made a ring with a coral stone engraved with the sign of Jupiter to protect himself from witchcraft and to overcome his enemies. The stone was placed on a piece of parchment on which the symbols for Virgo and Mercury were inscribed.

The widespread belief in magic is evident in how people attempted to counter witchcraft with another magical technique. To the modern reader, the defence against witchcraft looks like witchcraft itself. If cream would not churn into butter, one could put a red-hot horseshoe into it. The heat drove the evil out. A woman who was having trouble making cheese due to bewitchment was told to rub salt and water on the backs of the cows, and then put some of the salt in the milk pail before milking. To remove a curse from a bewitched pig, one could cut its ears off and burn them. In another case, the afflicted pig's ears were burned, without mention of removing them first. When many animals were afflicted, burning one alive could stop the death toll. The intentional cruelty of the counter-magic was often worse than the cruelty of the alleged witchcraft.

Identifying the witch was the next step. There were several techniques used to draw out the guilty party. Often it was a matter of confirming the identity of someone already suspected. One could burn some of the thatch from the person's house, which was meant to either bring the witch to the scene of the crime or remove the curse from the bewitched party. Burning the guts of an animal bewitched to death would cause the witch to experience burning pain. Amy Duny was suspected of causing the illness of a child. A physician suggested hanging the child's blanket in the fireplace all day. Anything suspicious that lodged itself in the blanket was to be thrown into the fire. An unlucky toad (a common witch's familiar) found there was held in the fire with tongs until it exploded. The child recovered and Amy was found with her face and legs scorched. Who is the witch in this instance? In some cases, suspected substances found in the accused's house, such as bread, salt, or ashes, would be fed to either the victim or an animal. In the famous Salem outbreak, a 'witch cake' was made from rye meal and the urine of one of the allegedly possessed girls. The cake was fed to a dog to ascertain whether or not the girls were bewitched. If so, the dog would have suffered in the same manner. The outcome of the experiment was not documented. In another case, a doctor recommended that an afflicted woman boil her urine with some nail clippings and hair, which would cause the suspected witch to bloat. It was unclear if the accuser was trying to affect a cure or simply identify the witch.

Another method of determining the guilt of a person was swimming, based on the medieval practice of judgement by ordeal. In most parts of Europe, the procedure was considered illegal, but it was sometimes used by the common people. The woman's wrists were bound together and tied to her ankles. One witness said the woman's right hand was bound to her left foot and her left foot was bound to her right. She was then thrown into a pond or river, preferably cold water. A woodcut of this process indicates that she was prevented from drowning by being tied to ropes held by people on the shore. [See Image #22, Woodcut of swimming a witch] The process was not intended to drown her. If she floated, she was guilty, because the water would reject a person who had rejected baptism. If she sank, she was innocent. Such practices illustrate the tenuous differences between superstition, religion, and magic.

One method of removing a suspected curse was to scratch or beat the witch. Drawing blood from the face was especially effective. In some cases, the scratching became a brutal beating. In 1604, 94-year-old Agnes Fenn was suspected of bewitching a man. Instead of reporting her to the authorities, she was brought to the man's chamber and asked to remove the curse. She alleged that when she refused, the men punched and pushed her, and stabbed her in the face. We know about this case because Fenn subsequently charged the men with slander for calling her a witch. Her case was reviewed in the Star Chamber court. One of the men interrogated for participating in the beating revealed that Fenn was attacked, at least to the point of being scratched. His denial of the men's attempts to use ritual magic techniques to remove her suspected curse serves as evidence that they were also suspected of using counter-magic:

> 'this dep't [deponent] saith that he or any other of the said company did not to his knowledge make any circle with any figures as is supposed. But he saith that there was a crosse with chalke in the floor of the chamber made in sporte as this dep't then verely thought & yet thinketh. But who did make the same this dept doth not truely knowe. Nether was the Comp[lainan]t tossed through any circle, or stabbed into the face either witch'th knife or dagger as is supposed. Neyther did this dept heare it said That the blacke divill should carry her away. Neyther did she bleed the quantity of a quarte, as

> is supposed. But true it is that her face was scratched a little. But by whom this dept doth not know certainely but thinketh that the depts ______ Sturlowe did scratch it. Nonethelesse she was not in danger of her life. For the usage of her was not so barbarous to put her life in danger, as is supposed.'[16]

Unfortunately, the judge's decision on the case has been lost.

The ultimate counter-magic was the death of the suspected witch. Some people believed that the witch's curse would not end until her life did. Her death was also a preventative measure against future problems.

Cunning-Folk

In most cases, the alleged witch harmed with a glance, a crust of bread, or a few muttered words. But there was another group of people who openly claimed occult knowledge and the ability to do magic, usually for beneficial purposes. Cunning folk, or wise men and wise women, were the names most commonly used in England for this category of people, but sometimes the term 'conjurer' was used as well, usually in a derogatory sense. The same types of practitioners were known all over Europe by different names. Many writers of the time thought that 'white witches', as they were sometimes referred to, were as bad as 'black witches'. The term white witch was a designation by those who condemned cunning folk, because they considered all magic had a demonic source. Demonologists commonly believed that if a person had the skills to heal, the person could also harm. Magical techniques used by cunning folk included charms, amulets, divination, and herbal concoctions.

In England, more men were cunning folk than women. Male cunning folk often practised their craft alongside another occupation, such as being an artisan, a school teacher, or a herdsman. Even some clergy were cunning folk. They were usually conversant in herbal remedies and were consulted to cure both sick people and animals. Their fees, if they even charged for their services, were more affordable than licensed physicians. In addition to medical cures, they helped clients to find lost and stolen goods, to identify the thief, and to tell the future. They assisted with treasure-hunting and constructed charms for love magic, gambling, and general protection. One of their occupations was identifying witches. They also treated bewitched people and livestock. A person might consult with a cunning person when he or she suspected witchcraft to be the cause of an illness or accident.

The cunning person would confirm the cause and then suggest a possible suspect, often a neighbour of the bewitched. Occasionally, a cunning person would perform an exorcism to relieve a possessed person of demons.

Witchcraft was often viewed as an innate or inherited ability, but the conjuration and construction of charms used by cunning folk were acquired skills. These skills could be handed down from one family member to another or learned from books. Cunning folk were more likely than the bulk of the rural population to be at least semi-literate. Sometimes they possessed handwritten or printed books of magical formulae and recipes, as well as almanacs and astrology manuals. The books themselves were sometimes considered quasi-magical. The English cunning man John Walsh complained that after constables confiscated his books, the fairies would not assist him in his services.[17] Apparently, the presence of the books was more important than the information they contained. A basic knowledge in astrology was common, even if it was only in relation to the proper time to harvest herbs. The cunning woman Mary Parish supplied a gambling charm for her client that consisted of a variety of periwinkle harvested at a particular astrological time while reciting a particular prayer. Astrology was also used in the construction of talismans for healing and protection. Richard Napier, an Anglican clergyman and a licensed physician, cured with astrological talismans. Part of his diagnostic technique was the casting of a horoscope for each patient to determine the effect of the heavens on the person's body.

Some cunning folk used a magic wand. Wands were used to look for hidden treasure. The well-known astrologer William Lilly used hazel divining rods to look for buried treasure in Westminster Abbey in the company of thirty other men, including King Charles I's Groom of the Bedchamber. For more information on the use of wands in relation to ceremonial magic, see the next chapter.

Scrying was another technique used by cunning folk. To scry, the person used a mirror, a basin of water, or some other reflective surface in which the client could see the face of a suspected thief or witch. A cunning man named Blumfield used a common mirror to show his customer the thief who stole his linen. The man confirmed that he 'did see the face of him that had the said linen'.[18] Some cunning men confessed to invoking spirits into crystals for the purpose of divination. The infamous 'Dr' John Lambe had a crystal ball into which he invoked the spirit Benias. On another occasion, a man picked up Lambe's crystal ball out of curiosity and saw a shepherd in it.

Two very common techniques employed by cunning folk were the key and psalter and the sieve and shears. Reginald Scot explained how to do both of these operations in his demonological treatise. He accused Catholic priests of performing the key and psalter:

> 'Popish preests … doo practice with a psalter and a keie fastned upon the 49 psalme, to discover a theefe. And when the names of the suspected persons are orderlie put into the pipe of the keie, at the reading of these words of the psalme … the booke will wagge, and fall out of the fingers of them that hold it, and he whose name remaineth in the keie must be the theefe.'[19]

The sieve and shears was also related to religion, involving the aid of the apostles Peter and Paul:

> 'Sticke a paire of sheeres in the rind of a sive, and let two persons set the top of each of their forefingers upon the upper part of the sheeres, holding it with the sive up from the ground steddilie, and aske Peter and Paule whether A. B. or C. hath stolne the thing lost, and at the nomination of the guiltie person, the sive will turne round.'[20]

As these examples demonstrate, the line between folk magic, witchcraft, and medicine was very blurry in the premodern era. In most cases, it was just in the eye of the beholder. The intention of the practitioner appears to be the most important aspect. Witchcraft was not just the practice of magic, but was *maleficium*, the supernatural means of causing harm. Cunning folk and counter-magic were not viewed as witchcraft by the general population, because the intent of their efforts was not to harm, but was for the good of the community.

Cunning folk were seldom caught up in witchcraft accusations unless a cure went wrong, or they had some other falling out with a client. Nevertheless, within the five to twenty per cent of men who were accused of witchcraft, a relatively high percentage were cunning men. The tragic tale of Anne Bodenham of Salisbury is an example of how a cunning person could get into trouble with the law. She was an 80-year-old cunning woman who was hanged as a witch after many years of practice. She taught reading to children, cured diseases with charms, and found lost and stolen goods. Unfortunately, she got caught up in a dispute between a gentry woman, the wife of Richard Goddard, and the woman's two step-daughters. It all started when Anne Styles, one of the Goddard's maids, was sent to consult Bodenham about a silver spoon, which had been stolen from the Goddard home. She returned another time to inquire about some money lost by the son-in-law. On this occasion, Bodenham took out a book, which the maid said contained a picture of the Devil, placed a round green glass on it, and lifted them both up to the sunshine. The maid looked in the globe and saw what various people were doing in her master's house. When she returned home, she verified their activities. One of the other maids said that Bodenham was 'either a Witch, or a woman of God', indicating the fuzzy line between sinner and saint.[21] Meanwhile, Mistress Goddard suspected that her step-daughter were trying to poison her. Styles was sent back to Bodenham to determine the truth. On her way back to the cunning woman's house, a little black dog ran ahead of her and 'brought her to the Witches house.' Bodenham confirmed the suspicion about poisoning, and offered to prevent it. She sent the maid to the apothecary to buy white arsenic, which she intended to burn to prevent the poisoning, a kind of sympathetic magic. Nevertheless, Mr Goddard wanted to know where the poison was hidden in his house and sent the maid back again to find out. Styles reported (after her incarceration) that this time Bodenham engaged in ritual magic. She drew a circle, swept over it with her broom, drew a second circle, and looked again in her glass. She stood in the circle and invoked demons in a soft voice. A spirit appeared in the shape of a little boy, which turned into something like a snake, then into 'a shagged Dog with great eyes'. She burned some stinking material in a pan of coals to disperse the demon, then showed Styles in the scrying glass that the poison was under the step-daughter's bed in a white paper. Bodenham then sent Styles to a meadow to gather vervain and dill, which she dried and powdered. She gave the powder, some of the leaves, and her nail clippings to the maid to take to her mistress to put in the drink of the step-daughters. The potion was supposed to rot their guts and make their teeth fall out. Mrs Goddard also procured a charm from Bodenham to protect her from danger. The Goddard household freely availed themselves of her services, which were all services available from a cunning person. But the story of the demons appearing in a circle transformed Anne Bodenham into a witch.

The elaborate plan got out of hand when the step-daughters found out that they were suspected of trying to poison their step-mother. They inquired at the apothecary about who had purchased poison lately, and he named the maid, Anne Styles. Mistress Goddard told the maid to run away and 'shift for her selfe' before the justice of the peace came to make inquiries, because she knew it would reflect badly on her household. The son-in-law became involved at this point and had the maid intercepted on her way to London. To save her own skin, Styles told a tale about making a pact with the Devil at the behest of Bodenham. She accused the cunning woman of bewitching her and threw many elaborate fits to demonstrate her position as a victim. Bodenham was arrested and put in prison for three weeks until the court met. Styles continued to have 'such strange fits that drew both pity and admiration from the beholders'. In the end, Anne Styles was set free as a victim of the witch; Anne Bodenham was hanged. In this case, Bodenham was used as a scapegoat for family squabbles.

Even the practice of identifying witches could backfire on a cunning person. Jochim Emecke was a cowherd and healer in a northern German town. In 1635, he was consulted about an outbreak of disease in local livestock, and he accused a local woman of causing it. As a result of his naming the witch, both the woman and Emecke were subjected to the swimming test. They both floated, which meant they were guilty. The authorities then used interrogation and torture to determine the 'truth'. Both of them were executed. The accused woman was burned as a witch, and Emecke was beheaded for the lesser offence of employing magic and abusing the name of God.

Cunning craft was a site for the crossover of popular magic to learned magic and vice versa. The important thing to remember is that magic was accepted as possible, whether it was used to heal or to harm. Some magic was considered the work of demons, while other magic was acceptable either as the work of God and the angels or as sympathetic magic.

Conclusion

There is no substantial evidence that the people accused of witchcraft in the premodern period were either Devil worshippers or followers of a pre-Christian fertility cult. Nevertheless, both accusers and those accused of witchcraft believed in the power of magic. This is evident not only in the number of accusations that arose from the village, but also in the number of people who resorted to cunning folk or used counter-magic to manage suspected witches. Some of the accused may have even thought that their curses and spells could cause harm to their neighbours. This would explain why a woman might confess under interrogation. The accused could not deny the feelings of guilt, anger, and vengeance that could lead to misfortune. It is even possible that old, poor women cultivated a reputation for witchcraft, because it was one of the few resources they had. The fear of reprisal would have encouraged her neighbours to treat her decently. For the most part, village women were executed as witches without any evidence of actually attempting magic. In the next chapter, we will examine how elite men actually practised ritual or ceremonial magic without any consequences.

Chapter 6

The Circle is Cast, Ceremonial Magic

'Know that your words have won me at the last
To practice magic and concealèd arts.
Philosophy is odious and obscure,
Both law and physics are for petty wits,
Divinity is basest of the three —
Unpleasant, harsh, contemptible, and vile.
'Tis magic, magic that hath ravished me!'[1]

Christopher Marlowe, a rival of William Shakespeare, wrote *The Tragicall History of the Life and Death of Doctor Faustus* in the sixteenth century. The Faust character was based on the legend of the German magician and alchemist Johann Georg Faust, who boasted that he could reproduce all the miracles of Jesus. The tales that grew up around him were part of the literature about the Devil that was popular in German culture after the Reformation. Marlowe was no doubt trying to cash in on a hot topic of the day. In the play, Faustus rejects the usual choices of a well-educated man: philosopher, lawyer, physician, and divine. Instead, he chooses the 'art' of magic, implying that it takes a knowledgable man to command the spirit world. The woodcut on the cover of the published version of the play depicts a wealthy man, judging by his rich attire, standing in a circle drawn on the floor, which is inscribed with astrological symbols. [See Image #23, Frontispiece, *The Tragicall History of the Life and Death of Doctor Faustus*] He holds a book in one hand and a wand in the other. More books are on a shelf nearby, which speak of both the man's education and wealth. The only element that connects the image to witchcraft is the demon standing outside the circle. Marlowe's readers would have known that Faustus was practising magic rather than witchcraft. Written in the middle of the witchcraft persecution era, the play depicts the magus as a servant of the Devil, but the men who experimented with conjuring up demons believed that they were controlling them, not being controlled by them.

The 'pure' form of ceremonial magic, if there ever was such a thing, has been continually bastardised and demonised throughout history. Modern Wicca, aided and abetted by Hollywood movies and novels about the occult, continued the evolution of magic by entangling the practices of ceremonial or ritual magic with the concept of the premodern witch. We will look more closely at this process in the last chapter. First, let us try to draw some defining boundaries between witchcraft/sorcery and ceremonial/ritual magic. The borderline between the two is indistinct at best and indistinguishable at worst. Ritual magic, no doubt, borrowed ideas and practices from the societies in which it evolved; folk magic, in turn, gleaned bits and pieces of the literate practices and turned them into shorter rituals, which did not require literacy, expensive materials, and detailed preparations. Some folk practices and superstitions were considered witchcraft, because they were used for the purpose of causing harm or they were understood as resulting in *maleficium*. But for the most part, witchcraft was a social construction not a reality. Definitely not a religion. Nonetheless, witches were configured as devil-worshippers, who either did things that were impossible, such as flying to the sabbat and having sex with demons, or that were improbable, such as making ointments from dead babies and suckling demonic familiars. Outside of poisoning, which, last time I checked, does not require a pact with the Devil, most of what witches were accused of would not have worked anyway. If you have any luck causing hail by stirring water with a stick, let me know. For the most part, the techniques attributed to witches did not require literacy, and most of the accused, who were female, were not trying to practise any sorcery.

Ceremonial magic, on the other hand, was a literate form of magic, which was actually practised, or at least experimented with. Magicians were almost exclusively educated, elite men, including aristocrats, physicians, clerics, and lawyers. This is the same class of men who practised alchemy in the early modern period, the forerunner of modern chemistry. A magus needed to be able to read the Latin manuscripts that held the instructions and the long invocations. A knowledge of astrology was also useful, and theological training came in handy to consecrate materials, both of which were learned in the university setting. Although not strictly necessary, an understanding of natural philosophy was also helpful. While some elite women received a private education equal to a man's, females were not allowed to attend the public grammar schools where Latin was taught, nor were they permitted in universities.

The objectives of ritual magic ranged from the noble aims of attaining knowledge, mastering the arts, learning languages, improving the memory, and achieving union with God to the lowly purposes of discovering stolen goods, achieving victory in battle, gaining favour at court, inciting lust, causing impotence, gaining invisibility, and even killing the pope. Magic was also employed in treasure hunting, which was a very popular past time in early modern Europe. Without banks to deposit money into, people often buried their valuables in the form of coins and jewels. Ruins of monasteries and castles, as well as barrows and wayside crosses, were popular locations to dig for treasure. Magic could help locate the place where the treasure was buried and also subdue any spirits that might be guarding it. There were also rituals for obtaining a familiar spirit, usually the spirit of a dead person rather than the animal familiars of English witches. There was even a spell to call up a beautiful virgin fairy, Sibilia, for the purpose of 'common copulation'. The purposes of magic were only limited by a person's imagination. But in spite of the elaborate preparations, ritual magic was probably not any more successful than the spells of witches.

Ritual magic predates Christianity. The ancient rituals were not transmitted word for word down through the centuries, but there is a lot of continuity in the methods. Magic is a perennial practice that changes configuration depending on the culture in which it is practised. After the collapse of the Roman Empire, it adapted to Christianity. We have very good information concerning the ancient form of ceremonial magic in the Greek Magical Papyri. The rituals contain the same elements that appear in the early modern ceremonies. Long complex invocations, prayers, hymns, and exorcisms combined magic and religion, or more accurately, used religious elements for magical purposes. Technical information included the making of talismans, wands, knives, swords, ink, pen, parchment, perfumes, and all the other paraphernalia necessary for the appeasement of the spirit world. The classical rituals often included animal sacrifice to placate the spirits, and some of the ingredients for the rituals required the death or mutilation of members of the animal kingdom, most commonly roosters, bats, cats, and toads. Elaborate preparations of the space, the tools, and the magician were important. The practical aspects of the instructions emphasised fasting, chastity, ritual bathing, and the wearing of ceremonial garments of clean linen, preparations that were similar to the ancient priesthood.

These same elements can be found in Judaic religious rituals as well. The Old Testament instructs an officiant to dress in linen: 'He shall put on the holy linen coat, and he shall have the linen breeches upon his body, and shall be girded with a linen girdle, and with the linen mitre shall he be attired: these are holy garments.' (*Leviticus* 16:4) The names of angels were also borrowed from Jewish apocalyptic literature, specifically the *Book of Enoch*. Enoch was allegedly the great-grandson of Noah. The *Book of Enoch* is the origin of well-known angels, such as Michael, Gabriel, Raphael, and Uriel. The *Book of Enoch* also contained astronomical and astrological material.

The biblical King Solomon also played a role in ritual magic. He was the son of David, renowned for fighting the giant Goliath and for building the temple that housed the Ark of the Covenant. Solomon had prayed for help because demons were interfering with the construction of the temple. In response, God sent the angel Michael with a magic ring engraved with the pentalpha, which had the power to subdue the demons and force them to use their supernatural abilities to build the temple. The legend of King Solomon was written in the *Testament of Solomon*. The book included a list of more than thirty demons, along with the words required to subdue them. This list was repeated in many other books of magical instructions. Several other texts were attributed to Solomon as well, including the *Key of Solomon*, the *Ars Notoria*, and the *Almandal*. None of the Solomon volumes were written until after the coming of Christ, but magical manuals were considered more authoritative if they could be traced back to some ancient source. In the *Clavicula Salomonis* or *Key of Solomon*, compiled in the twelfth or thirteenth century, good and evil spirits were harnessed to find hidden treasure, to locate missing and stolen goods, to become invisible, and to provoke lust. The *Ars Notoria* or *Notary Arts* was allegedly revealed to King Solomon by an angel in a dream. It contains prayers to saints and angels for divine knowledge of the liberal arts, which included grammar, rhetoric, logic, arithmetic, music, geometry, and astronomy. The *Almandal* was a manual for the invocation of angels, including how each angel would appear.

Jewish tradition also contributed the secret names of God, which had been given to Moses on the mountain. Two of the names for the Old Testament god became very popular in ritual magic. AGLA is an acronym for *Atah Gibor Le-olam Adonai* or Thou art mighty forever, O Lord. The other is the sacred name that should not be spoken: YHWH for *Yod He Wau He*, commonly pronounced as Yahweh or Jehovah. In magical texts, this is referred to as the Tetragrammaton or the word of four letters. In Reginald Scot's *Discoverie*, one can see the use of both of these holy names in the magician's circle. [See Image #24, 'How to inclose a spirit in a crystal', in *Discoverie of Witchcraft*]

The names of God were keys to interpreting the Torah. In the thirteenth century, a poor Spanish rabbi named Moses de Léon published a group of books called the *Zohar*. At the time, they were presented as ancient texts written in the second century, when Jews were persecuted by the Romans. They may have incorporated oral traditions, but scholars believe that they were written by de Léon himself. The practice that was developed from these texts, known as Kabbalah, is the mystical interpretation of the Torah. The overall substance of the work concerns man's relationship with the divine. Unity with the godhead could be achieved by moving up through the ten *Sefirot*, which are aspects or emanations of the divine. The practical Kabbalah attempts to extract occult information from the Hebrew scriptures via the practice of numerology or gematria. A numerical value is attributed to each of the letters to reveal divine meaning. Renaissance magicians later incorporated some of the concepts of the Kabbalah into magic.

By the middle ages, magical texts were a synthesis of Babylonian/Persian, Egyptian, Greek, Roman, Jewish, Gnostic, and Arabic traditions and sources. Texts containing magical instruction were later referred to as *grimoires*. The term is derived from the French word *grammaire*, referring to books written in Latin. It did not become popular in England until the mid-nineteenth-century revival of magic, but I use it as a convenient designation for manuals of magical instruction. In addition to instructions for ritual magic, *grimoires* often included charms, amulets, spells, and recipes. Even after the books were available in print, men continued to write their own copies. Not only could they record what excerpts were of particular interest to them, but the handwritten manuals were considered more effective. The book itself had magical power.

The early modern *grimoires* contained many elements of Christian liturgy. This is not surprising considering that learned magic was kept alive throughout the middle ages by monks, friars, and clerics. In the early middle ages, the clergy were the most literate members of society. There was a surplus of clerical persons in the middle ages, who were largely underemployed and unsupervised. Many priests did not have full-time parish duties and many young men were accepted into monastic orders. Not only were they literate and had time to experiment, but copying and illuminating manuscripts were common elements of a monk's duties. They had both the time and the means to transcribe *grimoires*. The liturgical aspects of early modern magic were no doubt added by this group of men during the early middle ages. The clerics Christianised the rituals in the same way that Augustine and Aquinas had Christianised Plato and Aristotle respectively. The theological underpinnings of magic would have been important to the monks. Clerics also had knowledge of exorcism and consecration, which continued to be key elements in the magical rituals. Priests were often employed to conduct a mass to consecrate magical objects.

Ironically, the belief in divine intervention strengthened the possibility of magic rather than dismantling it. As the manuscripts were circulated through monasteries and universities, the copiers and editors added bits and pieces of information, probably gleaned from their own experiences and experiments, as well as items from the oral tradition of folklore. The results are often quite eclectic. In most cases, we do not know how much men tried to carry out the instructions in the manuals. They may have dabbled out of curiosity or a sense of inquiry and experimentation. On the other hand, their interest in the texts may have been strictly academic or theological. We do know, however, from men's personal journals and correspondence, that many of the techniques outlined in the *grimoires* were attempted.

Not only was access to literacy restricted in the premodern period, but the necessary books to practise magic were a luxury, which further limited who could be a magician. The rituals themselves were also expensive, employing costly ingredients and paraphernalia. Operations were complex and technical, requiring lengthy preparations, not the type of magic attempted by the village witch. One example will suffice. The ink used for writing the various characters and letters for the ritual had to be specially prepared, exorcised, and consecrated. One set of instructions directs the magician to place water from a river into a new, varnished pot along with a powder made from gall-nuts, Roman vitriol (copper sulphate), and gum arabic (from the acacia tree). The mixture was then boiled over a fire made with sprigs of fern gathered on St John's Eve and twigs of vines gathered on the full moon in March. A fresh batch was required for each operation. Just waiting for the appropriate astrological moment could mean months of planning. Magicians also favoured the use of parchment on which to write, which was made from the skin of animals. Even after the fifteenth century when paper became a less costly option, *grimoires* still recommended using virgin parchment, made from young animals not yet sexually active, or unborn parchment, made from aborted animal foetuses. All of the tools had to be ritually made and consecrated, including the pen used to write with, the knives, swords, wands, incense, and virgin wax candles.

In addition to preparing the tools, the magician had to prepare himself. In its purest form, ritual magic was just that. The preparations were ritualistic, insisting on the purity and chastity of the practitioner. In medieval *grimoires*, magicians were advised to attend the ritual wearing the clerical surplice or stole for protection from demons. In one set of instructions, the operator was directed to fast for nine days, to be moderate in speech, and to dress in special, clean clothing. He was to attend mass for each of those nine days, placing his magic book on the altar. Before the book was even opened, the magus had to sprinkle it with holy water and say seven psalms and the 'litany' over it while kneeling toward the east. Confession, prayer, and meditation were all aspects of getting ready to cast the circle. Latin invocations and supplications were pages long. Not for the faint of heart. And not for the part-time cunning man, who also had a trade to attend to. The time required to prepare for magic meant that the magician was a man with a lot of leisure time on his hands, someone from the upper echelons of society.

After days, months, or even years of preparation, the magician could finally cast the circle. The magic circle is one element of ritual magic that has survived centuries of transmission and has been adopted by modern witches. In classical sources, circular movements were used to purify an area, often with libations of water and wine. This was usually in association with summoning up ghosts from their graves. In premodern practice, the circle was usually for the protection of the magicians, and the demons appeared outside of the circle. In some cases, a separate circle was made for the demons to occupy. The circle was also a place of power, which enhanced the ability of the magician to focus his mastery on controlling the demons. The circle could be very simple or extremely elaborate, including specially built platforms or rooms purposely constructed. The necessary figures could be drawn on a cloth or directly unto the floor or ground with ashes or chalk.

One set of instructions directed the magus to strike the ritual knife into the centre of the proposed site and measure a circle nine feet around it. Another circle was to be made behind the first. Between the two, pentacles were to be drawn with the various names of God, such as AGLA, the Tetragrammaton, El, and Adonai. Crosses were made in the circumference of the first circle. Behind the second circle, a square was made to hold a pot of tools and a sword. When all was ready, a fire was lit and a specially consecrated candle was placed in a lantern. Then the participants entered the circle (it is unclear which one), closed the 'gateway', and perfumed themselves with incense. Conjurations were made facing the east. The magicians then stood ready with pen and ink to write down the messages from the spirits.

Another simpler set of instructions told the would-be magician to go to a private spot in the woods, draw a circle 'four square' with a naked (unsheathed) sword, make a pentacle in every corner, and stand in the east to begin the invocations. The sixteenth and seventeenth century *grimoires* are full of the appropriate symbols and words to be written in the circle. These could be inscribed in the circle itself, drawn on parchment and held in the hand, or fastened unto the clothing. In addition to AGLA and the Tetragrammaton, crosses and pentacles were the most popular symbols. Pentacles, or pentangles, are technically five-pointed stars, but the manuscripts often say pentangle but show a hexagram or six-pointed star, commonly called the Star of David, which is now associated with the Jewish community.

Not every magician followed the instructions to the letter. In fact, some of the people attempting to perform ritual magic probably did not have any written instructions. Casting a circle was not normally in the repertoire of the village witch, but magical instructions were experimented with by male and female cunning folk, who often adapted the elaborate instructions contained in *grimoires*. The tailor and part-time cunning man William Wycherley told authorities that he used a circle called 'Circulus Salamonis'. In the circle, he invoked a spirit called Baro, using a sword, a sceptre, and a ring inscribed with the word Tetragrammaton. The cunning man John Walsh used a circle, two wax candles, and a cross of virgin wax to invoke fairies. He purified the ritual space with frankincense and Saint Johns' wort. In the previous chapter, we examined the case of Anne Bodenham, who had learned her skills under the notorious 'Dr' John Lambe. The servant girl who testified against her said she used her staff to cast a circle, which she fumigated before calling up the Devil. Her alleged magical practice could have been embellished to make a stronger suit against her as a witch. The same witness said that the spirits she called up looked like ragged boys, who danced in the circle with the cat and dog. Hard to discern between fact and fiction in any of these cases. The Italian sorceress Anastasia 'la Frappona' confessed to making a circle with charcoal, into which she entered and fumigated the 'spirit of love' with incense. She also did image magic inside the circle, pouring oil of turpentine over a wax figure in the shape of a man and piercing it with three pins. She was attempting to attract a particular nobleman as a lover. A similar experiment took place in 1630, led by a Franciscan monk by the name of Diego. He had made a ritual knife out of iron, according to some magical instructions. He spread cypress ashes over the floor, into which he drew three circles that intersected. The circles were consecrated to demons. At the entrance to each circle, he drew symbols of angels and demons. Candles, also inscribed with special symbols, were placed at the centre of each circle. In one of the circles, Diego read invocations from a *grimoire* while his companion knelt in one of the other circles. Goose quills and blank paper were available for the demons to write on. Unfortunately, the demons could not make it that evening.

Even accused witches occasionally employed the device of the circle. After Margery Staunton was refused some milk, she squatted down on the ground outside the woman's house and inscribed a circle with a knife. She dug several holes inside the circle and declared that she was making a 'shityng house for her self'.[2] The woman who had denied her request subsequently fell sick. It is impossible to know if Mother Staunton understood the symbolism of the circle or whether she was just making a crude gesture associated with excrement. But her actions were interpreted in a magical manner due to her notorious reputation for grumbling curses after being denied her wishes.

As we can see from these examples, there were many ritual tools used for magic. Knives, swords, and wands were used to cast the circle, to protect the participants against the spirits, and to carry out other magical operations. In Reginald Scot's anti-witchcraft treatise, he included an illustration of the ritual knife that was used to cast the circle, with Alpha inscribed on one side and Omega on the other. [See Image #25, Conjuring Knife, in *Discoverie of Witchcraft*] The cunning man mentioned above, William Wycherley, tried to use an unconsecrated sword for treasure hunting. He reported that while the men were digging for the treasure, a black horse came and scared them away. Apparently, the ritual preparation of the tools was crucial to success.

The use of a wand first appears in Homer's *Odyssey*. The god Hermes used his golden wand to transport souls to the underworld. In the same tale, Circe uses a wand to turn Odysseus's crew into swine. The seventeenth-century cunning woman, Mary Parish, spent a considerable amount of time searching for two different sticks to serve as wands for divining or opening the ground when treasure hunting. One was a common smooth hazel; the other was a 'she' witch hazel, which is actually a type of elm. The wands then had to be consecrated by a Catholic priest. The angels delivered another wand to Parish and her partner Goodwin Wharton that had been manufactured in heaven; it was carved from a unicorn's horn. Other instructions suggested that the hazel wand should be cut from a young tree with a single stroke at sunrise on a Wednesday (the hour and day ruled by Mercury). The rods were then to be inscribed with characters of Mercury and consecrated with some sweet incense.

One of the most important elements of ceremonial magic was words. In the middle ages, the majority of the invocations were in Latin, probably due to the heavy borrowing from liturgical language. By the early modern era, the elaborate conjurations and invocations of ancient rituals had been supplemented with prayers. The Paternoster, the Ave, the Creed, and bits of scripture were used to command the spirit world. Sacred words, saints' names, and the Trinity were added along with the use of holy water, holy oil, and palms blessed by a priest. One Anglican priest thought that the words 'hocus pocus' used by magicians were a corruption of the Catholic phrase *hoc est corpus*, Latin for 'this is my body', which is used by the priest during the Eucharist. The words were probably corrupted by the illiterate congregation, which did not understand the Latin used in Mass. For the theologian, the words of consecration said over the Eucharist are not the cause of the transubstantiation, but rather a signal to the divine for the intervention necessary to make the conversion from wine to blood and bread to flesh. However, this subtlety was probably lost on the average communicant. To further complicate matters, Thomas Aquinas had argued that the rituals of the sacraments operated by virtue of the operation not the operator. *Ex opere operato* (meaning from the work being worked) put more value on the words and actions of the priest conducting the ritual than on the spiritual status of the priest or the participants. As a result, the words themselves took on a numinous meaning. It is hard to determine how much magic was influenced by religious practices and how much religion was moulded by magical techniques. But it is pretty clear that they both had the same roots in the supplication of spirits. In exorcism, the priest commanded demons to leave a person's body; in magic, the magician commanded demons to appear and grant his desires. Both operations depend on the belief that the demons are real and that they can be controlled.

Necromancy

Ritual magic can be roughly broken down into necromancy, theurgy, and image magic. Similar to all other aspects of magic and witchcraft, there are no clear divisions between the various strands. Necromancy literally means the raising of spirits of the dead. Traditionally, this was to consult the spirits for the purpose of divination or knowing the future. In Chapter 1, we saw how Odysseus used necromancy to seek advice from the spirit of a dead person. In the story of Saul and the witch of Endor, related in Chapter 2, the sorceress used the art of necromancy to call up the spirit of Samuel for the purpose of revealing the future to Saul. During the witchcraft persecution era, the term necromancy was used in a derogatory fashion to describe any form of 'black magic', also referred to as 'nigromancy'. The spirits conjured up were usually considered demons rather than spirits of dead humans.

Operations sometimes included the blood of sacrificed animals, and the goals were not always altruistic. This form of magic was used for locating buried treasure, for inducing love or hate, and for causing harm or disease.

The opponents of magic considered that all magic was underwritten by the Devil. However, for the magicians who were attempting these rituals, the difference between necromancy and witchcraft was that the magician was in control of the demons. He summoned and subjugated them for the purpose of serving him in whatever endeavour he was pursuing. The witch, on the other hand, was a servant of the Devil. Ritual magicians commanded spirits; they did not obey them. Evil spirits were treated quite harshly: 'if the Spirit be pertinacious, obstinate, and will not appear' then the conjurations were to be 'stronger to stronger, using Objurgations, Contumelies, Cursings, and Punishments, and suspension from [the demon's] Office and Power'.[3] Banishing the spirits was the final element of necromantic rituals. If the demons were a nuisance, as in the case of guarding hidden treasure, the magus could banish them with words such as 'I excommunicate thee and deprive thee from all thy dignities to the deepest pit in Hell and there shalt thou remain in everlasting chains, in fire and brimstone, where shall be weeping and gnashing of teeth forever.'[4]

Necromantic rituals frequently called on higher powers, such as angels, saints, and Christ, to assist in controlling and binding the demons. As I have pointed out several times, magic and religion were not necessarily separate practices. Richard Napier was the rector of Great Linford, Buckinghamshire, England, where he practised medicine. He used divine power to control the demonic spirits. He also invoked the angel Raphael into a crystal for additional information concerning his patients. He used the following invocation:

> 'I charge thee thou wicked & unclean spirit or spirits by what title soever thou be called, I charge & command thee by the living god, the true god, & the holy god & by their virtues & powers which have created both thee & me & all the world, I charge thee by these holy names of god Tetragrammaton + Adonay + Saday + Sabaoth + Jehova + ____ + *Omnipotens* + *Sempete*___ + *Dominis Dominantiu* + *Rex regnum* + by thou virtues & powers & by all their names by the which god gave power to man both to speak or think.'[5]

Napier maintained that his practice was religious not magical. He desired 'that gift divine supernatural of virtue celestial … to heal in [God's] powerful name.'[6] Astrology, angel magic, and physic sat comfortably together. It was necessary to obtain God's or at least the angels' protection from the inferior sort of spirits. However, this did not make the process angelic.

Theurgy

Theurgy, or angel magic, was the invocation or petitioning of angels on their own account, rather than as a controlling mechanism over demons. For the fourth-century philosopher Iamblichus, theurgy was a way for man to tap into divine power and become closer to God. In the eyes of the men practising it, theurgy was a type of 'white magic'. Religious devotion, magic, and mysticism were all part of the practice. The benevolent angels were not commanded and controlled like demons, but were supplicated and invoked with 'gentle & convenient' speech.[7] Rituals were more like petitioning than summoning.

Heavenly knowledge was sometimes attained through ritually induced visions. In the *Fourth Book of Occult Philosophy*, the unknown author described how to 'receive an Oracle from the good spirit'. The magician had to be 'chaste, pure, and confess'd' and dressed in 'clean white garments'. On the first Sunday of the new moon, he was to make a circle 'with a sanctified cole' inscribed with the names of angels and God. With incense burning, he was directed to face the east and recite a particular psalm. The ritual was supposed to be repeated for six days. On the seventh day, he again entered the circle and anointed himself

> 'with holy anoynting oyl, by annoynting his forehead, and upon both his eyes, and in the palms of his hands, and upon his feet. Then upon his knees let him say the Psalm aforesaid, with Divine and Angelical names. Which being said, let him arise, let him begin to walk about in a Circle within the said Circle from the east to the west, until he is wearied with a dizziness of his brain: let him fall down in the Circle, and there he may rest; and forthwith he shall be wrapt up in an ecstasie, and a spirit will appear unto him, which will informe him of all things.'[8]

Fasting, burning incense, and walking in circles until exhausted probably induced a trance-like state conducive to having dreams and visions.

Scrying

Both demons and angels could be controlled and accessed via a technique called scrying. Scrying was the practice of looking into a reflective surface, such as a crystal, a mirror, or a bowl of water, to see images. The scryer might see visions in the surface of the water or mirror, or the spirit might inhabit the magic ball. The Greek Magical Papyri give instructions for several methods. The ancient practitioners of these arts believed that different liquids drew different spirits. Rainwater accessed the gods of the heavens; spring water summoned ghosts of the dead from the earth, thereby making scrying a form of necromancy. The Greeks used olive oil on the surface of the water, over which spells were uttered. Augustine also believed that some magicians used blood, which would summon up demons. The Greek natural philosopher Pliny the Elder discussed a 'holding stone' used by magicians to entrap ghosts.

The ritual element of scrying came in the form of sacrifices, invocations, and burning of incense. In the ancient world, the usual offerings of wine, honey, milk, and cakes were made. Black rams were typical sacrifices, but black cattle were also used. In one case, three black puppies were used to call up Hecate. (Please, please, do not try this at home!!) Demons and the god Hades were also summoned. Other ritual features that could be included were scrying at astrologically propitious times, such as the conjunction of Venus and Jupiter in a particular phase of the moon. Scrying might be done within the magic circle with a mirror specially made on the first hour of a Friday under a waxing moon. Specific spirits were sometimes invoked, such as Adam's first wife, Lilith, who was considered a Hebrew night demon.

Edward Kelley, the scryer who worked for the renowned Tudor mathematician and magician, John Dee, used a quartz sphere, or crystal ball, which is currently on display in the British Museum. The pair of magicians also used a jet black obsidian mirror brought back from Mexico after Hernando Cortés's conquest. Apparently, objects of volcanic glass were used by Aztec priests for divination. A magical disc in the same display cabinet was used by Dee to set his 'shew stones' on while scrying. It is a twenty-three centimetre wax disc engraved with pentangles and magical names. Beryl stones are also mentioned in ancient texts for scrying. Richard Napier had a 'beryl glass' into which he invoked the angel Raphael. Mr Blumfield, a cunning man of Essex, used a common mirror to show his clients the faces of the suspected thieves. The cunning woman Mary Parish of London used a glass of water, which she kept fresh with lemons.

Magical ointments for the scryer's eyes were also used, perhaps to interfere with normal vision. The cunning woman Mary Parish claimed that she had used an ointment made from a lapwing killed in June at a particular astrological hour. This may have been gleaned from the well-known magician Agrippa, who said that he knew how to make a similar ointment from the blood of a lapwing, a bat, or a goat. He also claimed to make a salve from the gall of a man and the eyes of a black cat, but he did not offer the details. Perhaps just as well.

Traditionally, the scryer was a child. In the Greek Magical Papyri, the observer was to be a boy-medium, who had not had sex with a woman. Rather disturbing that 'with a woman' needs to be added to this qualification, but it was pederastic Greece after all. In one set of instructions, the stipulation was made that the boy should not have been used for scrying before. A fifteenth-century commonplace book belonging to Robert Reynys describes a ritual for divination using a boy between seven and thirteen years of age. A red thread was wound around the child's thumb and the acronym AGLA was inscribed on the fingernail. Angels were expected to appear in the boy's nail. John Dee experimented using his 7-year-old son Arthur to peer into the crystal. These child mediums may have been under hypnosis or put into a trance state. The reason for choosing children was that innocence and purity were believed to be necessary to communicate with the spirit world. Good health, intelligence, and beauty were also favoured in the medium. Mary Parish and Goodwin Wharton discovered that a woman could achieve the same purity as a virgin via her unborn child. Mary was able to see the angel Uriel in a glass of water whenever she was pregnant (which was often). Generally, females were not favoured as mediums, although the blind seer Tiresias used his virgin daughter to describe the ghosts he called up.

Accusations of sacrificing young boys in order to perform necromancy were also made in the classical era. The Roman poet Lucan described the witch Erichtho ripping foetuses out of wombs to lay on her altar in order to draw the ghosts. Many such accusations were made against real historical characters as well. This may be the underlying source of the charges made against the Pappenheimer family, discussed in Chapter 7. Perhaps it is not a giant step from using a virgin boy as a scryer to sacrificing children for divination to stealing unborn babies from their mothers' wombs for nefarious purposes.

Image Magic

The third strand of ritual magic has been called image magic by the historians studying this material. This is the aspect of magic that was most often borrowed by the less literate members of society, such as cunning folk. The power of the heavens was drawn down into amulets, talismans, and other magical objects. Both licensed physicians and local healers used these devices. When the English astrologer William Lilly was taking care of his master's wife, he discovered a small bag of gold and iron amulets that she wore on her body. Lilly referred to these as 'sigils', which contained inscriptions of the planets Jupiter and Venus. The unlicensed physician and magician Simon Forman made a gold ring set with coral, to be worn on the little finger of his left hand. It was designed as protection against witchcraft and devils. He wanted to gain favour in his profession and success over his many enemies. We have already discussed King Solomon's ring used to control demons. Prayers, invocations, and fumigations were all employed to invoke astral powers into the talismans.

Astrology was an aspect of both necromancy and theurgy, but image magic drew very heavily on astrological knowledge. Astrology by itself is not magic. The occult influence on both people and objects attributed to the stars and planets is what makes astrology magical. The astral power emanating from the heavens could be captured in rings, talismans, and images. Astrological knowledge was kept alive by Arabic scholars in the Islamic world in the early middle ages. The collapse of the Roman Empire had cut off communications with much of the Arabic world. Then the Crusades made relations between the Christian West and Muslims even more difficult. However, the Crusades also renewed contact with the Islamic world. The other point of contact was in the Iberian Peninsula and southern Italy, where the Islamic culture remained strong throughout the middle ages. Spain did not complete the conquest of Muslim territory until the late fifteenth century. Also, beginning in the eleventh century, the universities in Bologna, Paris, Oxford, and Cambridge were established. Scholars had a renewed interest in the classical texts, especially Aristotle's as we have seen in the case of Thomas Aquinas. Between the eleventh and thirteenth centuries many Greek and Arabic texts were translated into Latin. After Spanish Christians captured Toledo, Islamic, Judaic, and Christian scholars worked together. Out of this eclectic mix came a volume known as the *Picatrix*, probably composed in Spain in the eleventh century and then translated from Arabic into Spanish and then into Latin. It was a compilation of technical information on magic and astrology from older sources, many of them from the Near East. It became a key text for early modern magicians. This fuelled a further interest in astrology, which was promoted in royal courts as well as the universities.

Natural Philosophy

Natural philosophy is, quite literally, the philosophy of how nature operates. It was the forerunner of modern science. Premodern philosophers and magicians did not have the same understanding of science that twenty-first-century people do. Whereas modern science is quantitative, natural philosophy was qualitative. Modern scientists measure the material world in an attempt to understand it. In the ancient and premodern era, the world was explained in terms of its qualities, such as hot and cold and wet and dry. More importantly, for our purposes, natural philosophers were concerned with the effects that those qualities could have on other elements.

The classical Greek philosopher Plato had a huge impact on the ancient and early modern understanding of the universe. His theories continued to be the basis for natural philosophy until the sixteenth century, when various well-known men such as Copernicus, Descartes, and Newton would challenge those ideas. For the Greeks, all of nature was permeated by both soul (*psyche*) and reason or mind (*nous*). This meant that the world was not only alive but was also intelligent and purposeful. Nature was viewed as a living organism. The interconnectedness between the heavenly realm and the earthly realm was like a sort of kinship. Plants, animals, and minerals were affected by the astral sphere of stars and planets. Plato's philosophy can be expressed in terms of the macrocosm and the microcosm. The macrocosm, which is the spiritual realm including the heavens, was linked to the microcosm, which is the earthly realm of matter. This connection enabled man to tap into the powers of the macrocosm. Because plants, animals, and stones shared in this divine interconnectedness, they could be used to cure diseases and as protective amulets. Connections were sometimes hidden or occult, but they had the potential to be discovered and tapped into.

The title page of Robert Fludd's *Utriusque cosmi maioris scilicet et minoris metaphysica, physica atqve technica historia* (1617–1619) has a representation of this idea. [See Image #26, Illustration of macrocosm and microcosm] Fludd was an English neoplatonist and physician, who attempted to explain the relationship between man and the cosmos. The image depicts a man, representing the microcosm, in the centre of the macrocosm, consisting of the stars and planets, which are denoted by their astrological signs. The sun and moon above the man's head represent spirit and soul. The human body was considered a miniature universe that reflected the properties of the heavens. The five points of contact of the man within the circle (head, two hands, two feet) mirrored the five senses and contributed to the pentacle becoming the ultimate magical symbol. The theory of macrocosm and microcosm was also summed up in the phrase 'as above, so below', which was expressed in the *Emerald Tablets* attributed to Hermes Trismegistus, an Egyptian sage thought to predate both Plato and Moses. 'That which is below is like that which is above & that which is above is like that which is below to do the miracles of one only thing.'[9] Plato's theories had not been diminished with the advent of Christianity, because nature, of course, was created by God. Understanding the secrets of nature meant a better understanding of God. Nature was a divine implement and had purpose.

Of course, any philosophy of nature had to be reconciled with the Bible. God not only created the universe but was an active force in the world on a daily basis. This would be strengthened after the Reformation by Protestant doctrine, which promoted the idea of providence. There was no such thing as chance. Everything happened with God's permission and direction. For magicians, magic was a way to ascend to divine union. The belief was that once the magician revealed the wonders of the natural world, he would have even more faith and love for God. The shift from the divine being immanent in nature to outside of nature would not happen until the fifteenth and sixteenth centuries. The concept of God as 'Clockmaker' and nature as a well-oiled machine with mechanical laws that had been established at creation only gradually took shape in the seventeenth century. A more organic view in which nature was identified with the divine was more prevalent during the height of the witchcraft era.

This worldview is what allowed for the belief in magic. The magician knew where to look in nature for magical effects and how to use those effects for good or evil. In other words, real magic was natural not supernatural. The magical aspect of this philosophy arose from the belief that the occult properties of the stars and planets could be drawn into objects in the material world. The magician could harness the power that was in the natural world, including the heavens, as opposed to working wonders that were antithetical to nature and caused by demonic means. Amulets, talismans, and other image magic were not viewed as witchcraft, because they were based on assumptions about the physical and divine properties of the materials used. The magician was simply tapping into the occult properties of natural elements. Manipulation of the material world could access and employ the spiritual world. There were natural affinities between various substances, such as metals, stones, plants, animals, colours, and the heavenly bodies. For example, iron, used for swords, was under the power of Mars. The ancients did not know that Mars was covered with iron oxide dust, which makes it appear red. Rather, Mars was the Roman god of war, so things to do with war — martial things — were under his influence. After Christianity, it might have been acceptable in some circles to associate the planet Mars with iron, but certainly not with the god. The stars and planets were also related to the 'doctrine of signatures', which proposed that the occult character of natural substances could be identified by outward appearance. God had left a clue about what properties or uses natural substances possessed.

Natural philosophy got a boost in the Renaissance when more works by Plato starting arriving from the East. One of the key concepts of Renaissance humanism was emphasis on a return to original sources and ancient texts. A group of scholars called neoplatonists worked on translating these texts from the original Greek to Latin, which was the academic language of the West. The most prolific scholar was Marsilio Ficino. He was the son of a physician and studied philosophy and medicine before he obtained the patronage of a wealthy and powerful Italian patron, Cosimo de' Medici of Florence. The head of the Medici family employed Ficino to translate Platonic texts into Latin. Cosimo gave Ficino a house near Florence, into which he invited other humanists to discuss Plato's work. The circle of philosophers became known as the Platonic Academy. Ficino later became ordained as a Catholic priest.

Medici was constantly on the outlook for new material. In 1460 one of his agents, a Byzantine monk, brought him a text allegedly written by Hermes Trismegistus. Cosimo asked Ficino to immediately direct his attention to translating the new manuscript. The legendary figure was a compilation of the ibis-headed Egyptian god of wisdom, Thoth, and the Greek messenger god, Hermes, known by the Romans as Mercury. Later analysis determined that the manuscript was written in Greek-speaking Egypt in the first or second century CE, but at the time, scholars believed that it had influenced Platonic and biblical ideas, not the other way around. Originally published as the *Pimander*, the body of work eventually became known as the *Corpus Hermeticum*. Unlike the *Picatrix*, the *Corpus* was a theoretical and philosophical treatise on magic, particularly concerning the quest for knowledge and union with the divine. Because the Renaissance neoplatonists believed that Hermes was a model for Moses and Plato, the texts paved the way for a renewed acceptance of Platonic concepts, which did not conflict with Christian precepts.

The Renaissance neoplatonists, influenced by the *Corpus* and the classical neoplatonists, encouraged a metaphysical understanding and exploration of nature. Ficino built on the idea of a world soul outlined by Plato to explain how the heaven and earth corresponded. The world soul gave form to the world and acted as an intermediary between spirit and matter. The world was filled with magical forces that operated through sympathies and antipathies. Ficino developed the idea of a cosmic spirit that permeated the entire universe in the form of a fine corporeal substance. This was what provided a channel between the astral bodies and the earthly bodies. Some things had more pure cosmic spirit than others. Ficino considered wine, white sugar, gold, music, and the scents of cinnamon and roses as particularly potent. (I am sure that if he had experienced chocolate from the New World, he would have included it on his list.) Using astrology and correspondences, the magician could attract divine spirit for spiritual growth or more mundane purposes.

The *Corpus* was not a how-to manual for magic, but it offered authority for the Renaissance magicians to pursue their investigations. In 1489, Ficino published *Three Books on Life.* In the third book of *De Vita*, he supported the idea that ritual could activate occult properties in nature. Stones and herbs sympathetic to the stars could be used to channel the powers that God had implanted in nature. Other scholars added more practical information to the philosophical concepts. Giovanni Pico della Mirandola, a disciple of Ficino, integrated the ideas put forward in the Judaic Kabbalah with the concepts in the *Corpus Hermeticum*. The purpose was not magic, per se, but rather union with the divine. The practical aspects of the Kabbalah included meditation on the several names of God in order to produce ecstasy. But the magician had to be careful not to be ensnared by demons. The practical Kabbalah used the angels as protection against the evil spirits.

Another major contributor to Renaissance magic was the German scholar Henry Cornelius Agrippa von Nettesheim. He published *De Occulta Philosophia* or *Three Books of Occult Philosophy* (1531–1533), which outlined the technical aspects of astral magic. Agrippa was attempting to defend magic as a natural science. Rather than an explicit how-to manual for ritual magic, the work provided a wealth of information on the properties of the heavenly bodies and their earthly correspondences in stones, plants, and animals. Agrippa contributed the idea of inscribing a pentagram at each of the four cardinal points of the ritual circle, which would be adapted by modern Wiccans. The Catholic church placed the book on the Index of Prohibited Books, which aided in its success. The *Fourth Book of Agrippa* was added to publications after his death, but was probably not his work. It deals with more practical and demonic aspects of ritual magic.

Fantasy and Imagination

Imagination has had a long association with magic. Plato considered *phantasia* or fantasy as one of the divisions of the soul. The human imagination facilitated the manifestation of Platonic 'Ideas' into real objects. The five physical senses of sight, hearing, touch, taste, and smell collect data from the world around us, which the imagination interprets into images, memories, and actions. When Augustine Christianised the work of Plato, he maintained this aspect of the philosopher's concept by identifying imagination as a tool that helped the soul achieve union with God. Because humans had free will, they could direct the images formed through the use of imagination. The negative aspect of this concept was the belief that imagination could work on others, as well as the individual. This explained how a witch could cause harm by merely a glance or a wish. For the ritual magician, the imagination aided in drawing down the influences of the heavenly bodies, thereby creating a bridge between the macrocosm and the microcosm. Imagination worked in conjunction with the will to produce the effects of magic. Agrippa advised the magician to 'vehemently, imagine, hope, and believe strongly' for success.[10] And the *Corpus Hermeticum* stated: 'For imagination is nothing but begetting.'[11] In *Magic and Masculinity*, I argue that early modern magicians used ritual magic to self-fashion their identities. This is one of many aspects of magic that has continuity with modern witchcraft.

Popular Use

Over time, the procedures of ritual magic were bastardised and butchered until the not-so-educated magician was merely following a fairly simple recipe for magic. The fragments of necromancy that were practised by witches, cunning folk, and the less educated lacked the rigour of the original ceremonies. Over the years and through many transmissions, they became more demonic and less dramatic, reduced to mere actions rather than rituals. As we have seen, one aspect of ritual magic was the inscribing of pentacles, figures, and Hebrew names of God on parchment to be used inside the magic circle. This aspect filtered down to lower magic. In its investigations, the Venetian Inquisition often found scraps of paper inscribed with crosses, characters, and symbols that were used as charms for safety, love magic, and invisibility spells. It appears that these ideas were wide-spread and long-lived.

Take for example the magical ritual for invisibility. From the Greek Magical Papyri to Harry Potter, the desire to become invisible appears to be a relatively common fancy for humans. In a fifteenth-century manual discovered in Munich, instructions in Latin outlined how to make a cloak of invisibility. The following excerpts were transcribed and translated by the historian Richard Kieckhefer.

> 'under a waxing moon on a Wednesday, in the first hour of the day, having remained chaste for three days beforehand, and with cut hair and beard, and dressed in white, in a secret place outside of town, under a clear sky, on level ground, trace a circle such as appears here, with a magnificent sword, writing these names and everything shown along with them.'[12]

The magician fumigated the circle with frankincense, myrrh, and other incense starting and ending in the west. The circle was then blessed with salt and water while reciting a particular psalm. Kneeling in the east, the magus conjured up four 'powerful, magnificent, illustrious spirits' to appear 'with utmost humility, bound, constrained, and sworn to carry out' his commands. The invocation was repeated four times at each direction. When the spirits appeared, the practitioner requested 'a cloak of invisibility, which should be thin and incorruptible, so that when I wear it no one can see me or sense my presence.' In return, the magician traded the white garment he was wearing. The spirits were dismissed with the words 'Go in peace' and the magus left the circle with his sword. But we are not done yet.

> 'On the third day, return there with the cloak, and you will find your garment, which you will take. Be sure to remember; if on the third day you do not return, or you do not take the garment left there, on the fourth day you will find nothing, but in seven days you will die. Having taken it on the third day, you will burn it in the same place. And know that when you burn it you will hear great lamenting and complaining.'

Now there is just one more step, which seals the ritual as a Christian one: 'take blessed water and sprinkle the cloak, saying, "I conjure you, cloak, by the Father and the Son and the Holy Spirit, and by this water, that whenever I put you on, no one may sense my presence or see me … ."'

Compare this ritual to the actions of an Italian monk in 1584, who was hoping for easy access to women. He obtained three skulls from the graveyard of his monastery. He planted a bean in each mouth and eye socket, then covered the skulls in holy ash. The skulls were watered every day. The monk hoped that the beans would grant invisibility when eaten. A century later, on the other side of the continent, the cunning woman Mary Parish of London conducted a similar experiment. Her partner Goodwin Wharton caught three black cats. At the appropriate astrological moment, the cats were killed and the hearts removed. A pea was placed in each heart and the hearts were planted when the moon was waxing. The pea was supposed to make a person invisible when held in the mouth. Unfortunately, the peas needed to be consecrated by a Catholic priest, which was hard to do in Anglican England. Similar recipes for invisibility can be found in many *grimoires*.

These last two recipes appear to operate on the basis of natural correspondences rather than the aid of any spirits, good or bad. But authorities who were policing magic were suspicious that the magicians were actually making a pact with demonic spirits, who required something in return, say a person's soul. The more nefarious aspects of ceremonial magic rituals raised suspicions about both intentions and methods. Both the theories and practices of known magi, such as John Dee and Marsilio Ficino, were circulated amongst the demonologists, Inquisitors, and judges who would make decisions about the procedures. Even a critic of the witchcraft accusations such as Reginald Scot was aware of the *grimoires* that were circulating. Scot published many of the aspects of necromancy in an attempt to make the practitioners look foolish. By drawing attention to the rituals, he may have contributed to undermining the belief in the efficacy of natural magic. Even if the men who practised ritual magic throughout the late middle ages and into the Renaissance were not persecuted, the discussion of ceremonial magic increased the consciousness of demonic magic in the minds of authorities. The result was that all magic was condemned as witchcraft in the early modern period. Next we will look at the repercussions of this interpretation.

Chapter 7

The Tree of Life and Death, Persecution through Prosecution

The treatment of alleged witches in the early modern period has often been referred to as a holocaust or, at the very least, the victimisation of women. Terms such as 'witch hunt' and 'witch craze' are common. But was it? Persecution is a type of victimisation, usually marked by hostility toward, and maltreatment of, a person based on political, religious, sexual, or racial prejudices. Prosecution, on the other hand, is a legal procedure, usually conducted according to a set of rules sanctioned by the state to address crime and maintain social order. The problem in definition occurs when persecution is legalised, as it was in Nazi Germany and still is in many parts of the world. When witchcraft is defined as a legitimate method of committing a crime, then the witch is a criminal, who can be prosecuted under the law. If witchcraft is defined as devil-worship, then the witch can be persecuted for religious beliefs, even if no crime is committed. These conditions, which existed in early modern Europe under the monopoly of monotheistic Christianity, were further complicated in a society where sexual acts were legislated by the state. Fornication with the Devil then became a crime as well as heresy. The end result was prosecution under the law for activities that could not possibly have resulted in the alleged crimes. The law was used to persecute the imaginary figure of the witch, who, unfortunately, was embodied in real people.

So far we have examined two intertwined aspects of witchcraft prosecutions and persecutions: accusations from the village level, born out of popular culture and belief in the supernatural; and concepts about diabolical witchcraft promoted by the educated elites. These are commonly referred to as 'bottom-up' and 'top-down' theories concerning the causes and repercussions of witchcraft. The bottom-up approach stresses that the initial accusations of witchcraft depended on belief in magic and witchcraft at the lower end of the social structure. Most accusations originated in the village setting and were commonly levelled by one woman against another and then supported by the community. For the most part, it was local suspicions and village quarrels that resulted in accusations. As we have seen, ideas about the Wild Hunt and belief in the supernatural were widespread in popular culture, which facilitated the prosecution of the witch by authorities.

In the early days of witchcraft historiography, the top-down theory was the only one. The idea that witches were systematically hunted by church and state authorities was common. Accusations of witchcraft were allegedly used by the people in power to control the masses. According to this theory, the persecutions ended because of the emergence of rational scientific thought. This argument has since been completely debunked. Proponents of a modified top-down theory would now argue that the crime and sin of witchcraft did not exist until the secular and ecclesiastical authorities put laws and guidelines into place. Both criminal courts and church institutions, such as the Inquisition, provided opportunities for members of society to come forward and make accusations. This theory acknowledges that the majority of accusations were generated, or at least supported, at the village level, but argues that peasants would not have initiated the mass hunts that were carried out by the elites. The top-down theory also argues that sometimes the controls that were put into place regarding witchcraft accusations and prosecutions actually protected suspects from lynchings and mob rule. Most historians in the twenty-first century would take the middle way: witchcraft prosecutions were not a result of either a completely bottom-up or top-down set of circumstances. There is no single, straight-forward explanation. The belief in and the handling of witchcraft had many subtleties and regional differences.

Nevertheless, there would not have been indictments and trials of witches, and the wealth of records that they left, if there had been no laws in place to address magic and witchcraft. The inquisitorial process as opposed to the accusatorial process, discussed in Chapter 2, was combined with the legal and illegal use of torture that contributed to the large hunts that took place. The squabbling about religion and politics that was happening at the top end of society, in addition to war, famine, and disease, was the background noise that fuelled the fear and anxiety surrounding the subject of witches. Without the laws that were implemented by the state and the policies put in place by both the Catholic and Protestant churches, witch hunting would not have reached such epidemic proportions.

Classical Roots

As we have seen, magical practices of various sorts had been illegal ever since the ancient Greeks and Romans. As Christianity developed in the late days of the Roman Empire, prayers to the pantheon of classical deities also fell under the rubric of magic. The secular Roman authorities had been concerned with magic that caused harm and with crimes committed by supernatural means. But Christianity inherited not only the Roman restrictions on magic but also the Judaic prohibitions. The Hebrews had condemned magical practices on the basis that they were a form of adoration of other gods. And we have seen how Augustine demonised the Roman gods. The overriding concern of the Christian authorities in relation to magic became heresy.

Premodern Law

Throughout the middle ages, witchcraft was mainly under the jurisdiction of the ecclesiastical courts, which were concerned with correcting a person's beliefs, especially beliefs that the church considered 'superstitious' or pagan. Penance was the most common resolution. Accusations of witchcraft might arise in a secular court, if a person suspected he had been harmed by sorcery. In a largely agrarian society, the secular courts tended to be local and communal. The lord of the manor held court to adjudicate disputes in his domain. The purpose of justice was to restore peace to the community. If damages had been incurred, the guilty party was made to compensate the plaintiff. The process was not controlled by lawyers, and the law was accusatorial not inquisitorial. There was more emphasis on rehabilitating the accused back into the community than there was on retribution and punishment.

In the late middle ages and continuing into the early modern period, the process of statehood and the centralisation of authority began. The state took over many areas of social control that had previously belonged to the church. The new courts were more punitive and abstract than the restorative and personal nature of the manorial courts. This could work to the benefit of the accused, if the person was a victim of local prejudices and personal vindictiveness. Instead of concern for the functioning of the manorial community, the broader purpose of justice was to deter crime by demonstrating the consequences.

There was no pan-European law that dealt with magic and witchcraft. Witchcraft was configured differently in different areas and treated differently from region to region, even within one state. Generally speaking, laws against witchcraft and magic in the early modern period were part of the secularisation and separation of church and state that was happening in this era. But in some instances, the church and state worked together even more closely during the Reformation and Counter-Reformation. The law could take the form of an English circuit court, with educated judges appointed by the Crown and a jury of local men; a Scottish commission, consisting of local clergy and landowners; the French *parlement*, with lawyers trained in Roman law; the Spanish and Roman Inquisitions, with judges trained in both ecclesiastical and secular law; or a small village court with a single judge or a jury of peers.

England

In England, witchcraft was mostly a secular concern. Legislation dealt with the crimes committed via witchcraft rather than any heretical belief underwriting sorcery. The first witchcraft statute was issued under Henry VIII in 1542. It addressed witchcraft and sorcery in relation to the destruction of people and goods, in other words, *maleficium*. Cunning folk, who found lost and stolen property, and magicians, who invoked spirits, were also sanctioned, but the so-called witchcraft acts were seldom used against them. The law was repealed during the reign of the boy-king Edward VI, and not reinstated by his elder half-sister Queen Mary I. In 1563, murder by witchcraft became a felony punishable by death under Elizabeth I. If a witch only sickened or lamed people or cattle, she served one year in prison and time in the pillory. But the second offence of *maleficium* warranted the death penalty. When James VI of Scotland came to the English throne as James I in 1603, the law was made more severe. The first offence of *maleficium* could result in death. More importantly, a clause was added concerning the entertaining, employing, feeding, or rewarding of any evil or wicked spirit. This covered any demons raised by ceremonial magic, but more specifically addressed the witch's familiar. This clause moved the crime from causing harm to simply being a witch because of the relationship with a familiar, which was considered an incarnation of the Devil. Witchcraft became a victimless crime.

None of the English legislation incorporated any ideas about the sabbat or the pact with the Devil. This was a Continental concept that took much longer to surface in English cases. Prosecutions for witchcraft were mostly limited to accusations of *maleficium*. There were between 500 and 1,000 executions in the whole period. Judicial torture in criminal cases was not a part of English common law as it was in the Roman law, which had been adopted by most of Europe. The witchcraft acts in England were not repealed until 1736, at which time they were amended to address the fraudulent aspects of pretending to perform witchcraft or conjuration.

Although centralisation of the government had begun in the middle ages in England, as well as the rest of Europe, there is a danger in seeing the state, headed by the monarch, as an all-powerful machine devoted to rooting out witchcraft and heresy. The Crown, guided by the Privy Council, was dependent on its agents of state authority to carry out its proclamations and statutes. The local authorities played a major role in the policing of social order in the early modern era. Local judges, justices of the peace, sheriffs, churchwardens, and parish clergy often had different agendas or different opinions than the Crown. In many cases of witchcraft, we see that the local authorities had more power than the state in managing prosecutions. This was especially relevant to witchcraft, because accusations usually came from within the community. When something bad happened, such as illness of a person or livestock, a woman who was quarrelsome, had a bad reputation, or was a general nuisance was often targeted as a scapegoat. The woman was accused by someone she knew in the neighbourhood. At that point, the person had limited options. If she was a woman with some means or the right connections, she could countersue her accusers for slander. This was what happened in the case of Agnes Fenn, discussed in Chapter 5. Flight may have been an option in rare cases. Dame Alice Kyteler managed to flee to England when the accusations against her got out of hand. But Dame Alice was a woman of means, with influential friends and family. Most of the accused women were poor, which is why they were accused in the first place, because they were constantly begging and grumbling.

Formal accusations of witchcraft first went to the local justice of the peace (JP). These were usually men of some education and standing in the community. They were not necessarily educated in the law or practising lawyers or judges. It was an honorary position that only satisfied the ego, not the pocketbook. The justice of the peace was one of the 'gatekeepers' in witchcraft accusations. He could shut down the accusation or investigate it. While the JP gathered depositions from the community concerning the allegations, the accused woman would be held in gaol or some other temporary confinement. Before her trial, she would be examined under oath by the JP and perhaps examined for a witch's teat by several respectable women. If the justice of the peace felt there was sufficient evidence against her, she would be held until the next court date.

The local clergy also played an important role. In general terms, the parish minister could stir up concern about witchcraft with his sermons, which could make people think about *maleficium* in cases of misfortune rather than natural causes or just plain bad luck. More specifically, a minister or priest could shut down formal accusations with his advice. Sometimes a concerned citizen would approach the clergy about a suspected witch. For example, Ralph Josselin, a vicar in Essex County, was consulted by one of his parishioners about possible witchcraft. In his journal, he reported that:

> 'one J. Biford was clamoured on as a witch, and M' C. thought his child ill by it; I could no way apprehend it, I tooke the fellow alone into the feild [*sic*], and dealt with him solemnely, & I conceive the poore wretch [the woman accused of witchcraft] is innocent as to that evill.'[1]

Sometimes the church was more lenient with its parishioners than the state was with its subjects. For example, in 1555 Joan Tirrye of Taunton, Somerset, was examined by the Catholic church court after giving medicine to a neighbour's wife and to some cattle, which she thought were bewitched. She said that fairies 'taught her such knowledge that she getteth her living by it'.[2] She confessed to dancing with the fairies in the nearby meadow, a statement that could easily be construed as attending a sabbat. But this incident happened during the reign of the Catholic monarch Queen Mary I. The witchcraft statute of Henry VIII had been repealed and the Bishop's Consistory Court dealt with cases of magic. Tirrye was told to stop believing in the illusion of fairies, reminiscent of the advice in the *Canon Episcopi*, and to desist from her healing practices. The church wanted the sinner to see the error of her ways and repent rather than be executed as a witch.

The community also played a large role in witchcraft accusations and indictments, not only as accusers, but also as searchers, watchers, and witnesses giving depositions. Women were involved as much or more than men, especially in the early stages of a case. They were ideally situated to witness alleged witchcraft as attendants at sick-beds, as midwives, wet-nurses, and general care-givers. Females were the heart of the community information system. They attended births and prepared bodies for burial. They were responsible for the preparation of food and managed small livestock. And they were active in the marketplace as both buyers and sellers.

After gathering information and depositions from the community, the justice of the peace decided whether or not to go forward with the accusations. The first hurdle an accused English witch had to get over was the local Quarter Session courts. They were held four times a year, usually at the county seat. The court was not authorised to try felonies, which included witchcraft, but they could present the accused for trial at the

Assize court. Presentments at the Quarter Sessions were heard by a Grand Jury, consisting of twelve men chosen from the minor gentry. These were not lords or aristocracy, but were property owners and substantial men in the community. The jury never included women, even if they held land in their own right, which they could do in England. Not exactly a jury of one's peers, since ninety per cent of the accused witches in England were poor and female. If the Grand Jury decided that the case was valid, they issued a 'true bill', and the person was formally indicted and held over for trial. Names of witnesses were documented at that time.

The next step was the Assize court, which was held twice a year. Two educated and trained judges travelled to the counties from London on various circuits. This is another example of the centralisation of the judicial system that could circumvent local prejudices. The Assize court was held in front of a Petty Jury consisting of twelve men chosen by the sheriff. These men were from the middling sort, yeomen farmers and artisans, which made them somewhat closer to a jury of peers. There was no legal counsel for the accused. When the court was in session, the depositions previously taken by the local justice of the peace were read. The jury decided the guilt or innocence of the accused, and the two judges passed the sentence. No doubt the learned judges had a lot of influence on the jury's decision.

The exception to the English model of witchcraft prosecution was the Matthew Hopkins case, which took place between 1645 and 1647 during the civil war. [See Image #27, Woodcut of 'Matthew Hopkins Witch-finder General'] This case is a good example of how the absence of state courts could affect the outcome of a witch hunt. The circuit courts out of London were suspended during the Civil War, and justice was in the hands of local justices of the peace and large landholders, who had more latitude in their judgements. It was England's largest episode of witchcraft. Approximately 240 people were accused and 100 of them were hanged. The episode started out like so many others in England. Elizabeth Clarke of Manningtree, in Essex County (discussed in Chapter 4), was a poor single woman, whose mother had been accused of witchcraft years before. She was crippled, with only one leg. Among other things, she was accused of murdering the son of Susan Edwards. The baby's wet-nurse lived close to Clarke's house. Not only was Susan's husband, Richard Edwards, the largest landowner in the area, but her step-brother was Matthew Hopkins, who became involved in the case as a self-styled witch hunter. After the initial accusation, other residents of Manningtree and nearby Mistley started remembering strange illnesses and miscarriages. Clarke was first questioned by some of the townsfolk, to whom she admitted that she associated with several other women who were already under suspicion. John Stearne, a staunch Puritan who fancied himself a gentleman and became Hopkins's partner in crime, was told about Clarke's confession. The community thought he could help bring the women to justice, since he had connections with Sir Harbottle Grimston, a local magistrate, who was also a strong Puritan and Parliamentarian. Grimston issued a warrant to Stearne to initiate an investigation and to obtain names of any other witches from Clarke. Matthew Hopkins, a bored young gentleman new to the area, who had been spoon fed on the fear of the Devil, volunteered to help Stearne in his mandate. Clarke was arrested, searched for a witch's teat, and watched for three days and nights to see if any of her familiars came to her. The old lady was bound to a chair in the middle of the room while six 'watchers' observed her. On the third day, four imps appeared to all the witnesses: a cat, two dogs, and a rabbit. Clarke also confessed to having sex with the Devil. In her confession, she implicated the other women in town who were already suspect. Clarke and her accomplices were removed to the cells beneath the ageing Colchester Castle to await trial.

Other members of the several communities involved came forward with more accusations of witchcraft against the women. While Hopkins and Stearne gathered their evidence, a new accusation of witchcraft arose in the nearby town of Thorpe. Another warrant was issued and Margaret Moone was searched and watched. The positive reception that these accusations received from the magistrates encouraged other citizens to come forward with more accusations. The 'gatekeepers' failed to close the gate. Witchcraft suddenly appeared everywhere in the area. Old community squabbles, stresses of the civil war, and an overriding fear of the Devil merged to set in motion a train wreck. Hopkins, Stearne, and judges such as Grimston confirmed the worst fears of the villagers. The men in authority allowed the accusers, the searchers, the watchers, and the witnesses to get out of control. Because these cases were outside of the central court system, mild forms of torture were used, including sleep deprivation, watching, and swimming. The 80-year-old vicar John Lowes was forced to run back and forth for several nights until he was out of breath, 'till he was weary of his life'.[3] Since that still did not make him confess, he was thrown in the moat at Framlingham Castle where he allegedly floated, a sure sign of being a witch. More Continental elements made their way into the confessions, including a pact with the Devil and demonic sex. Hopkins and Stearne made use of the wording in James's legislation, which allowed for a person to be guilty of witchcraft for merely conversing with a familiar. As investigations by the two men continued, and spread to other counties, they started to meet with some opposition. In 1647, Hopkins was forced to retire from his self-styled position as witch finder because of poor health. He died of tuberculosis in August 1647 in Manningtree, where the hunt had started. After that, Stearne also lost interest in the proceedings and went back to his home in Lawshall. This episode actually contributed to a decline in witchcraft executions in England, as authorities saw the dangerous repercussions of zealous investigation.

Scotland

Scotland followed the Continental model of witchcraft rather than the English model. In relation to the population, the number of trials and executions was high. Almost 2,000 trials were recorded and as many as half of these ended in executions. Rather than small, local episodes over a long period of time, the cases tended to be larger and more highly concentrated in certain areas. Most trials in Scotland took place on the coastal areas and close to the border with England. Easy access to Edinburgh meant access to legal recourse. In contrast, the Highlands, which were the dominion of the Gaelic-speaking clans, were untouched by trials. There are no records to explain how magic was dealt with there. This is similar to the situation in Gaelic areas of Ireland and Wales. Resistance to outside influences and reliance on clan justice probably played a role in managing the witch without recourse to legal means.

The first Witchcraft Act of 1563 secularised offences that had previously come under the jurisdiction of ecclesiastical courts of the church of Rome. This was not so much a turn away from religion as it was a function of a change in religion. Religion actually played a key role in witchcraft prosecutions in Scotland. The sins of adultery, incest, and bestiality were also brought under secular jurisdiction. Under the direction of the theologian and author John Knox, the Scottish parliament instituted Calvinist Presbyterian-style Protestantism in 1560. The reigning monarch at the time was the young Catholic queen, Mary Queen of Scots, who was residing in France with her first husband King Francis II. The Scottish nobility was strongly Protestant and, eventually, Mary was forced to abdicate the throne in favour of her young son by her second husband, Henry Stuart, Lord Darnley. As a boy, the future James VI was firmly under the control of the Protestant Privy Council. The new kirk, the Scottish word for church, was governed from the bottom up, rather than the top down organisation of the Catholic institution.

Each local kirk was managed by a group of elders and the local minister. They were answerable to the regional presbytery. The presbyteries, in turn, were accountable to the General Assembly, which was the highest authority in the church. The success of the Presbyterian church in Scotland created a power vacuum in the area of social control, including sexual behaviour. Issues that had previously been dealt with by the Catholic ecclesiastical courts were now up for grabs. In addition to suppressing sexual misdemeanours, the kirk was eager to root out any practices that they considered remnants of Catholic 'superstition'.

After the North Berwick trials involving James VI, discussed in Chapter 3, an individual commission from the Privy Council or Scottish parliament was necessary to prosecute a person for witchcraft. Most commissions were requested by landowners and clergy. Similar to the situation in England, suspects were reported from within the community to the local authorities, in this case the Kirk Session. The elders and the minister decided whether to dismiss the case, banish the person from the community, or take legal action. Before obtaining a commission from the Privy Council to hold a trial, they gathered evidence from neighbours and interrogated the accused, who was usually confined during this stage of the process. Local ministers often obtained confessions and gave evidence at trials. Although torture was not legal, the local kirk and community often employed it. The witch could be watched or walked incessantly so that she could not sleep. The process of pricking to locate the Devil's mark could become a form of torture. Thumbscrews, burning with hot irons, and good old-fashioned beatings were also employed. The Kirk Session wanted a confession before obtaining the commission, which meant that the trials were merely formalities rather than justice. Then the witch would be tried locally rather than being transported to Edinburgh.

A major outbreak of accusations, which has been termed the 'Great Scottish Witch Hunt', happened in 1661 and 1662, at the moment in history when King Charles II was restored to the English throne following the Interregnum in England. During Cromwell's Protectorate, the English had insisted on acting alongside the Scots as commissioners, which had a moderating effect on witchcraft accusations. The Restoration ended that arrangement and allowed the Scots to once again approach the topic of witchcraft in their own way, which included the belief in the sabbat and the pact with the Devil, similar to beliefs more prevalent on the Continent. In the space of a year and a half, more than 600 individuals were accused, resulting in perhaps as many as 300 executions. The hunt started in East

Lothian, with more than 200 suspects. The accused were treated harshly. One woman was stripped naked and laid on a stone and covered with a hair cloth for twenty-eight days and nights. Others were dressed in hair shirts dipped in vinegar while in gaol, which caused the skin to peel away. The Privy Council issued many commissions for trials to local authorities. The accused were very typical: old, poor women; sexually promiscuous females; and those with reason to be vengeful. There were no underlying political vendettas going on, and the social rank of the accused did not move up to the elites as it did in the large Continental trials. The judges eventually became sceptical and started granting acquittals, which slowed down the momentum of the hunt. However, it took longer for the Privy Council to reach the same level of scepticism and to stop issuing commissions. Finally, in April of 1662, the Council issued a proclamation that said a person could not be arrested as a witch without a special warrant from the Council. The local authorities had been obtaining confessions before they even applied for a commission to try the witch. This put an end to the illegal methods used to extract a confession from a suspect. Pricking and torture were forbidden. In this episode of witch hunting, the authorities were both to blame for letting the accusations get out of control, and were the ones to pull the plug. Note that the accusations were fuelled by the beliefs at the village level. It is possible that left to their own devices the locals would have persecuted and lynched the suspects without the judicial machinery in place.

Ireland

As mentioned above, the Gaelic speaking areas of Scotland, Ireland, and Wales did not suffer the same sort of witchcraft persecutions as the rest of Europe. Or, the treatment of witchcraft has not left any historical records. From what evidence we have, it appears that instead of a concept of the demonic witch causing *maleficium* and worshipping the Devil, the witch was mostly configured as a 'butter-witch', who stole or damaged milk products or interfered with fertility of cattle. The figure of the witch was not threatening enough to move people to have recourse to the law. In Gaelic Ireland, fairies were more likely to inflict harm on people and cattle than witches were. Fairies were managed by the cunning folk, often through the use of protective charms. An Irish Witchcraft Act was implemented in 1586 as part of the programme to anglicise Ireland. The activities of cunning folk were illegal under the provisions of the statute, but the authorities tended to overlook them as they did in England. In the areas of Protestant plantation, the English and Scottish settlers brought the idea of the malefic witch with them and pursued accusations, which went before the judiciary. However, cases rarely went to the stage of prosecution. In Ulster, witchcraft was arbitrated by the Presbyterian church courts, who were more interested in policing the morals of their congregation. Ecclesiastical courts handed down light punishments for magical activities, as they attempted to impose their version of Christianity on the Irish Catholic population.

France

In France, there was no statute issued from the Crown that specifically dealt with witchcraft as a crime. This meant that judges could apply arbitrary decisions on individual cases. The lawyer and demonologist Jean Bodin, who thought that witchcraft was a *crimen exceptum,* had written his treatise as a guide for judges in 1580. It was not the official stance of the government, but the three kinds of acceptable proof outlined by Bodin were generally accepted: tangible evidence, such as potions and powders or a written pact with the Devil; confession given when not being tortured (but this could follow torture); and the testimony of a reliable witness, which excluded the testimony of one witch against another. The lower village courts had to refer any capital cases to the provincial court of appeal, called a *parlement*. There were nine of these courts in France, with the *parlement* of Paris being the most important and influential. The cases that went to *parlement* were heard by a panel of judges rather than a single judge who heard local cases. One of the advantages of the referral to a higher court was that the appeal courts were not influenced by local grievances and prejudices.

After 1625, all witchcraft cases had to be appealed to the *parlement* in Paris. The appeal system had a significant effect on the number of executions. There was a high rate of acquittal. Between 1540 and 1640, the Paris *parlement* reviewed more than 1,000 cases and only sentenced 115 witches to death. However, 395 individuals received the lesser sentences of galley service or banishment. The provincial *parlements* were equally lenient. Even before the mandatory referral to Paris, the *parlement* treated abuses of the judicial system harshly. In 1601, a hangman was sentenced to life service on the galleys for his part in the death of more than 200 persons. He had used the illegal pricking test to identify witches. It was also a member of a provincial *parlement* of Bordeaux that eventually terminated the Basque trials conducted by Pierre de Lancre, which were getting out of hand.

There was a higher percentage of men accused in France than in other areas such as England and Germany. Many were shepherds who employed magical techniques, such as using the host or toad venom to either harm or protect livestock. It appears that in many cases they acted as cunning folk. The trial often centred on the fee that was charged for removing a curse. The other common category of men accused was the clergy, who were targeted for improper use of sacramentals and causing possession, as in the case of Urbain Grandier discussed in Chapter 5.

Small witch hunts erupted all over France in the 1640s. Witches were blamed for the bad weather and were often handled by locals outside of the law. Local authorities were reticent to interfere with the public demand for justice. They were unable to police local lynchings or illegal procedures, such as swimming. The *parlement* was also ineffective because it could only control cases that came through the courts. When these situations came to light, the local magistrates were punished or dismissed. After the Affair of the Poisons, Louis XIV issued an edict that essentially reclassified witchcraft as fraud. Execution for witchcraft could only be carried out with his personal signature. Penalties were also established for those who pretended to be magicians and sorcerers. Heresy, particularly related to sacrilege, was still punishable by death.

Holy Roman Empire

The Holy Roman Empire was a conglomeration of more than 300 independent principalities, duchies, bishoprics, and free cities, which encompassed most of Europe. Present day Germany, Austria, Switzerland, Belgium, Alsace, Lorraine, northern Italy, and parts of Poland and the Czech Republic all came under the jurisdiction of the Holy Roman Emperor, who was elected by a select group of Electors. The Empire did not function as a state, and there was no central control. This fragmentation and decentralisation contributed to the fact that seventy-five per cent of all the European executions for witchcraft took place in this territory: 25,000 to 35,000 in a 100 year period between 1560 and 1660. The Holy Roman Emperor Charles V, who also happened to be King Charles I of Spain, had put the *Constitutio Criminalis Carolina* in place in 1532, a form of Imperial or Roman law code. The clause concerning witchcraft states that anyone causing harm via witchcraft should be put to death by fire. If the person uses sorcery or magic without causing harm, that is, without *maleficium*, the person should be punished otherwise. But the distinction between the two types of magic was too difficult for judges and jurists to understand, and the law did not help to reduce punishment. According to the *Carolina*, courts of small territories were supposed to get advice from universities in dealing with witchcraft prosecutions. But even when they did, this did not always act as a control, because the universities were familiar with the demonologists' ideas and encouraged convictions based on diabolism. The *Carolina* was issued as a legal guideline, but there was no administration in place to ensure that the code was implemented in the various principalities. There were no circuit judges as there were in England. There was a central imperial court, the *Reichskammergericht*, but it was not a mandatory appeal court like the French *parlement*.

There were vast differences in the treatment of witchcraft from one area to the next in the Empire. In general, the larger territories were well-governed and showed more restraint than the smaller ones. For example, Friedrich V, the prince-elector of the Palatinate, followed Weir's advice and banned witch hunting in his area. However, in the small duchy of Lorraine, where the demonologist Nicolas Remy was the Attorney-General, there were 1,500 to 2,000 executions. Victims included court officials, physicians, and courtiers.

The worst panics were in three archbishoprics: Trier, Mainz, and Cologne. The archbishops served as both secular and church leaders with a heightened sense of moral obligation, particularly during the Counter-Reformation. The ecclesiastical rulers used secular authorities to prosecute suspects. The demonologist Peter Binsfeld was instrumental in a huge witch-craze that started in the archbishopric of Trier. [See Image #28, Image of sabbat from leaflet titled *Trier Hexentanzplatz*] There had been severe hailstorms and poor harvests throughout the 1580s and 1590s, which had destroyed the vineyards. Bad harvests translated into sick cattle and children as well. Misfortune on an extreme scale appeared unnatural, and the general population looked for a reason. Witchcraft fit the bill. Archbishop Johann von Schönenberg was anxious to rid the diocese of Protestants, Jews, and witches. He used the newly-established Jesuit college to incite suspicions. The hunt extended up the social ladder to dozens of parish priests, burgomasters, government officials, and even nobility. Dietrich Flade, who was opposed to the use of torture, was included in this hunt, as discussed in Chapter 5.

After 1590, the witch hunt spread northeast to the archbishopric of Mainz. The archbishop of this diocese was one of the seven Electors who helped choose the Emperor, making his voice politically important. The territory was rich and vast. Approximately 1,800 witch burnings took place under three different archbishops, so it was not a single zealous personality that was to blame. In this instance, it seems that the torturing and convicting of witches happened at a local level. The vast territory was fragmented and lacked central authority. Instead, local nobility held on to traditional rights of self-government. The Reformation had exacerbated the situation because although the head of state was a Catholic archbishop, many of the citizens and most of the nobility were Protestant.

In Cologne, Ferdinand of Bavaria was the prince-elector and archbishop. He employed witch commissioners, who terrorised the region. Between 1626 and 1634, 2,000 people were sentenced to the stake. This is the jurisdiction in which the Jesuit Friedrich Spee operated as a confessor and wrote the *Cautio Criminalis* in protest.

The prince-abbot of Fulda, Balthasar von Dernbach, also enthusiastically embraced the Counter-Reformation campaign. However, his attempts at implementing the provisions of the Council of Trent, such as the public whipping of clergy's concubines, did not go over very well, and he was forced to resign. But he had the decision overturned, and subsequently became a fierce witch hunter. One of the first accusations was levelled against Anna Haan, the wife of the man who had been instrumental in his forced resignation. Because the family were substantial members of the community, they appealed the conviction. The judge in the case, Balthasar Nuss, was eventually executed for his role in the atrocities. This case spilled over into Bamberg where Anna's son, Georg Haan, was the chancellor. Under a zealous Counter-Reformation bishop, the suffragan bishop Friedrich Förner started a witch hunt, delivering a series of sermons against magic and witchcraft. A combination witch house and torture chamber was built specifically for the hunt. Dr Haan and his whole family were burned at the stake: his wife, daughter, and son, as well as his son's wife and her mother and father, who was the wealthiest man in the prince-bishopric. This can truly be labelled a hunt, targeting political and religious enemies, as opposed to an outbreak of witchcraft that started at the village level and was subsequently supported by elites.

Before we leave the Holy Roman Empire, let's look at one more heart-breaking case. In 1600, the duke of Bavaria in south-east Germany attempted to initiate a national witch hunt. The hunt started with the Pappenheimer family.[4] At the time of their arrest, the Pappenheimers were cleaning privies for a living, a line of work that was on par socially with being an executioner. The mother, Anna, was the daughter of a gravedigger, another lowly occupation. She was also licensed to beg part time to supplement the family income. Anna, her husband, Paulus, and the two eldest of their three sons, 20-year-old Michel and 22-year-old Gumpprecht, were accused by a condemned outlaw of murdering seven pregnant women. The family was tracked down and arrested in Abensberg. After being tortured, they admitted to several crimes as well as witchcraft. The council of state had the family carted to Munich, with plans to make an example of them in regards to the problem of vagrancy and crime on the highways. They were manacled and incarcerated in the Falcon Tower gaol. The youngest son, 10-year-old Hänsel, was put in the same cell as his mother. He was questioned first, being the weakest and most vulnerable. When he would not give the answers that the authorities were looking for, he was flogged until he agreed with their suggestions. Yes, his brothers did murder women so that they could cut the hands off the unborn babies in the mothers' wombs.

The father Paulus was the next to be questioned. He was lifted on the strappado three times to make him confess to murdering twelve persons, burning down villages, and stealing money from the church. Two days of torture caused the oldest son Gump to confess to a long list of sins, whatever he could think of to make the persecution stop. Michel endured the strapado no less than twelve times, while he insisted on his innocence. When adding weights to his feet, thereby dislocating his shoulders, did not extract the required responses, a burning torch was held under his armpits. Under threat of another round of the strappado, Michel confessed to setting fires, stealing from churches, and killing pregnant women, using the powder made from the babies' hands to kill cattle. But the interrogators were not satisfied with these detailed revelations. Where did the family dispose of the stolen church goods? The Jews. Not only did they buy the booty, but they offered to buy stolen children as well. This was completely acceptable to the anti-Semitic authorities. No evidence was sought in the form of dead bodies, burned buildings, desecrated churches, or missing children. In other words, no *corpus delecti*.

Anna Pappenheimer was the last to be questioned. She confessed to flying to the sabbat, sex with the Devil, and signing a pact with her blood. After this confession, the interrogators turned their attention to witchcraft and re-tortured Paulus and the two older boys until they confessed to being in the service of Satan. Under pressure to reveal more 'information', both Anna and Paulus accused a miller and his family, who had long been the subject of rumours in their neighbourhood that they were witches. The miller was tortured to death without confessing. The miller's wife was submitted to the strappado five times before her spirit broke and she confessed to being a witch. However, even after three more days of torture, she would not incriminate her dead husband or her daughter, nor would she name accomplices. Given this level of loyalty and fortitude, one can only imagine what suffering finally caused her to condemn her daughter to the stake by telling her persecutors that her child was a witch. Other associates of the Pappenheimer family were arrested and questioned. Repeated torture added more and more names to the long list of witches. One woman alone named ninety-nine persons to contribute to the more than 400 suspects. Fortunately, an all-out hunt was not made to find these people and take them into custody.

The 'trial', if one can call it that, took place in the public square outside of the town hall. Confessions were read aloud. For such horrendous crimes, simple execution was not deemed enough punishment. Red-hot pincers were used to rip six pieces of flesh from each of the condemned person's arms and bodies. Then the executioner cut off Anna's breasts. The party was carted to gallow's hill where Paulus and the two older sons were broken on the wheel. Paulus was then impaled on a stake, a punishment that even then was deemed barbaric. The youngest son, Hansel, was forced to sit with the sheriff on his horse and watch while his family was burned alive. He later suffered the same fate. This episode, including unrestricted torture, was approved by the demonologists Del Rio and Remy. Universities were consulted and legal opinions were sought. This case would have evolved into a major hunt except the privy councillors interfered and terminated the persecutions.

The Inquisition

In modern popular culture, the Inquisition, with a capital I, was the most notorious institution for witch hunting. However, historians have shown that this Roman Catholic institution was much more lenient than many secular courts and actually discouraged accusations of witchcraft. There were three Inquisitions in operation in the early modern period during the height of the witch craze, in Spain, Portugal, and Italy. There were no Inquisitions north of the Alps, even in Catholic countries such as France or the parts of the Holy Roman Empire that remained Catholic after the Reformation. We should not confuse other church courts, such as an annual visitation by a bishop to his diocese to reinforce heterodoxy, with the formal Inquisition. The large hunts that took place in the archbishoprics of the Holy Roman

Empire discussed above did not involve the Inquisition. The archbishops acted of their own accord.

The Inquisition was first established in the middle ages in response to the threat of heresy from the Cathars. Following the Albigensian Crusade in the thirteenth century, a tribunal was set up to identify and punish heretics. In the late middle ages, Inquisitors operated mostly in southern France and northern Italy. The Inquisition was not designed to hunt witches; it was implemented to root out heretics. Inquisitors were chosen from the monastic orders, most commonly Dominicans and sometimes Franciscans. These orders were not cloistered but moved around preaching and offering the sacraments. They answered directly to the pope, not to the archbishop of the area in which they were active. Inquisitors were outside of the usual hierarchy of the church, which descended from the pope down through the archbishops, bishops, and priests. They were vested with full powers of *inquisitio*, or the right to investigate. An Inquisitor would be appointed to a specific geographical area. Although they were empowered by the pope, Inquisitors relied on support from the local secular authorities as well as local clergy. However, the actions and decisions of the Inquisitors often aroused opposition from local authorities. It was because of this lack of support that Heinrich Kramer had difficulty in the Tyrol area and subsequently wrote the *Malleus Maleficarum*.

The Spanish Inquisition

In 1478, the new rulers of the two Spanish kingdoms, Isabella of Castile and Ferdinand of Aragon, requested a full-time Spanish Inquisition from Pope Sixtus IV. Although the Spanish Inquisition received its authority from the pope in Rome, it operated independently. The Crown had a lot of influence. The Inquisitors were appointed by an Inquisitor General, who was appointed by the Spanish monarchs rather than the pope. There was a ruling council, called *la Suprema*, which consisted of four clergy under the direction of the Inquisitor General. The institution's initial concern was former Jews and Muslims, who had to convert to Christianity if they wished to stay in Spain. Converted Jews were known as *conversos*; converted Muslims were called *moriscos*. The government was concerned that the converts might not have been sincere about their conversions and were still practising their old faith. By 1512, sorcery and divination were also under the jurisdiction of the Inquisition.

Suspected heretics came to the attention of the Inquisition either from denunciations from someone in the community, who could remain anonymous, or through a confession to a local priest. If the priest felt he could not absolve the person, he or she was sent to the Inquisitor to confess any part in heretical activity. Sometimes people came under investigation after being mentioned in relation to another case. The Inquisitor would then be the one to initiate an investigation. The parish priest would be interviewed about church attendance and neighbours might be asked about the person's reputation. Witnesses were questioned under oath to determine if a full investigation was warranted. If there was sufficient evidence, the accused would be brought in for questioning. Without being told what charges were laid against her or him, the suspect would be asked to confess to any violation of religion he or she might have committed. Inquisitors engaged in detailed and lengthy cross-examination of suspects in a series of audiences. The accused were even provided with legal council at no charge. The defence lawyer was appointed by the Inquisition and was encouraged to tell the accused to confess and seek penance. Confession also meant that the person's property was not confiscated. Any discussion between the lawyer and his client had to take place openly in front of the Inquisitor. The process could take weeks or even months, particularly if the accused denied any guilt. The option of interrogatory torture was a last resort in obtaining a confession. It was only supposed to be used when there was a strong presumption of guilt and a suspicion that the accused was not telling the truth. There were strict guidelines to follow. A trial was held after the interrogation of the suspect and the gathering of information from witnesses. The jury included the Inquisitors, a representative from the local bishop, and advisors on legal and theological matters. The verdict was based on a written report of all the material. The jury could request interrogatory torture if the case lacked evidence. But the Inquisition was generally sceptical about the truth exacted through torture and made limited use of it.

The church was more concerned with penance than with punishment. However, as discussed below, penance instead of execution could be quite harsh. The person could be sentenced to several years in gaol or galley service on a ship. Both held high risks of death by disease or malnutrition. Banishment was also an option. If a person was lucky enough to just receive penitence as punishment, the penitent had to wear a *sanbenito* whenever out in public, a special garment that declared his or her position as a sinner to the community. The apron-like article was usually yellow with a double cross on it. [See Image #30, Sketch of a heretic wearing a *sanbenito*] After the penance was served, if it were not for life, the *sanbenito* was hung on display in the parish church indefinitely, with a label stating the person's name and crime. When the Inquisitor made his annual visitation, he would check the condition of the articles and replace any that were falling apart. The person was also excluded from any form of office or importance in the society. The person could not bear arms or travel on horseback.

Early in the sixteenth century, there were outbreaks of witchcraft in Spanish Navarre. The government of Navarre had sent a special commissioner to look for heretics. The commissioner had taken two young girls with him who could supposedly identify a witch by looking into her eyes. As a result of this campaign, hundreds of people were questioned and an unknown number were executed. In 1525, a secular judge travelling through the area arrested forty witches and had most of them put to death. When the episode came to the attention of *la Suprema* in 1526, the Inquisitor General called a meeting to address some of the concerns raised from confessions. They reviewed the trials and issued instructions concerning witchcraft, advising caution. They were quite sceptical about the alleged capabilities of the witch and ordered the authorities to put more emphasis on education and rehabilitation than punishment. There was also a prohibition against confiscating property in witchcraft cases. The instructions contained so many cautions that there were only a few executions for the rest of the sixteenth century.

The region known as the Spanish Navarre was directly opposite the mountainous area of the French part of Navarre, the Basque province of Pays de Labourd. That was where the French judge and demonologist Pierre de Lancre had investigated an outbreak of witchcraft in 1609. That frenzy of witch hunting had spread from the Spanish Basque region. An abbot in the town of Zugarramurdi requested *la Suprema* to investigate accusations of witchcraft in December 1608. In January of 1609, a commissioner was sent to start the investigation. He reported to the Inquisitors stationed at Logroño, one of the nineteen regional courts of the Inquisition. As a result of his investigation, four women were brought to Logroño for interrogation. They were kept in a secret prison (the Inquisition had its own gaols and did not use the secular facilities) and eventually confessed without torture. The women's confessions included accounts of visits to the sabbat. While they were incarcerated, one of their gaolers had overheard a conversation amongst them that indicated they had only confessed to get out of gaol, not because they were really witches. Shortly thereafter, six other people voluntarily travelled to Logroño so that they could retract the confessions that they had made publicly in the parish church. They were also put in prison and questioned. The Logroño Inquisitors made their report to *la Suprema*. The ruling council directed the Inquisitors to continue their investigation to determine if the suspects went to the sabbat in their dreams or in reality. If the women travelled there in reality, *la Suprema* wanted some concrete evidence. For example, if ointments were mentioned to assist in flying, the Inquisitors and their agents were supposed to obtain the ointments and have them checked by an apothecary. They also wanted to know if the crimes confessed to by the witches actually occurred by checking with the villagers. The Inquisitors spent six months questioning the ten suspects and became convinced that they had uncovered a diabolical cult. One of the things that convinced them of the truth of the suspects' statements was that they were all in agreement about the events, even though they were questioned independently.

After months of questioning the ten witches and reporting to *la Suprema*, one of the Logroño Inquisitors went on a visitation of their region. This was an annual event. In each location, he read the Edict of Faith, which listed the many varieties of heresy, and gave a sermon about the dangers of wandering from the faith. Then the congregation was invited to denounce anyone suspected of heretical activities or opinions, including having a familiar, invoking demons, casting magic circles, making a pact with the Devil, or possessing forbidden books (which could include the Bible in the vernacular). The witnesses remained anonymous, so there were no repercussions for telling on one's neighbour. The local priests were instructed to continue preaching against the diabolical sect after the visitation, which they did eagerly, describing all the details of the sabbat.

After the travelling Inquisitor returned to his headquarters in Logroño, five witches voluntarily came forward to the local priest. This led to the arrest of thirteen more people, including a monk and a priest. In other villages, the Inquisitor discovered that witches were enticing and kidnapping children and taking them to the sabbat. In his report to *la Suprema*, the visiting Inquisitor claimed that he had evidence against 280 witches and many children, who had attended the sabbat. More arrests were made and the tribunal now had thirty-one witches to deal with in their secret prison, including the first ten who had been there for more than six months. In most cases of an annual visitation, there was an Edict of Grace offered. A repentant heretic could turn herself in and receive reconciliation with the church. More importantly, her property would not be confiscated. In this instance, the Edict of Grace was postponed until after the *auto de fé*.

The *auto de fé*, meaning 'act of faith', was a public ritual where accused heretics were sentenced and penitents were reconciled to the church. Besides those convicted for witchcraft, there were other people condemned for

Judaism, Mohammedanism, Lutheranism, bigamy, and heretical utterances. The ritual was usually held once a year. Special scaffolding was erected in the public square or plaza, which was most often in front of the cathedral. [See Image #31, Painting of an *auto de fé*] In this particular instance, there were an estimated 30,000 observers at the *auto de fé*. The evening before the sentencing, a procession took place to the site by all the important officials. On the morning of the event, the condemned heretics processed barefoot into the square, following dozens of church officials and civic authorities. The accused were dressed in *sanbenitos* and heretics' mitres or conical hats, and carried unlit candles. After a mass and a sermon, the sentences of the condemned were read. The spectacle was an opportunity for the guilty to demonstrate their penance, as well as for the church to publicly confirm its values. The church did not have the authority to execute heretics. Instead, the condemned, consisting of unrepentant and relapsed heretics, were 'relaxed' to the secular authorities, which took the responsibility of burning them alive at the stake. The person had the chance to confess right up to the last second. If they did, they were mercifully strangled or garrotted before the fire was lit.

Thirty-one people from the village of Zugarramurdi and surrounding area were part of the *auto de fé*. Before it was held on 10 November 1610 in Logroño, some sort of epidemic ran through the prison. A 90-year-old stone-deaf woman was the first victim of the mysterious illness. As more witches died, the Inquisitors concluded that the Devil was responsible, because he was trying to interfere with the women's testimonies. Only eighteen of the peasants, shepherds, and farm labourers were alive by the time of the trial. Included in this number were two clerics: a monk and a priest. Of the thirteen who died in prison, five were burned in effigy, because they had not repented. The other eight had been pardoned for confessing and repenting, and had been given a Christian burial. Ten of the remaining witches confessed. Six, who denied their guilt, were burned alive at the stake. The two clerics were interrogated under torture, because there was doubt about their statements. They maintained their innocence, but were banished to galley service for five years.

Instead of ending the witch craze, the *auto de fé* stimulated more confessions and accusations. Even before the trial and execution of the first group of thirty-one witches, the clergy were reporting many problems in the Basque villages. Franciscan, Dominican, and Jesuit friars were sent on a preaching crusade into the affected area. Their preaching did not prevent witchcraft, but instead stirred up another witch craze. When *la Suprema* did not send out an Inquisitor to investigate immediately after the *auto de fé*, the general population started to take matters into their own hands. Suspects were publicly persecuted. They were garrotted in the manner of the Inquisition's method of torture, stripped and ducked repeatedly in the river, and stoned. Houses were destroyed and property was damaged. The villagers imprisoned suspects without food or drink. Some people were tied to trees all night. Others had their feet put into freezing water while they were in the stocks. Accusations were kept alive by reports from children aged six to twelve, who claimed that they had been transported to the sabbat by witches. Some children even denounced their own parents. The children were coaxed, bribed, and threatened to support the accusations.

Several people became concerned with the growing witch hunt. One was the bishop of Pamplona, in whose jurisdiction this was happening. Another was a Jesuit friar who had been preaching and hearing confessions in the area. The man who would ultimately turn things around was one of the Inquisitors who had been involved throughout the process of the investigation, trial, and *auto de fé*. Alonso de Salazar Frías had studied canon law at the Universities of Salamanca and Siguenza, and had had a very illustrious career in the church before his appointment as an Inquisitor in 1609. He had been quite sceptical of the proceedings and the evidence used to convict the witches, but he was a junior member of the Logroño tribunal so did not have much authority. In 1611, Salazar was sent out on one of the annual visitations with an Edict of Grace. He was very sceptical of the stories told by the alleged witches. He took an empirical approach to evidence, conducting experiments with twenty-two jars of ointments that were allegedly for flying or were powders from the Devil, all of which proved fake. Some alleged poisons were also tested by apothecaries on animals. Several witches confessed that they had made the unguents out of harmless materials, such as pork fat and chimney soot, in order to satisfy the demands of the investigators. Young girls who confessed that they had sex with the Devil at the sabbat were examined by midwives and found virginal. And the location of an alleged sabbat was kept under surveillance all night, with no sign of the witches who had confessed being there.

Salazar reported directly to the Inquisitor General that there was no proof of any witchcraft. He believed that 'there were neither witches nor bewitched in a village until they were talked and written about'.[6] As a result of his investigation, the instructions for dealing with cases of alleged witchcraft were amended in 1614. After Salazar's report, *la Suprema* took a very cautious approach to accusations of witchcraft. They tended to view witchcraft as delusion or superstition rather than devil-worship. Inquisitors were advised not to believe everything about witches as described in treatises such as the *Malleus*. If the Devil was so deceptive, perhaps he had also deceived the authors. Nonetheless, outbreaks of witchcraft continued to erupt in northern Spain. Local authorities tried to circumvent the authority of the Inquisition, but in most cases *la Suprema* managed to intervene and prevent burnings. In this case, the centralisation of the Inquisition and its insistence on concrete evidence saved many lives. Further prosecutions were prevented by an Inquisitor sent by *la Suprema* to administer amnesty and determine the truth of the alleged sabbat activities. As a result of this episode, there were no more executions in Spain by the Inquisition for witchcraft.

The Roman Inquisition

The Inquisition in Italy was established after the Reformation, when the Catholic church was concerned about the threat of Luther's new sect, especially in the north. There was no hope of re-establishing the Inquisition in the Holy Roman Empire where Kramer had operated in the middle ages. The *Carolina* did not even address heresy. There were too many conflicts and divisions in the Empire. In 1542, Pope Paul III used the successful example of the Spanish Inquisition to set up a special committee of cardinals to oversee the prosecution of heretics in Italy, formally known as the Congregation of the Holy Office of the Roman Inquisition. Rather than individual Inquisitors operating independently, the central committee of cardinals directed the work of the Inquisitors. In the first thirty years, the institution was mainly concerned with destroying Protestantism. Trials for magic and sorcery were rare. After the Italian Protestant movement was suppressed, interest gradually shifted to cases of magic.

The Roman Inquisition's main concern about magic was the misuse of sacramental elements, such as the wafer used in the Eucharist, holy water, and holy oil. In the face of Luther's heresy, the Catholic church was worried about the misappropriation of ecclesiastical rites and symbols. They did not want outside competition with legitimate clerical procedures. Many of the trials involved the clergy, who had access to sacramental paraphernalia and knowledge of rituals and prayers. Priests were sometimes accused of performing masses or baptisms over magical objects. Church authorities were concerned that magicians were worshipping demons by kneeling, burning incense, wearing priestly garments, and otherwise showing them reverence that should have been reserved for God. In 1586, Antonio

Bellinelli, a Franciscan friar from Naples, confessed (without torture) to using incense, holy water, and consecrated candles to invoke spirits according to the rituals in *The Key of Solomon*. His purpose was love magic and the discovery of hidden treasure, not *maleficium*. Nevertheless, he was hanged and his body burned for his nefarious activities.

The church was also concerned with suppressing superstitious beliefs in popular culture, including love magic, fortune-telling, divination, treasure hunting, and magical healing practices. These were activities of the cunning person or white witch, which were of more interest to the Inquisition than the demonic witch. Love magic was treated severely. Specialists in love magic were typically urban prostitutes, who hoped to attract or keep wealthy clients. Love spells combined liturgical elements, including prayers to saints, with pagan elements, such as prayers to the moon and stars. In 1519, the illiterate enchantress Anastasia 'la Frappona' of Modena allegedly lit a blessed candle in front of an image of the crucifix before she conducted prayers. Completely naked, she knelt down with her hair unbound on the rooftop to invoke the powers of the heavens. The Inquisition viewed her actions as paganism and idolatry. She confessed to using many techniques to arouse love, involving stones that had been in a dog's mouth, earth from a graveyard, frog's blood, knotted string, wax images, the heart of a cat, menstrual blood, and even focaccia. She used ritual fumigation to raise a demonic spirit to create love between two people. The Inquisitors were concerned about her abuse of sacramental items such as holy oil and other items that had been consecrated on the altar by a priest, as well as the fact that she used her love potions to seduce a married man into adultery. She was also accused of trampling on the cross and making a pact with the Devil. Anastasia repented and abjured; she was sentenced to ten years exile. She was supposed to fast on bread and water for the rest of her life and to pay for the expenses of her trial. An unknown Flemish artist rendered his vision of a woman performing a love spell around 1470, which contains similar elements. [See Image #32, 'The Love Spell']

Maleficium, which was the main concern of secular courts, was a minor concern in Inquisition records. The general population believed that illness and misfortune could be caused by supernatural means, but there were very few denunciations to the tribunal solely for causing harm by witchcraft. When accusations of *maleficium* were included amongst other charges, the authorities chose to focus on the heretical aspects of the case and virtually ignored the *maleficium*. In cases of illness allegedly caused by witchcraft, attending priests and physicians were called in to give opinions as to whether or not the cause was natural or supernatural. The usual assumption of the tribunal was that illness was natural unless it could be proven otherwise. Even if it was agreed that an illness was supernatural, it was difficult to prove that the suspected person had made a pact with the Devil in order to cause it. The Devil could have acted on his own accord. Without evidence that the witch abused the sacraments or overtly worshipped the Devil, *maleficium* was not considered heretical.

The Inquisition also gave more credence to empirical evidence and the opinion of physicians than the judges in northern Europe. Some young women confessed that they had been to the sabbat and had sex with the Devil, a very common and expected confession in northern cases. In this case, midwives were brought in to examine the girls for virginity. Accusations of witchcraft were kept in check because a witch's testimony was not used to accuse others, as it was in the Holy Roman Empire, especially relating to attendance at the sabbat. The sabbat was considered a delusion, not a place where a witch met fellow witches, whom she could then denounce. The Devil's mark was also not taken as evidence. Diabolical witchcraft or devil-worship were not the main focus. The Holy Office ensured that the guidelines put in place were followed. In one case, the administrator of a castle in the area of Orvieto arrested four women suspected of witchcraft. They were treated so harshly that two of the women died in gaol. At least one of the women was raped. When this episode came to light, the judge in the case was sent to the galleys for seven years. The surviving women received compensation.

The branch of the Roman Inquisition that operated in Venice was a little different. Italy was not a unified country at that time, just a geographical area composed of independent city-states and duchies in the north, the Kingdoms of Naples and Sicily in the south, and the Papal States in central Italy. Rome and the Papal States were not only the spiritual authority for all of Catholic Europe, but they were also territorial and economic rivals of Venice. Because of this friction, Venetians did not always welcome interference from Rome and the situation came to a head in 1518. Papal inquisitors operating in Europe at that time were vestiges of the medieval Inquisition, appointed individually by the pope. The Roman Inquisition had not been instituted yet. Inquisitors acting in the area of Val Camonica had executed some sixty men and women; many more were in prison awaiting trial. The secular authorities were upset that the trials were moving ahead quickly without their input. They were also concerned that the accused were being promised leniency if they confessed and were then executed anyway.

The Council of Ten, the governing body of Venice, ordered the trials to be suspended until they could investigate them. This invoked the involvement of the papacy, who appointed the papal ambassador to handle the situation. In spite of the temporary suspension of proceedings, some of the Inquisitors continued to arrest witches. The Council of Ten lost patience with the church officials, and the pope condemned the interference of the secular authorities. But by then it was 1521 and the Vatican was more concerned with Luther and his followers than it was about a few witches. To balance the interests of the Republic of Venice with the interests of the Roman Catholic church, Venetian representatives were appointed by the government to act in conjunction with papal representatives. This arrangement protected the interests of the state and guaranteed the Inquisition secular support.

After the Roman Inquisition was formed in 1542, the Inquisition in Venice acted as a safeguard against the mass execution of witches that happened in the Holy Roman Empire. There were only 500 cases examined over a 100-year period. One of the distinguishing characteristics of the Venetian Inquisition was its lack of interest and belief in the sabbat. Elements such as incest, cannibalism, and the pact with the Devil were virtually absent from denunciations, because these were aspects of the witches' sabbat. In a 100-year period, the sabbat was only mentioned in six cases, none of which resulted in arrests. In one instance, a female *benandante* told the tribunal about her night battles against witches and denounced two women as witches. She was found suspect of heresy for believing that women could take the form of cats and fly to the sabbat, as well as believing that the caul protected a person from harm. This sceptical attitude to the reality of the sabbat prevented the type of mass prosecutions experienced elsewhere, which was based on the concept of a demoniacal sect of conspirators. The Devil's mark, allegedly received at the sabbat, was not considered as evidence that a person was a witch.

Conditions in Gaol

In both Inquisition investigations and secular accusations, trials did not usually take place immediately. The authorities needed time to collect depositions from witnesses and interrogate the suspect, sometimes with the use of torture. In many areas, the judges travelled out from the main city to the countryside, where most of the accusations arose. A suspect could stay in gaol for a few days or for several years, just awaiting trial and sentencing. The incarceration period acted as a form of duress, which could result in confession. Most areas did not have a gaol that had been specifically built to house prisoners for the long term. Facilities were more often meant just to temporarily hold a person awaiting trial. The location could be the dungeon under a castle or a separate outbuilding. Cells tended to be dark, damp, and cold. Prisoners slept on stone floors with a little filthy straw. Sometimes they were shackled. In the private gaols used by the Inquisition, the person could be confined for weeks or months, wondering when they would have an opportunity to plead their case in front of the tribunal. Anne Foster, who was denied some mutton from a sheep farmer, was accused of killing his sheep and burning down the man's barn using witchcraft. In gaol, she was chained to a post. In the night, the Devil came in the form of a rat to suck her blood, at which time there was a most lamentable and hideous noise. And devil-rats were not the only thing to fear. Two guards in Germany confessed to raping female suspects while they were in prison. No doubt this happened more often than reported. Richer suspects were susceptible to extortion and blackmail by their custodians. Generally, the cost of incarceration, as well as the trial expenses, were the responsibility of the accused. In many cases, food was not given to the inmates unless someone brought it or paid for it. Many people died in gaol from 'gaol fever', brought on by the cold, damp, and malnutrition. Demonologists attributed the deaths in gaol to the Devil, even when the death was clearly suicide.

Torture

While in gaol, the witch was often tortured. The extreme violence directed toward witches needs to be viewed in context. Certainly, torture is sadistic, but it was not particularly misogynistic. Authorities were torturing witches not women. And torture was not reserved just for suspects of witchcraft. It was also used in other capital offences in this period, especially treason and spying. The church had started to allow the use of interrogatory torture in the thirteenth century when heresy had become a problem. Torture was viewed as a method of examination rather than a form of punishment. Demonologists promoted the use of torture in the case of witchcraft on the basis that it was a secretive crime with very few, if any, witnesses. In most parts of Europe, a conviction depended on confession, and torture persuaded the person to this end. England was the exception to the rule; confession was encouraged but was not necessary in order to issue the death sentence. The Crown used torture in cases of treason, but it was not legal in the treatment of witchcraft.

On the Continent, a set of rules was developed about the use of torture, supposedly for the protection of the innocent. Emperor Charles V's legal code, the *Carolina,* limited the form and duration of torture, the frequency, and the severity. Torture was only supposed to be applied if the judge or inquisitor already had a fair amount of proof of guilt. However, the amount of proof required was less stringent than for other crimes. Normally, two eye witnesses to the crime were required as evidence. For witchcraft, the statement of one eye witness was enough. Pregnant women and children were supposed to be exempt from torture, but we know that the rules were sometimes broken (like the bodies of the victims). Confessions given under duress were to be reiterated outside of the torture chamber within twenty-four hours. Unfortunately, the denial of confession usually meant the person was re-tortured until she was willing to confess while not being abused directly.

The judges and inquisitors were present in the torture chamber, supervising the proceedings and questioning the suspect. The man applying the torture was usually also the executioner and sometimes also the gaoler. In parts of the Holy Roman Empire, the executioner was also a witch finder. The first step in the process was often just exposure to the torture chamber or a display of the implements of torture. In this way, the witch was threatened with the possibility of violence. Other procedures that do not qualify as torture per se would have been intimidating and shameful for the accused. Witches were often stripped, shaved, and searched as part of the investigation process. Examiners were looking for hidden spells or talismans as well as the Devil's mark. In England, this intimate searching was done by other women, quite often midwives or respected matrons. They were looking for the witch's teat used for feeding the familiar. The teat was frequently found in the genitals. On the Continent and in Scotland, the invasive probing was usually done by the male torturer. The mark or scratch that the Devil made on a witch was identified by pricking. The mark was allegedly insensible and would not bleed when pricked. If the person did not feel any pain or if the mark did not bleed, the test was taken as empirical evidence of a pact with the Devil. Suspected witches would sometimes ask to be pricked in order to prove their innocence. The torturer or professional pricker used pins up to three inches long. In addition to the pain of the actual thrust of the pin, the victim would suffer shame at being stripped naked and shaved, as well as the loss of blood from all the places pricked that were not Devil's marks.

Professional witch prickers, employed by magistrates, were active in the middle of the seventeenth century in Scotland and in England during the aberration of justice as a result of the civil war. The most notorious Scottish pricker was John Kincaid, who was frequently used by the Presbyterian kirks. He had been active in the 1640s and had acquired a reputation for the quick and successful identification of witches. The obvious way to get around the consequences of being pricked would be to scream in pain every time the needle was applied. But the pricker tricked the victim by inserting the needle into an area of the body that the suspected witch could not see. When asked where the pain was, she was told it was not where the pricker was putting the needle. Kincaid was involved in the big hunt of 1661 as a professional pricker, but he eventually went too far. In 1662, he was arrested for pricking without a warrant from the magistrate. The Privy Council investigated and concluded that he had been abusing his power. He was tried for fraud and deceit in 1663. After nine weeks in the Tolbooth of Edinburgh, he was released due to his old age and infirmity. Too bad witches were not treated as mercifully as their adversaries. Reginald Scot and Friedrich Spee had warned readers about the tricks played with this technique in the sixteenth century. [See Image #29, Trick Bodkin] Scot gave instructions on how to make the false bodkin, which could be thrust into the body without causing harm. The haft of the instrument was hollowed out so that the blade could slip into it. A sponge held in the hand, soaked with a little blood or wine, gave the appearance of the blade being driven into the flesh. As the bodkin was pulled away from the person's body, the blade fell out of the haft to complete the deception.

One of the first implements of torture used, especially for women, was the thumbscrews, called pennywinkis in Scotland. They crushed the tips of the fingers or toes in a vice-like mechanism, usually until the blood ran. Use of this device was not limited to the weaker sex. A letter survives from 1628 in which the burgomaster or mayor of Bamberg, Johannes Junius, explained his circumstances to his daughter. He wanted to assure her that although he had confessed to making a pact with the Devil, having sex with a succubus, and dancing at the sabbat, he was completely innocent. He described how the executioner had put the thumb-screws on him until the blood ran out of his fingernails. For four weeks after, he could not use his hands. He pointed out how bad his hand-writing was as evidence of this fact.

The strappado was most commonly documented as the method of torture used on witches. The person was hoisted into the air by a pulley attached to the arms, which were tied behind the back at the wrists. Fifteen to thirty minutes was the recommended time for the first application; one hour was the maximum allowed. But there is at least one instance recorded of a woman in Germany who was left suspended in the air for five hours. She reported to her persecutors that during that time she had learned how to fly. If being lifted off the ground did not cause enough pain to result in confession, weights were added to the feet, which would contribute to the dislocation of the shoulders. Fifty to one-hundred pound weights (twenty to forty-five kilos) were tied to the ankles. In other cases, the person was lifted then dropped suddenly and repeatedly, thereby wrenching the shoulders out of the sockets. Junius told his daughter he endured this eight times.

Without dwelling on man's inhumanity to man, I will mention just a few other techniques used. Leg presses or screws, also known as 'Spanish boots', squeezed the calf and broke the shin bone. Sometimes the pressure was so great that marrow spurted out. The person could be tormented with the use of red hot pinchers to rip out pieces of flesh. Water torture involved the person being force-fed huge volumes of water by putting a tube or funnel down the throat. In addition to causing extreme discomfort, the process could lead to death. The body cannot process that much water. Osmosis causes the cells to explode. The Spanish Inquisition used the *garrotes*. Eight ropes were bound around eight different parts of the body and tightened by turning rods until the ropes cut into the flesh. The *echelle* was a kind of ladder or wheel that stretched the body. As in the strappado, the wrists were tied behind the back and raised behind the body. The feet were tied to a rotating log, which was wrenched forward, thereby dislocating the shoulders. The rack served a similar function, sometimes with spike-covered metal rollers that increased the pain by digging into the back. In severe cases, kneecaps and elbows were also irreparably damaged. Death must have been a welcome respite. Unofficial and illegal torture was also practised. As we saw in the Hopkins' case, alleged witches were walked, sleep deprived, and swam. In the Basque witchcraft hunt, the local villagers employed several illegal methods on suspects. In addition to the strappado and forced drinking of water, they bound the person to a bench with ropes that were tightened by twisting sticks. There are even reports of victims being strewn with fire, pitch, and brandy mixed with gunpowder.

Once the process of torture was started, the authorities in charge were reluctant to stop until a confession was forthcoming. After all, how could a person justify abusing another human being in this manner who turned out to be innocent? A confession was mandatory to pass a verdict of guilty, but it was also mandatory to vindicate the use of torture in the first place. Validation of the process was important or the abusers would have lost faith in their process. A very vicious circle.

Punishment

Torture was not considered a form of punishment, just an interrogatory technique. The guilty witch still needed to be punished after confession. The wheel, which was used in the Pappenheimer case, was used as a form of punishment rather than torture. The condemned was fastened to the wheel and beaten with a club until all his joints and bones were broken. In some cases, the person was left there to die of exposure or starvation.

Execution was the ultimate penalty. In most cases, the sentence took place within a few hours, or not more than a day or two, after the verdict. Witches in England were hanged not burned at the stake. The only exception to this was when a woman killed her husband by witchcraft, which was considered petty treason. In 1645, Mother Lakeland of Ipswich confessed to being a witch for twenty years and having two little dogs and a mole as familiars. She bewitched her husband who 'lay in great misery for a time' before he died.[5] She also confessed to killing a man and his child, killing a maid servant who would not lend her a needle, and burning a ship that a man was supposed to be master of, because the man would not marry her granddaughter.

In Scotland and on the Continent, witches were burned at the stake. If the person confessed, they were garrotted before the fire was lit, as a show of mercy. Recalcitrant suspects were burned alive. Burnings were public performances by the authorities to display their power. It was hoped that the consequences of witchcraft would deter the crime. If this sounds rather harsh, we should consider the other forms of execution employed in the premodern period: drawing and quartering, drowning, breaking on the wheel, burying alive, and decapitation.

Execution was not the only way a person could be punished for magic and witchcraft. The least harmful physical method, but the most harmful spiritually, was excommunication from the church. This not only denied the person access to heaven, but also excluded her from the community of the church, which was the centre of social and economic life throughout the middle ages and well into the early modern period. The next least harmful punishment was private or public penance. This might mean that a person had to go on a pilgrimage or put a new roof on the church or pay a fine to a charity. These were obviously reserved for the more wealthy members of society. Regardless of social standing, public humiliation could be recommended. This could include standing on display outside the parish church during services, perhaps with a placard hanging around the neck naming the applicable offence, such as love magic or bean casting. Time in the pillory or stocks was also a form of public humiliation, often after public whipping through the streets. In addition to the physical pain caused by restriction in the pillory, people often threw things at the offender. Some sentences could result in death indirectly. Galley service was extremely harsh and long prison sentences were almost equal to a death sentence. However, the Roman Inquisition reduced gaol sentences for good behaviour and, if a person was ill, the sentence could be completed under house arrest. There is also some evidence that if someone became physically unfit for galley service, the sentence could be changed to a less harsh punishment.

Conclusion

In areas where the judicial system was centralised, there were usually fewer executions than in areas where cases were heard by the locally administered courts. Scepticism in the evidence to prove witchcraft also developed more quickly by the educated elites than it did in the villages. However, the criminalisation of the figure of the witch, as opposed to the crime of *maleficium*, was largely due to the influence of church and state, from the top down. The criminalisation of the witch was part of the broader criminalisation of women and poverty that was taking place in the early modern period, which included attacks on adultery, fornication, infanticide, vagrancy, and begging. This was not a misogynistic programme of witch-hunting as woman-hunting, but rather a reflection of the increasing concern about morality and economics, which frequently affected women more than men.

Throughout the second half of the seventeenth century and into the eighteenth century, the accusations and prosecutions for witchcraft declined and finally stopped. This was a gradual process, which happened at different rates in different places. There were many contributing factors, which did not affect geographical areas in the same ways. On the legal playing field, there was increasing judicial scepticism, stricter standards of evidence, and restrictions and prohibitions concerning the use of torture. Judges began to think that the crime of witchcraft was unprovable, even if they still believed that it was possible. Economic changes contributed to the eventual decline of accusations. Urbanisation in the face of proto-industrialisation increased education and literacy, which had the potential to reduce beliefs that the elites condemned as superstitious. The mass migration to the cities also contributed to the instability of the village society, which had been the breeding ground for witchcraft accusations. As we saw during the height of the witchcraft persecutions, accusations depended on a suspect building a reputation over many years. Improved medical conditions and access to medical facilities also offered other explanations and cures for illness. Religion also lost its stranglehold on the population. The attack on the church by men such as Voltaire and the Enlightenment *philosophes* attempted to dethrone superstition with reason. Their campaign was as much about the Catholic church as it was about magic and witchcraft. However, by the time Voltaire was writing, the witchcraft trials had already wound down. As the church lost influence on the population's daily lives, the belief in the demonic declined. Fundamentalist Christianity had been a fertile place for the Devil to spawn.

The decriminalisation of witchcraft did not mean that the belief in witches disappeared. It would take longer for disbelief in demonic intervention to become widespread. Rural villagers would still use the supernatural to explain misfortune. Because of the lack of judicial solutions, sometimes suspected witches were lynched or persecuted. Continuing belief in the supernatural was evident in the ongoing recourse to cunning folk. Alongside the continuing belief in the spirit world was a comic presentation of the witch. The stereotypical image of the Halloween witch had been fully developed before the end of the persecution era. In a satirical illustration by William Hogarth in 1762, a preacher in the pulpit dangled a female witch riding on a broom with her black cat familiar. The hooked nose, pointy hat, and flying cape would all become characteristics of the modern witch. [See Image #33, Depiction of Satirical Witch in *Credulity, Superstition, and Fanaticism*] The witch in the woods, stirring potions in her cauldron, would become the subject of romantic fairy-tales.

The magic practised by elite men did not disappear either. Ritual magic had never been prosecuted to the same degree as witchcraft. Social status, determined by gender, education, and wealth, had protected magicians from the stake. It was this aspect of magic that would be carried forward from the late-sixteenth century into the twentieth century. After magic was purged of its demons, new pseudo-sciences such as spiritualism and animal magnetism found their place in the new occult. The supernatural aspects of traditional Christianity were forsaken in favour of fraternities such as the Freemasons, which maintained elements of both religion and ritual magic. One of the mystic children of that union was Wicca, whose birth we shall examine next.

Chapter 8

By the Light of the Full Moon, Pagan Witchcraft[1]

The first problem in defining modern witchcraft is to find a term that will satisfy everyone. 'Wicca' usually refers to a particular variety of the modern phenomenon and is often considered a religion by its practitioners. The phrase 'pagan witchcraft' is also employed to paint a wider stroke that encompasses many other people who consider themselves on a 'pagan' spiritual path, as opposed to spirituality within one of the world religions. They may not adhere to formal Wiccan rituals. *Paganus* in Latin simply means 'of or belonging to a country community'. In the Roman Empire, the term was often used to refer to the tribes that populated the territory outside of Europe. As a result, the word took on primitive or barbarian connotations. During the institutionalisation of Christianity, it was used to refer to the religions of the ancient world as well, including Greece, Rome, and Egypt. Hinduism and Islam were tarred with the same brush. In the twentieth century, it was applied to pantheistic or nature-based spiritual movements. Personally, I think the term 'neopaganism' is a more all-encompassing term to differentiate the earth-based spirituality, which was largely developed in twentieth-century America, from the pre-Christian pagan religions and traditions, whether classical or primitive. Indeed, there are even some Wiccan 'churches', but Wicca, pagan witchcraft, and neopaganism are more aptly described as philosophies or lifestyles than as religions. You will not get two pagans in the same room who agree on every detail of this amorphous entity. It is almost impossible to make broad generalisations about modern witchcraft, but most people who identify as witches in the twenty-first century are environmentally green, politically socialist, and pacifist. One might be vegetarian while the other hunts with a cross-bow; one might live in a cabin in the woods while another is a computer geek who lives in a high-rise apartment in the city. But put them all together on Samhain (otherwise known as Halloween), one of the eight yearly sabbats, and they will meld into one consciousness. This chapter will examine how this particular entity developed in England in the twentieth century by combining premodern magic with trends in popular culture.

Modern pagans often relate to the image of early modern cunning folk, perhaps because of the myth that witches were all wise women and healers. Based on this definition of a witch, some modern witches claim to be 'hereditary' witches, having learned their skills from an ancestor, commonly a grandmother. Certainly, it is possible, and likely probable, that skills of the cunning folk were handed down through the generations. But cunning folk were solitary practitioners; there were no guilds or covens of wise men and women. And, as we have discussed, cunning folk were not usually considered witches, even in the early modern era. Cunning folk were more likely to be employed to identify a witch, who might subsequently be prosecuted and executed, than to be identified as a witch. Cunning craft was the practice of operative magic, not a philosophy or a religious belief. And the modern organisation of Wicca is much more than the practice of herbal medicine and spells. The resonance that the modern witch has with early modern cunning folk probably has more to do with the back to nature movement and the rejection of modern science that happened in the 1960s.

In any case, modern Wicca has not continued in an unbroken line of descent from the premodern era. The content of Wicca has borrowed widely and eclectically from classical mythology and religion, premodern folklore, ritual magic, anthropology and archeology, Eastern philosophy and religion, and the ecological and environmental movements. Ancient and premodern ritual magic contributed: the magic circle; the importance of the four cardinal directions and the four elements of earth, air, water, and fire; ritual tools such as the knife, sword, and wand; invocations to gods and goddesses; the concept of the macrocosm and microcosm, with correspondences in the natural world; and the primacy of the pentagram as a functional symbol. The concept of the *grimoire* of rituals and spells was gleaned from medieval magicians. The formation of a formal group or coven, in which to perform these various elements, was taken from the Enlightenment period, which fully developed the idea of the secret society or, at least, the society with secrets, which sprang from the roots of freemasonry. The concept of the witches' sabbat had originated in the late middle ages, but the modern witches' sabbat is quite different in purpose and design.

The ideology of pagan witchcraft is a product of several cultural movements throughout the centuries, including the idealisation of nature, German Romanticism, and the revival of classical motifs. Renaissance neoplatonists had developed the idea of spiritual growth as a necessary component for magic, along with union with the divine as an end in itself.

Nineteenth-century occultists built on this framework of traditional ritual magic, with an emphasis on the spiritual development of the magician. The *Corpus Hermeticum* and the Kabbalah, discussed in Chapter 6, were two important sources for the development of twentieth-century witchcraft. The power of the human will became more important than the rituals and recipes from medieval texts for the performance of magic. Imagination and will power, which had been aspects of Renaissance magic, became the main focus of modern magic. Ceremonies were designed to arouse the divine within and connect with the divine without, which is immanent in the earthly realm.

The Ritual Form

Freemasonry is one of the most influential forerunners of modern Wicca. It was born out of the vestiges of ceremonial magic in the seventeenth century, as elite men shaped bits and pieces of occult ritual into a homosocial institution designed to reinforce their elite status. Many secret societies subsequently developed in the eighteenth and nineteenth centuries out of this model. During the middle ages, craft guilds and trade organisations had developed rules and regulations for their members. They had instituted pledges and oaths, held annual feasts and processions, and sometimes used ceremonial robes for special occasions. One of these trade organisations was the stonemasons. Lodges of working masons were all over Europe. Stonemasons travelled from city to city building cathedrals and castles. Their guild necessarily differed from the sedentary guilds of the middle ages, which were rooted in one place. When a mason showed up at a new location, the masons in charge of the project needed a way to determine the man's qualifications to work as a stonemason. As a result, the group developed secret signs in order to recognise legitimate members of the craft. They also developed a whole mythology around their origins, reaching back to biblical characters, particularly King Solomon, who is credited with building the Temple that housed the Ark of the Covenant. Freemasonry developed from the roots of these operative masons. In the sixteenth century, lodges in Scotland started accepting non-stonemasons into their organisations as benefactors. These 'speculative' masons were men who were interested in the alleged secrets and the occult lore of the traditional masonic lodge. By the seventeenth century, the fraternity of Freemasons was operating completely independently from the working masons.

As builders, stonemason's had knowledge based in mathematics, especially geometry. This resonated with the symbols used in ceremonial magic, such as the pentagram. Freemasons developed this framework of mystical symbolism even further. A secret handshake was accompanied by a special embrace between brothers in which the two bodies made contact at five points: foot, knee, breast, cheek, and hand to back. This would be developed into the five-fold kiss in Wiccan initiation. Secret passwords, initiations, and threats in case of a breach of secrecy were all part and parcel of the new fraternity. Symbolic tools such as the level, compass, and plumb were displayed on an altar in the lodge. Elements of necromancy were included in the initiation rites of death and rebirth. Part of the mythology of the masons was the story that Noah's sons had raised him from the grave to question him about building secrets. In the third degree initiation rite of freemasonry, the symbol of the coffin is employed. This is reminiscent of the sarcophagus associated with the cult of Dionysus, as discussed in Chapter 4. It is almost impossible to trace the cross-pollination of these sorts of ideas and symbols, particularly because the society of Freemasons was very secretive during its formation. What is clear is that pagan witchcraft borrowed many elements from freemasonry in the twentieth century, which had, in turn, taken many components from classical sources as well as early modern magic. The masonic closing phrase 'Happy have we met, happy have we been / Happy may we part, And happy meet again' was most likely borrowed from the expression 'Merry meet and merry part', which was reported as a parting cry of witches in Somerset in the seventeenth century. This is now part of the Wiccan closing ritual. The phrase 'so mote it be', used in freemasonry, was probably adapted from magic rituals found in premodern *grimoires.* Sometimes invocations ended with the Latin declaration '*fiat, fiat, fiat*' or 'so be it'. This was also adapted by modern witches. In England, freemasonry was known as 'the Craft', a designation that would be taken up centuries later by Wiccans. As discussed below, most of the men who were influential in the formation of modern witchcraft were Freemasons. Freemasonry was the foundation stone of Wicca (pun intended).

At the same time that the Freemasons were forming their speculative lodges in Scotland and England, another secret society was taking shape. The elusive Fraternity of the Rosy Cross or the Rosicrucian Society has a very interesting history. Two pamphlets were printed anonymously in Germany in the early-seventeenth century. The pamphlets claimed that there was a secret society of alchemists, who had been meeting since the middle ages. The purpose of the organisation was the spiritual reform of society through magical means. There is no evidence that such a group existed at the time the tracts were written. It probably all started as a sort of hoax. Nevertheless, the same men who were forming freemasonry lodges and dabbling in magic and alchemy were fascinated by the idea. Because the fraternity was so secret, men could claim to be Rosicrucians without revealing any details or actually belonging to the elusive society. By the Enlightenment era, the imaginary secret society had become an actual institution. High ranking members of the Freemasons became members of this elite group for the purpose of studying the Kabbalah, hermeticism, and ancient magical texts. The Fraternity of the Rosy Cross became a space for magical influences to be woven into freemasonry and subsequently into Wicca.

A major influence in this revival of ritual magic was the nineteenth-century Frenchman Éliphas Lévi. He combined his (aborted) training for the priesthood in a Catholic seminary with his occult knowledge gleaned from secret societies. He had been initiated into freemasonry and studied ritual magic texts extensively. He incorporated Kabbalah, Tarot, alchemy, mesmerism, and animal magnetism into his own personal version of magic, which would serve as the foundation for later magicians. Lévi's occultism was a critique of orthodox Christianity, which appealed to political and spiritual radicals. One of his major contributions to Wicca was the initiation of the pentagram as a symbol to invoke the elemental spirits into the ritual circle. Air was associated with the east, fire with the south, water with the west, and earth with the north. In ritual magic, the pentagram had been used as a symbol of protection from evil spirits, not as an invoking mechanism. In Lévi's version, the pentagram was drawn in the air at each quarter at the beginning of a ritual and drawn in the opposite direction at the end of the ritual to banish the spirits. He also used the pentacle in his illustration of the idol Baphomet, the 'Sabbatic Goat' that was allegedly worshipped by the Templars. [See Image #34, Illustration of the idol Baphomet, in *Dogme et Rituel de la Haute Magie*] Lévi's portrayal of the beast was designed as a symbol of the balance of opposites. He acknowledged that there were good and evil, as well as male and female, elements in the universe. The pentagram on the forehead was a symbol of light. Other elements of the image were taken from the Kabbalah.

Lévi also promoted the idea that the inverted pentagram, with one point down and two points up, was a sign of the Devil. As a result, many people in the twenty-first century understand the symbol of the pentacle as evil. However, Lévi had not been supporting devil-worship. He denounced any form of black magic or conjuring of spirits. The inverted symbol was further reinforced as a sign of the Devil by Arthur Waite. He modified Lévi's image of Baphomet to represent the Devil in his Tarot deck, with the pentagram on the goat's head inverted. [See Image #35, The 'Devil card' in Waite's Tarot deck] Waite's conception had a more negative effect in the occult world. The inverted pentacle had never been an aspect of premodern ritual magic, but a version of Waite's Baphomet would be adopted later as the official symbol of Anton LaVey's Church of Satan.

An admirer of Lévi's was the Russian-born occultist Helena Petrovna Blavatsky. She was an internationally renowned medium in the spiritualist movement of the mid-nineteenth century and became a major figure in the Western occult movement. She attributed her knowledge to a group of supernatural spiritual beings called Mahatmas, which she claimed to have come into contact with in the Himalayas of Tibet. Following a prolonged residence in India, Blavatsky promoted the concepts of karma and reincarnation, drawn from the Hindu and Buddhist traditions. In 1875, she established the Theosophical Society. Theosophy is a philosophy that literally means 'god-wisdom'. The idea of an immanent and impersonal deity was influenced by Renaissance ideas of hermeticism and neoplatonism, alchemy, and the Kabbalah. Earlier versions of this mystical philosophy had been developed by the German mystic Jakob Boehme in the seventeenth century. Boehme had introduced the idea of a female aspect to the Trinity, known as Sophia or Wisdom. Blavatsky stated that the purpose of the Theosophical Society was to investigate the mysteries of nature and the psychical powers of the human mind. In her book *Isis Unveiled* (1877), she advocated for a psychic approach to spirituality and the integration of Eastern philosophies with Western esotericism. Blavatsky popularised the Platonic notion of the divine world soul, which would later contribute to the Gaia hypothesis of James Lovelock and the concept of 'Mother Earth', discussed below. More than 100 branches of the society sprang up throughout Europe, America, and India, reflecting the dissatisfaction of intellectuals with conventional religion. The popularity of theosophy indicates that certain elements of society were looking for spirituality outside of the confines of Christianity. However, neither Lévi nor Blavatsky encouraged their followers to practise actual operative magic.

Freemasonry continued to be the fertile soil from which more serious occultists would sprout. In 1888, William Wynn Westcott and Samuel Liddell Mathers founded the Hermetic Order of the Golden Dawn, allegedly a descendent of the medieval German Rosicrucian society. Both men had been Freemasons and members of the *Societas Rosicruciana* in East Anglia in England, and shared an interest in theosophy. They developed the rituals for the new group with influences from the Kabbalah's Tree of

Life and the personal journals of the seventeenth-century Tudor magus John Dee. Rituals from the recently discovered Greek Magical Papyri were transformed into mystical rituals designed for spiritual enlightenment. Grounded in the structure of freemasonry, the society had similar initiation rites, ceremonial garments, and symbolic tools. Masonic lodges were replaced with 'temples'. Mathers contributed several elements to the rituals that would later be incorporated into Wiccan ceremonies. In addition to invoking the four elementals with a pentagram, as developed by Lévi, Mathers called upon the 'Lords of the Watchtowers' at each of the cardinal points. This was adopted from John Dee's concept of guardian angels, which were associated with each of the four directions, who could be called upon for help in magical operations. The practice of purifying the circle with water and fire by circumambulating clockwise was also incorporated into Mathers' rituals. Mathers associated the traditional tools of operative magic with the Freemasons' idea of symbolic tools. There had not been a system, or even consistency, in the use of props before. The wand was aligned with fire, the knife with air, the chalice with water, and the pentacle with earth. The sword was connected to the power of the mind. A member's personal tools were consecrated during the initiation ritual. In imitation of the Catholic Mass, a cup of wine and a plate of bread and salt were consecrated and placed on the altar. What early Wiccans would later accept as ancient pre-Christian rituals were actually put into place in the late-nineteenth century by a group of men who were mostly Christians. However, the Golden Dawn was not opposed to non-Christian beliefs. Influenced by the Theosophical Society and the work of Blavatsky, all religions and spiritual concepts were accepted as reflecting the same core wisdom. Also on account of Blavatsky's influence, women were welcomed into the Hermetic Order of the Golden Dawn.

Samuel Mathers was especially interested in the actual practice of ritual magic. He translated and published several medieval and early modern occult volumes, including *The Book of Abramelin*, the *Key of Solomon*, *The Lesser Key of Solomon*, and the *Grimoire of Armadel*. After the death of Blavatsky in 1891, he initiated a higher grade within the Golden Dawn for the purpose of engaging in operative magic. These members of the Rose of Ruby and the Cross of Gold, also referred to as the Rosy Cross (an obvious imitation of the Rosicrucian fraternity), attempted to conjure up spirits. During the initiation rite of this inner order, the goddess Isis and the god Pan were invoked. They were not worshipped as gods per se, but were invoked as aspects of divinity. The pair represented qualities of many other deities, including Egyptian, Christian, Judaic, classical, and elemental.

The actual existence of the deities was secondary to their role in assisting in the transformation of the magician. Twentieth-century magic was, and still is, magic of the self. These divine beings represented qualities that the celebrant desired, as well as reflecting the syncretic and symbolic nature of the society.

Regardless of the intention, the order was frequently seen as polytheistic, which was a concern to devout Christian members such as Arthur Edward Waite. In addition to being a member of the Golden Dawn, he was also a Freemason and involved in the *Societas Rosicruciana*. He translated Lévi's work, *Transcendental Magic, its Doctrine and Ritual*, along with publishing many occult texts on alchemy, freemasonry, hermeticism, and the Kabbalah. He is probably best known for his edition of the Tarot deck. Although he did not believe in the morality or efficacy of operative magic, he combed through manuscripts of medieval and early modern *grimoires* to produce a volume that would be used as a practical handbook of magic by many occultists, first published as *The Book of Black Magic and of Pacts* (1898) and still available in print as *The Book of Ceremonial Magic*. Waite eventually left the Golden Dawn to start his own group of Christian mystics, known as the Isis-Urania Temple. He maintained his Christianity, but his interest in the occult and his publications influenced future pagans.

Another member of the Golden Dawn, who was at the opposite end of the spectrum to Waite, was the soon-to-be notorious Aleister Crowley. Mathers had initially supported his membership in the Golden Dawn, although they had a falling out in later years. Crowley had had a traditional education at Cambridge University and travelled extensively on his rich inheritance. He studied both Western and Eastern mystical practices and was a major influence on modern witchcraft. When the Golden Dawn went through several schisms, Crowley branched out to set up the *Ordo Templis Orientis* (OTO). In the tradition of ancient origins, the OTO claimed to be descended from the Knights Templar. Eastern mysticism was combined with the alleged masonic secrets. The key elements of the Golden Dawn were kept alive in this new organisation. By the beginning of the twentieth century, Crowley was promoting the revival of a religion of nature. Rather than the god of Christianity, he proposed worshipping the Sun, as well as the male and female Life Force. He also supported the concept of the triple goddess as laid out by Robert Graves (see below). He used the inverted pentagram initiated by Lévi as a symbol of the descent of spirit into matter rather than as a demonic symbol. He added a number of ritual tools to the five outlined by Mathers: the scourge, a container of consecrated oil, a bell, a censer, and a spell book or personal *grimoire*. All of these elements would be adopted in Wicca.

In addition to actual rituals and invocations written by Crowley, one of his main contributions to modern witchcraft was the negative publicity that he attracted. He was a flamboyant character and played up his provocative personality. His open opinions on sex as part of magic and his bisexuality gained him a notorious reputation. His privileging of the idol Baphomet contributed to his reputation as a Satanist, which he was not. In his Gnostic Mass, Baphomet was named as the 'mystery of mysteries'. For Crowley, the figure represented the 'as above, so below' aspect of the universe. Crowley used this figure to symbolise the animal aspect of humans that was joined with the divine. Although the most common image of Crowley is as the Beast 666 from the *Book of Revelation*, he did not actually believe in the Devil, as defined by Christianity. But he did believe in demons. The rituals of the OTO put more emphasis on operative and demonic magic. Crowley claimed to have called up 316 demons in one evening!! His outrageous behaviour and opinions received a lot of negative press. Under his influence, ritual magicians were constructed as Satanists and sexual perverts, which would affect the later reception of Wicca.

Another negative voice concerning witchcraft was Montague Summers. He had been educated at Oxford and ordained as an Anglican priest, despite his sexual orientation as gay. After accusations of pederasty, he attempted to become a Catholic priest, but was refused. Nevertheless, he presented himself as a priest for the rest of his life. As a defender of the faith, he attacked early modern witchcraft as Satan worship, promoting Murray's idea of a pre-Christian cult, but with an evil twist. The atrocities allegedly committed by early modern witches were accepted as real, although Summers was forced to reject the extreme aspects of premodern witchcraft such as flying to the sabbat. But he firmly believed in the power of Satan and the existence of demons. His translation of the *Malleus Maleficarum* published in 1928 would be the only English version of the text until 2006. By promoting this rabidly misogynistic work of demonology as the most important text on witchcraft, he skewed the opinion of a whole generation of readers, particularly the feminist authors who would attribute so much (unwarranted) importance to the *Malleus.* His contribution to modern witchcraft came in the form of raising awareness of witchcraft as a secret evil society. In an age in which spiritualism was making headlines, the general public was easily convinced that witches were still operating in league with the Devil.

The Ritual Fabric

Before this project becomes a history of 'great white men', let's put the work of these men into cultural context. It is the historian's job to look at the past, but it is also a common occupation of the average human. In relation to the birth of modern witchcraft, there were three interconnected cultural forces that would affect the development of Wicca, all of which looked backwards: the idealisation of the countryside, the revival of folk culture, and the reverence for the classical era. This was the backdrop in which the people discussed above operated.

The idealisation of the countryside began at the end of the eighteenth century. This was one of the repercussions of the so-called scientific and industrial revolutions. An increasingly urban population yearned for what they perceived as the simple rural life of their ancestors. City dwellers romanticised the premodern peasants' hardships as a better lifestyle, filled with communal festivals and social harmony. Living close to nature was somehow viewed as resulting in more wisdom. Pastoral poetry and paintings reinforced the concept of a pre-industrial rural paradise. This trend would continue for a long time and would eventually contribute to the 'back to the land' movement of the 1960s. It can still be seen in the marketing of food and fabrics that are 'natural'. Natural is better, naturally. The idyllic setting of the countryside would provide rich soil for the concept of witchcraft as the survival of a pre-Christian fertility cult to grow.

The idealisation of nature was part of a broader movement that developed in the late eighteenth century and peaked in the mid-nineteenth century: Romanticism. The Romantic movement was in response to the rationalism of the Age of Enlightenment, which defined modernity. In an effort to recapture the supposed simplicity of a former era, scholars turned to folk culture. Folk art, folk customs, and folklore were all held in high regard, as opposed to being looked down on by intellectuals, as they had been earlier. In Germany, the Romantic movement was also partly driven by a search for a national identity that could unify Germanic people. Scholars looked for ancient roots from which to grow a nation. One of the more direct effects of this movement on modern witchcraft was a collection of folk tales published between 1812 and 1857 by the Grimm Brothers, Jakob and Wilhelm. Jakob Grimm popularised the concept of the German *Wilde Jagd* as a ride of the dead led by pagan gods. His theories were based on nineteenth-century folklore rather than premodern material that predated the conception of the witches' sabbat. In other words, the sabbat had already entered into folklore by the time Grimm recorded his fairytales. Grimm did not support the idea that the early modern witches portrayed in his tales were practising a pre-Christian fertility cult, but he understood the folktales as remnants of pagan beliefs kept alive in popular culture, without any empirical evidence of those beliefs from the ancient or medieval eras. In spite of what he believed or intended, his folktales were used later to support the idea of the witches' sabbat as a vestige of an ancient cult.

In England, the Folk-Lore Society, founded in 1878, promoted similar ideas. 'Quaint' folk customs were mined for clues to earlier cultures. Folklorists even threw some Druid mythology into the mix by associating Druids with Stonehenge. The monolithic stone structure had been constructed during the Neolithic and early Bronze Ages for some undetermined religious and/or social purpose. The prehistoric site was built thousands of years before the 'English' arrived on the island. In the fourth century BCE, the Greeks, using their own culture as a lens, interpreted Stonehenge as a temple to Apollo. Speculation about the Druid connection started in the seventeenth century. Even before the Romantic movement, there was an intense interest in the monuments of the past. The seventeenth-century antiquarian John Aubrey developed the idea that the Druids were responsible for building Stonehenge as well as Avebury. Druids had been priests of the Celtic religion before the invasion of the Roman Empire in the first century CE. The Druid theory was made popular in the eighteenth century by another antiquarian, William Stukeley. Stukeley was a member of the Ancient Order of Druids, which was an order that had been formed in 1781 along the lines of the Freemasons. There was no evidence to support the theory that Druids built Stonehenge, but it fit well with the Romantic movement of the era. The fabricated association between the Druids and Stonehenge continued. Druids have celebrated Summer Solstice inside the stone circle from at least the early 1900s. In the 1960s, they were joined by a much broader group of pagans and New Agers, who consider the site a source of knowledge and power. Both Stonehenge and Druidry were, and still are, seen as representing British heritage and culture. In response to scientific rationalism, the ancient past and its peoples were revered as possessing a deep, earth-centred wisdom.

Druidry was not the only thing recuperated from an ideal past. Rural traditions and customs, such as the Maypole, the Morris dance, and legends such as Robin Hood and King Arthur were interpreted as residual practices of pagan religion. A nature-based religion that embodied prehistoric customs suited the group of men who romanticised the English countryside.

These ideas would be taken up by writers such as the well-known Irish poet W. B. Yeats. Yeats was a member of the Golden Dawn, as well as the Theosophical Society. Men like Yeats did not reject Christianity, but they blended their religious beliefs with ideas from Graeco-Roman mythology, the Kabbalah, and folklore. This pagan revival was seen as a supplement to Christianity rather than a replacement for it. However, it opened the door for the invention of modern paganism.

Not only the folklorists were looking to the past for answers. The social anthropologist Sir James Frazer was one of many writers who looked to the ancient past in this period. In his very popular work *The Golden Bough* (1890–1915), which is still in print today in an abridged version, his aim was to celebrate modern rationalism and the progress of man from his primitive roots. He presented ancient myths and tribal customs from all over the world to formulate a theory about a long-lasting practice of sacrificing a dying and resurrected god, which he considered 'a barbarous superstition'. His not-so-hidden agenda was to debunk Christianity. However, his work did more to paint a romantic picture of the 'barbarian' past, which would be used by many poets and novelists in the twentieth century. And we all know that writers and filmmakers have more impact on popular opinion than academics do. Frazer stressed the ancient spirit of vegetation, which would be configured as the 'Green Man' by later folklorists. Wiccans also adopted the 'Green Man' as one of their god figures, just as they did the 'Horned God' promoted by Margaret Murray. Frazer inadvertently made several other contributions to modern magic. He popularised a definition of magic in which the human will was used to effect change, by bringing spiritual and supernatural forces under the control of the magus.

Mother Earth

The turn to nature had other repercussions, which would ultimately affect modern witchcraft. The most important of these was the formulation of a Great Goddess, often expressed as Mother Earth. The seed of this idea was in classical sources. The ancients had many gods and goddesses associated with various aspects of both nature and culture. Medieval writers had focused their attention on a handful of these classical goddesses, including the Roman goddess Diana. As we have seen, demonologists named Diana as the leader of the women who flew at night. The Renaissance humanists had raised awareness and appreciation for Graeco-Roman art, literature, and philosophy. That trend was continued throughout the early modern period by scholars, playwrights, and poets. The nineteenth-century Romantics also looked back to the classical era. The privileging of classical Greece, Rome, and Egypt was combined with the renewed reverence for Nature, with a capital N. The Romantic poets embraced the ancient deities of Greece and Rome as symbols of freedom and creativity. By the beginning of the nineteenth century, Diana was being represented in literature as the goddess of the moon and the forest rather than as a patron of the hunt. Authors waxed poetically about the enchantment of the moon and linked the night sky with the divine feminine. The English poet Percy Shelley wrote a lyric poem to the 'Sacred goddess, Mother Earth' who gave birth to all life.[2] The new divine mother represented both the green earth and the white moon in the night sky. Poets such as Shelley also promoted the god Pan as a representative of the wild and dangerous elements of nature. Pan embodied the idyllic and frivolous aspects of the countryside as well as the mysteries of the natural world. The child-like and playful nature of Pan was a foil to the brutish nature of the city, from which the Romantics dreamed to temporarily escape. Margaret Murray would shape Pan into the more universal Horned God.

Western Europe continued to look back to its roots in ancient Greece and Rome for inspiration throughout the twentieth century. This classical pagan revival not only renewed respect for the art, architecture, literature, and philosophy of the classical world, but the former disapproval of classical religion was revised. The ancient traditions were admired as celebrating both the natural world and the human spirit. The term pagan lost its derogatory connotations of incorrect religious beliefs and came to denote the ancient knowledge and imagined freedom that predated Christianity. More emphasis was put on the individual human spirit and a connection with the natural world. This tendency to treat the ancient pagan gods and goddesses as representations rather than realities would later be adopted by modern pagans. This contributed to the development of the concept of Mother Earth as the Great Goddess.

The new-found veneration of Mother Earth contributed to theories of primeval societies that were matriarchal or, at least, woman-centred. Archeologists and prehistorians contributed to this theory as well, portraying a peaceful society that lived harmoniously with nature and worshipped a female deity. Frazer had also supported the idea of either a single mother goddess, with a son who was also her consort, or a dual mother and daughter team, in the likeness of Demeter and Persephone. For our purposes, it matters little that Frazer got many of his facts about the ancient pagan past wrong. What is more important is the long-lasting affect his 'imagined paganism'[3] would have on the formation of modern paganism.

The French historian Jules Michelet also contributed to the notion of a mother goddess. This was part of his strategy in attacking the patriarchal institutions of the Catholic church and the monarchy. As an alternative to Christianity, Michelet suggested a pro-motherhood religion similar to the classical cult of Isis. Women were hailed as saviours of society, who could overturn the materialistic male regimes. In a poorly-researched volume on witchcraft, *La Sorcière* (1862), he presented medieval witches as repressed women practising an ancient pagan religion. He romanticised the sabbat as an assembly of disenfranchised peasants, who were seeking spiritual and economic freedom. The god worshipped at these feasts was the fertility god Pan. Michelet admitted that the ancient religion had declined spiritually during the persecution era, but he still preferred it to the Church of Rome.

One of the enduring ideas that he put forward was that witches were targeted because they were healers, whose skills were the basis of modern medicine. But before you get too excited about celebrating Michelet as a feminist, what he really wanted was a society where women stayed in the home and acted as healers as opposed to the institution of a matriarchy. Nonetheless, his ideas were taken up by other feminist authors. The social rights activist Matilda Joslyn Gage combined the idea of a universal matriarchy in the past with the notion that the witchcraft persecution era was a misogynistic holocaust. Without any evidence, she claimed that nine million women had been burned at the stake, an idea that was taken up later by other feminist authors and filmmakers. This was the sort of rhetoric that inspired radical reactions, which was what the suffragist wanted.

The American folklorist Charles Godfrey Leland took up Michelet's dislike of the Catholic church and the French monarchy. He had taken part in the French Revolution of 1848 and championed the type of people who lived close to nature, such as Native Americans and Gypsies. He claimed to have met a northern Italian woman named Maddalena in 1886. She was apparently knowledgable about local cunning craft and folklore, including tales of witchcraft. As a result of their association and the information she provided him, he published *Aradia* in 1899, which was allegedly the copy of an ancient manuscript containing the gospel of a group of witches in Tuscany. Aradia was the daughter of the goddess Diana, who was sent to Earth to teach peasants herbal lore, so that they could overcome the oppression of their feudal lords. Aradia's followers were told to meet naked in a remote place on the full moon and celebrate the goddess of the witches, Diana.

The text became very important to modern pagans, and the mythology was integrated into the Wiccan 'Charge of the Goddess': 'once in the month, and better it be when the moon is full, you shall assemble in some secret place and adore the spirit of Me who is Queen of all the Wise. You shall be free from slavery, and as a sign that you be free you shall be naked in your rites.'[4] Here was concrete proof of the witch religion, which had survived from time immemorial. Leland went on to assert that this religion was still being practised in remote Italian villages. Unfortunately, there is no secondary evidence to support any of his claims.

The author Dion Fortune was also an inspiration for later Wiccans. She was self-educated in occult studies and became a member of several organisations of the day, including the Golden Dawn and the Theosophical Society. She founded the Inner Light in 1928, which was built on a freemasonry model. Following the lead of Blavatsky, she personified the goddess Isis in ceremonies. She also honoured Pan as the godhead. Her novel *The Sea Priestess* (1938) would become a model for an ancient matriarchy overseen by priestesses.

In occult circles at least, the time was ripe for the poet Robert Graves. His non-fiction work, *The White Goddess* (1948), had a huge impact on modern witchcraft. He developed the idea of the triple aspect of the goddess, as Maiden, Mother, and Crone, relating to the three phases of the moon: waxing, full, and waning. No church had yet been constructed to this twentieth-century deity, but the idea of the Great Goddess had gained a foothold in the popular imagination as a symbol of anti-patriarchy and anti-modernity.

Archaeologists threw their hats into the ring as well, until this (unproven) theory made its way into textbooks on ancient Greek religion. In the late nineteenth century, female figurines from the Upper Palaeolithic and Old Stone Age periods had been commonly referred to as 'Venus figures', referencing them to classical statues. [See Image #36, A female Paleolithic figurine known as the Venus of Willendorf] Theories about the small idols had ranged from them being symbolic concubines placed in male graves to representing fertility fetishes. But at the beginning of the twentieth century, archeologists started to suggest that the female figures, with exaggerated sexual features, were representative of the ancient worship of a single goddess as supreme creatress.

The Birth of Wicca

Of all the characters to influence the formation of modern witchcraft, Margaret Murray is the most striking. She was an Egyptologist at the

University of London, an early feminist, and a member of the Folk-Lore Society. She branched out from her academic specialty to write about what she believed was the survival of an ancient pagan religion. In her first book, *The Witch Cult in Western Europe* (1921), she took up ideas presented in Frazer's *The Golden Bough* and ran a marathon with them. She drew selectively from early modern pamphlets of English witchcraft cases, demonological treatises, and printed trial records to present an argument that the early modern witches were actually practising a fertility cult that had survived from pre-Christian times. A decade later, *The God of the Witches* (1933) reinforced her previous thesis and presented the 'Old Religion' as celebratory. The god Pan, which had been floating around in nineteenth-century literature, was transformed into the Horned God. She referenced stone carvings and cave drawings taken from archeology to argue that the Horned God had been the focus of worship since the Stone Age. She brought the Celtic figure of Cernunnos into the picture to support her claims. Her academic credentials gave her an enormous amount of credibility, and later authors of modern witchcraft in the 1960s and 1970s would fully endorse her views. *The Witch Cult in Western Europe* was reissued as a paperback in 1962 by Oxford University Press, which automatically stamped it as respectable history. Her theories would eventually be completely debunked and destroyed by historians of witchcraft. Her critics demonstrated how she ignored any evidence in the sources she used that disagreed with her theory.

Nevertheless, Murray's configuration of a pre-Christian fertility cult provided a wealth of information for future Wiccans. According to Murray's reading of the evidence, early modern covens of thirteen witches met at sabbats held four times a year on the seasonal quarter days (Candlemas, Beltane/May Day, Lammas, and All-Hallows) to honour the Horned God. At the sabbats, the participants feasted, danced, sacrificed animals and children, performed magic, and engaged in sex. Members were either dedicated to the religion as children or initiated into it as adults. Her presentation of witchcraft as an oppressed religion, persecuted by the repressive Christian church, caused readers to sympathise with the imagined religion. Her presentation also played into the romanticisation of nature and folklore. Occultists at the time ate it up, and many Wiccans, to this day, use her writings to support their belief in witchcraft as an ancient faith handed down through the centuries. To further support the thesis, Murray wrote the entry for 'witchcraft' in the *Encyclopaedia Britannica*, which was not revised until the 1960s. As we have seen, Murray was not alone in her tendency to revive witchcraft as a pagan religion, but her work had an enormous impact on the future of modern witchcraft. The stage was set for the birth of Wicca.

The midwife was Gerald Gardner. Gardner was a colonial civil servant, who served in Ceylon, North Borneo, and Malaya until he retired to England in the 1930s. His interest in all things spiritual and mystic had been fed by his colonial experiences. While he was in the East, he explored tribal animism. Back home, he became involved with freemasonry, spiritualism, the Folk-lore Society, and the occult in general. He was a member of Aleister Crowley's arcane OTO, which he attempted to rejuvenate in England. The OTO had grown from the roots of freemasonry with influences from Lévi, tantric Indian practices, and the myths surrounding the Templars. Crowley's practices became a major influence on Gardner's spiritual path. Gardner was also on the governing council of the Ancient Druid Order. He developed a friendship with Margaret Murray, whose theory that early modern witches were the remnants of a pre-Christian pagan religion would have a huge effect on Gardner's presentation of the 'Old Religion'. In other words, Gardner was involved in every aspect of the occult and folklore available in England. He was also a nudist.

The absolute truth will never be known concerning Gardner's claims about witchcraft. Gardner probably invented Wicca the way he invented his title of Doctor of Philosophy, even though he never earned a PhD from the University of Singapore. He said that he was initiated into a coven of witches in the New Forest area of Hampshire in 1939 by a local woman he identified as 'Old Dorothy'. The term 'coven' was first recorded in the case of Isobel Gowdie of Scotland in 1662. However, it was not used to describe a group of witches until the nineteenth century. Old Dorothy's coven was allegedly a remnant of the ancient witch religion. The existence of this group has never been confirmed. Gardner said he was pledged to secrecy, but he apparently got permission from the group to record his experiences in a novel titled *High Magic's Aid* (1949). After the act concerning witchcraft was finally removed from the statutes in 1951, and Dorothy was presumably dead, Gardner told the whole 'truth' about witchcraft in the non-fiction *Witchcraft Today* (1954). Margaret Murray gave her blessing by writing the foreword. Whether Gardner was telling the truth about Old Dorothy and her coven or whether he invented the whole story to give his new cult a traditional origin, matters little. He was the man solely responsible for bringing the religion of witchcraft to the public eye.

Gardner's presentation of the 'Old Religion' is almost identical to Murray's portrayal. What Gardner added over time were the rituals. Aspects of the coven's rituals will be familiar to my readers: performing rituals naked; feasting and dancing; invocation of a god and a goddess; casting circles with consecrated knives or swords; the importance of cardinal points; ritual tools; and the celebration of seasonal sabbats. Belief in reincarnation, probably an addition from theosophy strengthened by Gardner's interest in Buddhism, was also included. A careful analysis of the information offered by Gardner suggests that he gleaned his rituals from the many occult volumes available at the time, including those of Waite, Mathers, Leland, and Crowley. The medieval *Key of Solomon* and *Goetia* also played a leading role. Crowley had developed a religious philosophical system in Egypt in 1904 called Thelema. The basic principle of the system was the Law of Thelema: 'do what thou wilt shall be the whole of the law'. This was adapted to the Wiccan Rede: 'do as ye will an ye harm none'. Gardner constructed his own *grimoire*, which he called 'Ye Bok of ye Art Magical'. Like early modern magic books, it was an eclectic mix of material from the above mentioned sources, as well as biblical verses and elements of the Kabbalah. The volume also gave instructions for the preparation of the ritual space and tools, invocations of the spirits, and information about the importance of nudity. Ironically, the most obvious influence on Gardner's rituals was ceremonial magic. In the premodern period, ritual magic had been practised by the repressive feudal lords and members of the Catholic church that the Murray theory condemned. The poor, repressed peasants, who were allegedly persecuted for maintaining their ancient religion, had never engaged in high magic.

A more detailed examination of the rituals confirms their eclectic origins. The new religion had three degrees of initiation, an obvious borrowing from freemasonry and the secret societies that developed from that fraternity. The initiate was brought to the circle bound and blindfolded. After giving the secret password, the person was presented to the four directions and then swore an oath of secrecy. The ritual tools included a sword, a black-handled knife, a white-handled knife, a wand, a censer, a pentacle, a scourge, and a set of cords. The cords were an addition by Gardner, to represent the binding of the new witch's will by taking her measure. Another innovation was the name of the black-handled knife as an 'athame', possibly derived from one version of the *Key of Solomon*, which used the term *arthame.* The blessing of the wine, achieved by dipping an athame held by a female witch into a chalice held by a male witch, was adapted from Crowley's sixth degree OTO ritual. It represented the union of male and female and was used as a substitute for the 'Great Rite', which was ritual sexual intercourse between priest and priestess. As a nudist, Gardner had no qualms about privileging the sacredness of sexuality and the naked human form. Rituals were performed 'sky clad'. The casting and blessing of the circle and protecting it with pentacles were all familiar elements drawn from prior ritual magic sources. His personal touch came in naming his new *grimoire*, the 'Book of Shadows', a name borrowed from an occult Sanskrit manual.

The seasonal rituals recorded in the Book of Shadows gleaned material from Crowley's Gnostic Mass, as well as material from outside of magical traditions, including verses from the poet Rudyard Kipling. As mentioned above, the speech from Leland's *Aradia* was transposed almost word for word into the invocation of the goddess, which emphasised the importance of the goddess over the god. In Gardner's version, the invocation was called 'Drawing Down the Moon', which was taken from Ovid's line in the *Metamorphosis* attributed to Medea: 'Thee, too, O Moon, do I draw down' (see Chapter 1).

What Gardner achieved in the 1950s in the presentation of the 'Craft', as he called it, was the synthesis of classical pagan concepts (rampant in the nineteenth century) with medieval ritual magic (embodied in the many secret societies of the nineteenth and twentieth centuries) and the imagined and idealised image of the early modern witch (as outlined by Leland and Murray). The 'witch' was reborn as a celebrant of a counter-culture fertility religion.

Doreen Valiente was one of the first disciples of Wicca. Before she met Gardner, Valiente had been exploring magic through Crowley's work, spiritualism, and theosophy. She was familiar with the work of Leland, Murray, and Graves. Gardner presented her in public as a hereditary witch, the daughter of a traditional witch family, to strengthen his claim of being initiated into the 'Old Religion' in the New Forest. Valiente contributed to the poetic content of the rituals recorded by Gardner, which by that time also included the solstices and equinoxes, thereby creating the eight sabbats of Wicca. She removed much of the content that had been borrowed from Crowley, because she feared that his reputation would damage the acceptance of the new religion. Her contribution to modern witchcraft extended to writing several books and journal articles on the subject. She also promoted Wicca through radio and television interviews. By the 1960s, there were many covens of witches in England, not all of which grew out of Gardner's initial group. Once the broom closet was opened, many people brought out their brooms to make a clean sweep of it.

By the 1970s, the centre of modern witchcraft had migrated to America. After travelling across the pond, the works of Murray and Gardner collided with a strong women's spirituality movement to create a more liberal, left-wing version of witchcraft. Radical feminists employed the idea that nine million women were executed as witches to aid in their fight against the suppression of women by patriarchy. The early modern women who had been burned at the stake fuelled a second feminist fire. The persecution of the 'Old Religion' was presented as part of the misogynistic programme to control women. The *Malleus* was brought out and dusted off as evidence of this top-down attack on women, particularly midwives and healers who threatened the male medical profession. The poor, old early modern village hag was held up as the ultimate symbol of feminism, an independent woman acting out against the evils of church and state. Needless to say, this fiction of the suppression of women was very popular with feminists. When British Wicca first made its appearance in America, it was embraced as a female mystery religion, which was often strictly Dianic, that is, exclusive of male participation. Dianic or goddess-worshipping covens have continued to this day, but a more inclusive model of modern witchcraft emerged under the direction of the California-born Miriam Simos.

Writing under her Craft name of Starhawk, Simos first published *The Spiral Dance* in 1979, which would become the American witches' bible. A second edition was published for the tenth anniversary and the twentieth-anniversary edition was released in 1999. Starhawk is a feminist trained in several strains of modern witchcraft in San Francisco. *The Spiral Dance* supports Murray's thesis, presenting the idealistic and romantic myth as fact. She tells her readers that the form of modern witchcraft has been 'handed down in an unbroken line since before the Burning Times'.[5] Starhawk makes a point of declaring that there was no set liturgy for Wicca, but she offers clear instructions for groups or individuals to perform rituals for the purpose of celebration, as well as operative magic. Many aspects of Gardner's rituals were retained and the reader is encouraged to start her own coven or to practise as a solitary witch. Although she may have been unaware of it, and she certainly did not do it single-handedly, Starhawk took up the work of the Renaissance neoplatonist Marsilio Ficino. She gave a psychological spin to Wicca that emphasised self-development, the power of the human will, and the divine within. Both the god and goddess have a place in her version of the Craft, but the goddess is privileged as the embodiment of earth, moon, sea and sky. Through Nature, the witch could connect with the larger, magical forces of the universe.

One could argue that Starhawk's approach to magic is more metaphorical than Ficino and Pico's, but in both versions, the interconnectedness of the cosmos are at the centre. She also stresses the human relationship with Nature, making witchcraft an environmentally-friendly spiritual path, which appeals to many people who shy away from the dogma of any religion, including Gardner's Wicca. She continues to support the Murryite theory of ancient roots, but adds a modern, activist strand to the worship of Mother Earth. Starhawk firmly believes in putting your money (or your body) where your mouth is. She encourages pagans to peacefully protest military and environmental issues. As a reaction to industrialisation and urbanisation, Gardner's witchcraft had been politically conservative; socialism in the 1950s was seen as a threat. Starhawk's witchcraft, on the other hand, borders on radical socialism, with a strong dollop of feminism. The American eco-pagan movement sees female liberation and protection of Nature as improvements in a patriarchal, capitalistic world. Instead of hiding in the New Forest, this version of witchcraft is willing to take centre stage in a range of international issues, including the proliferation of nuclear warheads. The political activism of American paganism was clear in February 2017 when witches cast a binding spell against the newly-inaugurated president, Donald Trump. Magicians across the country were encouraged to use a stubby orange candle, an unflattering picture of Mr Trump (does a flattering one exist?), and a Tower Tarot card. In the Tarot deck, the Tower card depicts destructive change. A Facebook page suggested that the spell be repeated every waning crescent moon at midnight until Trump's administration stepped down.

It should come as no surprise that this version of witchcraft was born in California. Both academics and hippies were exploring all aspects of mysticism and spirituality in the 1970s. Eastern religions and associated practices such as yoga and meditation were combined with the experimentation of psychedelic drugs and Jungian psychology. The pacifism of Gandhi and the shamanism of Carlos Castaneda were not at odds in this eclectic soup. Starhawk was formulating her version of witchcraft at the same time that James Lovelock was developing his Gaia hypothesis. He argues that the earth acts as a single organism, which could regulate the conditions required for her survival. His theory is largely embraced by the environmentalist community, as well as modern witches.

Neopagans Today

There are many, many variations of modern witchcraft today. Like Luther's movement of protest against the Church of Rome in the sixteenth century,

Gardner's counter-culture religion opened the floodgates to a never-ending array of possibilities. It is no longer necessary for a person to be initiated into an existing coven by an experienced priest or priestess. Many people learn about the pagan movement strictly through books, the internet, and the media, and start their own covens. Many others practise as solitary witches. And just as Gardner composed his new religion from an eclectic blend of sources, pagan witches do not hesitate to bring in whatever spiritual or religious elements suit their fancy. It is not unusual to see a pagan altar decorated with sweetgrass or sage from Native American traditions, statues of Hindu gods and goddesses, a representation of the Buddha, Tibetan prayer flags, Egyptian iconography, and a broom in the corner. Invocations to the Roman goddess Diana and the Celtic god Cernunnos sit comfortably beside each other. Participants in a ritual may come dressed as Druids or Vikings or Gypsies or not dressed at all. Flowing robes, capes, excessive jewellery, masks, and face paint are all equally probable. To be barefoot is almost mandatory, as the celebrant steps on sacred Mother Earth. Ritual is a performance, and creativity and imagination are encouraged as a means to tap into the inner sacred. Dancing, drumming, chanting, and meditating are all tools of the Craft. Pagans do not believe in God: they believe in all the gods and goddesses as an expression of the divine that is immanent in Nature. Since humans are part of the natural world, the divine is immanent in them as well. Nature worship, sexual liberation, and social justice are common values in the neopagan community. The modern witch is on a post-modern nature-based spiritual path.

With one eye over her shoulder …

Endnotes

Introduction:

1. Henry Cornelius Agrippa of Nettesheim, *Three Books of Occult Philosophy*, trans. J. Freake, ed. D. Tyson (St Paul, MN: Llewellyn Publications, 2004), Chap. II, p. 5.

Chapter 1: By Seed and Root, Classical Beginnings

1. Ovid, *The Metamorphoses*, trans. H.T. Riley (London: Bell and Daldy, 1872), Vol. 1, pp. 257-59.
2. As quoted by David Skrbina, in 'Beyond Descartes: Panpsychism Revisited', *Axiomathes*, 16:4 (2006), p. 393.
3. As quoted in Elizabeth M. Butler, *Ritual Magic* (University Park, PA: The Pennsylvania State University Press, 1949), p. 13.
4. As quoted in Christopher A. Faraone, *Ancient Greek Love Magic* (Cambridge, MA: Harvard University Press, 1949), p. 42.
5. Saint Augustine, Bishop of Hippo, *The City of God (De Civitate Dei)*, trans. W. Babcock (Hyde Park, NY: New City Press, 2012), Book VIII, p. 274.
6. R.B., *The Kingdom of Darkness* (London, 1688), p. 57.

Chapter 2: By Bud and Stem, Medieval Menace

1. The Biblical scholar Horace R. Weaver described the use of the Urim and Thummim as follows. A priest placed six stones, three white and three black, in a small sacred container. The white stones indicated 'yes' and the black stones indicated 'no'. Three stones were drawn in response to a yes or no type question. Three white stones represented a favourable answer; three black stones meant God did not agree. A mix of black and white indicated that God was not going to respond.
2. Gregory Bishop of Tours, *History of the Franks* (New York: Columbia University Press, 1916), Book II, Chap. 30, pp. 39-40.
3. Translation of *Canon Episcopi* from Henry Charles Lea, *Materials Toward a History of Witchcraft* (Whitefish, MT: Kesssinger Pub., 1890), Vol. 1, pp. 179-80.

4. As quoted in Dan Jones, *The Templars: The Rise and Spectacular Fall of God's Holy Warriors* (New York: Viking, 2017), p. 346.

Chapter 3: By Branch and Leaf, Demon Logic

1. Jean Bodin, *On the Demon-mania of Witches*, trans. R.A. Scott (Toronto: Centre for Reformation and Renaissance Studies, 2001), 'Author's Preface', p. 44.
2. Henry Boguet, *An Examen of Witches*, ed. M. Summers (New York: Dover Publications, 1929), 'Author's Preface', p. xix.
3. Boguet, *An Examen of Witches*, Chap. XIII, p. 35.
4. Heinrich Kramer, *The Malleus Maleficarum of Heinrich Kramer and James Sprenger*, trans. and ed. M. Summers (New York: Dover Publications, 1971), Pt. I, Ques. 2, p. 14.
5. Kramer, *The Malleus Maleficarum*, Pt. II, Ques. 1, Chap. 7, p. 121.
6. Boguet, *An Examen of Witches*, Chap. XVII, pp. 49-51.
7. Boguet, *An Examen of Witches*, Chap. XI, p. 29.
8. James VI, *Daemonologie in Forme of a Dialogie* (Edinburgh, 1597), Third Booke, Chap. V, p. 57.

Chapter 4: By Life and Love, Sexual Sabbats

1. All quotations from Boguet, *An Examen of Witches*, Chap. I-III, pp. 1-5.
2. As quoted by Richard Seaford, *Dionysos* (London and New York: Routledge, 2006), p. 71.
3. Saint Augustine, *The Works of Aurelius Augustine, Bishop of Hippo. A New Translation*, trans. M. Dods, Vol. 1, *The City of God* (Edinburgh: T. & T. Clark, 1871), Book VI, Chap. 9, p. 249.
4. Boguet, *An Examen of Witches*, Chap. XIV, p. 41.
5. Boguet, *An Examen of Witches*, Chap. XIV, p. 42.
6. Nicolas Remy, *Demonolatry*, trans. E.A. Ashwin, ed. M. Summers (Mineola, NY: Dover Publications, 2008), Bk. I, Chap. XVI, p. 57.
7. Remy, *Demonolatry*, Bk. I, Chap. XVI, p. 57.
8. Inquisitor Pierre le Broussard, as quoted by Julio Caro Baroja, *The World of the Witches*, trans. O.N.V. Glendinning (Chicago: The University of Chicago Press, 1961), p. 91.
9. Boguet, *An Examen of Witches*, Chap. XII, p. 32.
10. Boguet, *An Examen of Witches*, Chap. XII, p. 31.
11. Remy, *Demonolatry*, Bk. I, Chap. VI, p. 14.
12. H.F., *A True and Exact Relation of the Severall Informations, Examinations, and Confessions of the Late Witches, Arraigned and Executed in the County of Essex* (London, 1645), A2, p. 3.

13. John Sterne, *A Confirmation and Discovery of Witchcraft* (London, 1648), C3, p. 15.
14. Remy, *Demonolatry*, Bk. II, Chap. III, p. 100.
15. Boguet, *An Examen of Witches*, Chap. XXXI, p. 88.
16. Remy, *Demonolatry*, Bk. I, Chap. XXV, p. 74.
17. Remy, *Demonolatry*, Bk. I, Chap. XXV, p. 74.
18. Boguet, *An Examen of Witches*, Chap. XXII, p. 66.
19. James Carmichael, *Newes from Scotland, declaring the damnable life and death of Doctor Fian* (London, 1592), A4 verso.
20. Remy, *Demonolatry*, Bk. I, Chap. XVI, p. 59.
21. Stuart Clark, *Thinking with Demons: The Idea of Witchcraft in Early Modern Europe* (Oxford: Oxford University Press, 1997), p.18.
22. Remy, *Demonolatry*, Bk. I, Chap. XVI, p. 57.

Chapter 5: By Flower and Fruit, Popular Culture

1. As reproduced in *Witchcraft and Society in England and America, 1550–1750*, ed. M. Gibson (Ithaca, NY: Cornell University Press, 2003), pp. 37-40.
2. Henry Goodcole, *The Wonderful Discoverie of Elizabeth Sawyer a Witch* (London, 1621), B2.
3. H.F., *A True and Exact Relation of the Several Informations*, A, A3 verso, pp. 1, 6.
4. Goodcole, *The Wonderful Discoverie of Elizabeth Sawyer a Witch*, A4.
5. As quoted in H.C. Erik Midelfort, *Witch Hunting in Southwestern Germany, 1562–1684: The Social and Intellectual Foundations* (Stanford, CA: Stanford University Press, 1972), p. 139.
6. Joseph Glanvill, *Saducismus Triumphatus* (London, 1681), pp. 311-314.
7. Francesco Maria Guazzo, *Compendium Maleficarum: The Montague Summers Edition*, trans. E.A. Ashwin (New York: Dover Publications, 1988), Bk. I, Chap. VIII, p. 23.
8. As quoted in C. L'Estrange Ewen, *Witchcraft and Demonianism* (London: Heath Cranton Limited, 1933), p. 344.
9. As quoted by Gustav Henningsen, *The Witches' Advocate: Basque Witchcraft and the Spanish Inquisition, 1609–1614* (Reno, NV: University of Nevada Press, 1980), p. 86.
10. Anon., *The Examination of John Walsh* (London, 1566), unpaginated.
11. As translated and quoted in Ruth Martin, *Witchcraft and the Inquisition in Venice, 1550–1650* (Oxford: Basil Blackwell, 1989), p. 107.
12. John Phillips, *The Examination and Confession of Certaine Wytches at Chensforde in the Countie of Essex* (London, 1566), A2 verso.

13. Matthew Hopkins, *The Discovery of Witches* (London, 1647), p. 2.
14. Thomas Potts, *The Wonderfull Discoverie of Witches in the Countie of Lancaster* (London, 1613), R3 verso.
15. Boguet, *An Examen of Witches*, Chap. XXI, p. 57.
16. TNA, STAC 8/140/23, Fenne v. Grosse, Faltricke, Scarrborough, Sturlowe, Cok et al.
17. Anon., *The examination of John Walsh*, unpaginated.
18. Essex Record Office, Q/SR 67/45.
19. Reginald Scot, *The Discoverie of Witchcraft* (1584) (New York: Dover Publications, 1972), Bk. XVI, Chap. V, p. 277.
20. Scot, *The Discoverie of Witchcraft*, Bk. XII, Chap. XVII, p. 149.
21. The following quotes are from Edmond Bower, *Doctor Lamb revived, or, Witchcraft condemn'd in Anne Bodenham* (London, 1653), pp. 3, 6, 9, 15.

Chapter 6: The Circle is Cast, Ceremonial Magic

1. Christopher Marlowe, *Doctor Faustus*, ed. S. Barnet (New York: Penguin Books, 1969), pp. 27-8.
2. *A Detection of damnable driftes, practized by three Witches arraigned at Chelmisforde in Essex, at the Assizes there holden, whiche were executed in Aprill* (London, 1579), A8 verso.
3. Heinrich Cornelius Agrippa von Nettesheim, *Henry Cornelius Agrippa his fourth book of occult philosophy of geomancie, magical elements of Peter de Abano*, trans. R. Turner (London, 1665), p. 64.
4. British Library, MS1727, fol. 8.
5. Bodleian Library, Ashmole MS182, fol. 169.
6. Bodleian Library, Ashmole MS 182, fol. 167 verso.
7. Bodleian Library, Rawlinson D253, p. 55.
8. Agrippa, *Henry Cornelius Agrippa his fourth book of occult philosophy*, pp. 59-60.
9. This is a translation by Isaac Newton in Keynes MS, King's College Library, Cambridge University.
10. Henry Cornelius Agrippa von Nettesheim, *Three Books of Occult Philosophy*, trans. J. Freake, ed. and annotated by D. Tyson (St Paul, MN: Llewellyn Publications, 2004), Bk. I, Chap. LXVI, p. 206.
11. *The Way of Hermes: The Corpus Hermeticum*, trans. C. Salaman et al (Rochester, VT: Inner Traditions International, 2000), Bk. 5:1, p. 34.
12. Richard Kieckhefer, *Forbidden Rites: A Necromancer's Manual of the Fifteenth Century* (Gloucestershire: Sutton Publishing, 1997), pp. 59-60.

Chapter 7: The Tree of Life and Death, Persecution through Prosecution

1. *The Diary of the Rev. Ralph Josselin, 1616-1683*, ed. E. Hockliffe, Camden Third Series, VOL. XV. (London, 1908), Entry dated August 30, 1665.
2. Bishop's Visitation Act Books, Somerset Record Office, D/D/CA 21 and 22.
3. As quoted by Malcolm Gaskill, *Witchfinders: A Seventeenth-Century English Tragedy* (London: John Murray, 2005), p. 142.
4. For the complete story, see Michael Kunze, *High Road to the Stake: A Tale of Witchcraft*, trans. W.E. Yuill (Chicago and London: The University of Chicago Press, 1982).
5. *The Lawes against Witches* (London, 1645), p. 7.
6. Quoted by Gustav Henningsen, *The Witches' Advocate: Basque witchcraft and the Spanish Inquisition, 1609–1614* (Reno, Nevada: University of Nevada Press, 1980), p. 88.

Chapter 8: By the Light of the Full Moon, Pagan Witchcraft

1. This chapter owes a great debt to the extremely detailed and rich work of historian Ronald Hutton, *The Triumph of the Moon: A History of Modern Pagan Witchcraft* (Oxford: Oxford University Press, 1999).
2. Percy Shelley, *Song of Proserpine* (1820).
3. Hutton, *The Triumph of the Moon*, p. 131.
4. Starhawk, *The Spiral Dance* (San Francisco: Harper & Row Publishers, 1989), p. 90.
5. Starhawk, *The Spiral Dance*, p. 25.

Further Reading

Primary Sources

Agrippa of Nettesheim, Henry Cornelius. *Three Books of Occult Philosophy*. Translated by James Freake. Edited and Annotated by Donald Tyson. St Paul, MN: Llewellyn Publications, 2004.

Bodin, Jean. *On the Demon-mania of Witches*. Translated by Randy A. Scott. Introduction by Jonathan L. Pearl. Toronto: Centre for Reformation and Renaissance Studies, 1995.

Boguet, Henry. *An Examen of Witches*. Edited by Montague Summers. New York: Dover Publications, 1929.

Guazzo, Francesco Maria. *Compendium Maleficarum*. Translated by E.A. Ashwin. New York: Dover Publications, 1988.

Kramer, Heinrich. *The Malleus Maleficarum of Heinrich Kramer and James Sprenger*. Translated and Edited by Montague Summers. New York: Dover Publications, 1971.

Remy, Nicolas. *Demonolatry: An account of the Historical Practice of Witchcraft*. Translated by E.A. Ashwin. Edited by Montague Summers. Mineola, NY: Dover Publications, 2008.

Scot, Reginald. *The Discoverie of Witchcraft*. 1584. New York: Dover Publications, 1972.

Spee von Longenfeld, Friedrich. *Cautio Criminalis, or a Book on Witch Trials*. Translated by Marcus Hellyer. Charlottesville and London: University of Virginia Press, 2003.

Secondary Sources

Apps, Lara and Andrew Gow. *Male Witches in Early Modern Europe*. Manchester and New York: Manchester University Press, 2003.

Bailey, Michael David. *Battling Demons: Witchcraft, Heresy, and Reform in the Late Middle Ages*. University Park, PN: The Pennsylvania State University Press, 2003.

Behringer, Wolfgang. *Witches and Witch-Hunts: A Global History*. Cambridge, UK: Polity, 2004.

Bever, Edward. *The Realities of Witchcraft and Popular Magic in Early Modern Europe: Culture, Cognition, and Everyday Life.* New York: Palgrave Macmillan, 2008.

Briggs, Robin. *Witches and Neighbors: The Social and Cultural Context of European Witchcraft.* New York: Penguin Books, 1996.

Clark, Stuart. *Thinking with Demons: The Idea of Witchcraft in Early Modern Europe*. Oxford: Oxford University Press, 1997.

Copenhaver, Brian P. *Magic in Western Culture: From Antiquity to the Enlightenment*. New York: Cambridge University Press, 2015.

Davies, Owen. *Grimoires: A History of Magic Books*. Oxford: Oxford University Press, 2009.

Davies, Owen. *Popular Magic: Cunning Folk in English History*. London and New York: Hambledon Continuum, 2007.

de Certeau, Michel. *The Possession at Loudun.* Translated by Michael B. Smith. Chicago and London: The University of Chicago Press, 1990.

Decker, Rainer. *Witchcraft & the Papacy: An Account Drawing on the Formerly Secret Records of the Roman Inquisition*. Translated by H.C. Erik Midelfort. Charlottesville & London: University of Virginia Press, 2003.

Duni, Matteo. *Under the Devil's Spell: Witches, Sorcerers, and the Inquisition in Renaissance Italy.* Florence: Syracuse University in Florence, 2007.

Faraone, Christopher. *Ancient Greek Love Magic*. Cambridge, MA: Harvard University Press, 1999.

Gaskill, Malcolm. *Witchfinders: A Seventeenth-Century English Tragedy*. London: John Murray, 2005.

Ginzburg, Carlo. *The Night Battles: Witchcraft & Agrarian Cults in the Sixteenth & Seventeenth Centuries.* Translated by John and Anne Tedeschi. New York: Penguin Books, 1985.

Goodare, Julian. *The European Witch-Hunt.* London and New York: Routledge, 2016.

Henningsen, Gustav. *The Witches' Advocate: Basque Witchcraft and the Spanish Inquisition (1609–1614)*. Reno, NV: University of Nevada Press, 1980.

Hutton, Ronald. *The Triumph of the Moon: A History of Modern Pagan Witchcraft*. Oxford: Oxford University Press, 1999.

Jensen, Gary. *The Path of the Devil: Early Modern Witch Hunts.* Lanham, MD: Rowman & Littlefield Publishers, 2007.

Kieckhefer, Richard. *European Witch Trials: Their Foundations in Popular and Learned Culture, 1300–1500.* Berkeley and Los Angeles: University of California Press, 1976.

Kieckhefer, Richard. *Forbidden Rites: A Necromancer's Manual of the Fifteenth Century*. Gloucestershire: Sutton Publishing, 1997.

Kunze, Michael. *Highroad to the Stake: A Tale of Witchcraft.* Translated by William E. Yuill. Chicago and London: The University of Chicago Press, 1982.

Macfarlane, Alan. *Witchcraft in Tudor and Stuart England: A Regional and Comparative Study*. Prospect Heights, IL: Waveland Press, Inc, 1970.

Magika Hiera: Ancient Greek Magic and Religion. Edited by Christopher A. Faraone and Dirk Obbink. New York and Oxford: Oxford University Press, 1991.

Martin, Ruth. *Witchcraft and the Inquisition in Venice, 1550–1650.* Oxford: Basil Blackwell, 1989.

Maxwell-Stuart, P.G. *An Abundance of Witches: The Great Scottish Witch-Hunt.* Stroud, Gloucestershire: Tempus, 2005.

Maxwell-Stuart, P.G. *Witch Hunters: Professional Prickers, Unwitchers & Witch Finders of the Renaissance*. Stroud, Gloucestershire: Tempus, 2003.

Midelfort, H.C. Erik. *Witch Hunting in Southwestern Germany, 1562–1684: The Social and Intellectual Foundations*. Stanford, CA: Stanford University Press, 1972.

Murray, Margaret A. *The God of the Witches*. London: Oxford University Press, 1931.

Ogden, Daniel. *Greek and Roman Necromancy*. Princeton and Oxford: Princeton University Press, 2001.

Purkiss, Diane. *At the Bottom of the Garden: A Dark History of Fairies, Hobgoblins, and Other Troublesome Things*. New York: New York University Press, 2003.

Rapley, Robert. *A Case of Witchcraft: The Trial of Urbain Grandier.* Montreal and Kingston: McGill-Queen's University Press, 1998.

Roper, Lyndal. *Witch Craze: Terror and Fantasy in Baroque Germany*. New Haven: Yale University Press, 2004.

Russell, Jeffrey Burton. *Lucifer: The Devil in the Middle Ages*. Ithaca and London: Cornell University Press, 1984.

Russell, Jeffrey Burton. *Witchcraft in the Middle Ages*. Ithaca and London: Cornell University Press, 1972.

Schulte, Rolf. *Man as Witch: Male Witches in Central Europe*. Translated by Linda Froome-Döring. Basingstoke, Hampshire: Palgrave Macmillan, 2009.

Sharpe, James. *The Bewitching of Anne Gunter*. New York: Routledge, 2000.

Sneddon, Andrew. *Witchcraft and Magic in Ireland*. Basingstoke: Palgrave Macmillan, 2015.

Somerset, Anne. *The Affair of the Poisons: Murder, Infanticide and Satanism at the Court of Louis XIV*. London: Phoenix, 2003.

Starhawk. *The Spiral Dance: A Rebirth of the Ancient Religion of the Great Goddess.* (1979) 10th Anniversary Edition. San Francisco: Harper & Row Publishers, 1989.

Thomas, Keith. *Religion and the Decline of Magic.* New York: Charles Scribner's Sons, 1971.

Timbers, Frances. *Magic and Masculinity: Ritual Magic and Gender in the Early Modern Era*. London and New York: I.B. Tauris, 2014.

Timbers, Frances. *The Magical Adventures of Mary Parish: The Occult World of Seventeenth-Century London*. Kirksville, MO: Truman State University Press, 2016.

Willis, Deborah. *Malevolent Nurture: Witch-Hunting and Maternal Power in Early Modern England.* Ithaca and London: Cornell University Press, 1995.

Witchcraft and Magic in Europe: Ancient Greece and Rome. Edited by Bengt Ankarloo and Stuart Clark. Philadelphia: University of Pennsylvania Press, 1999.

Witchcraft and Magic in Europe: The Eighteenth and Nineteenth Centuries. Edited by Bengt Ankarloo and Stuart Clark. Philadelphia: University of Pennsylvania Press, 1999.

Witchcraft and Magic in Europe: The Period of the Witch Trials. Edited by Bengt Ankarloo, Stuart Clark, and William Monter. Philadelphia: University of Pennsylvania Press, 2002.

Zika, Charles. *The Appearance of Witchcraft: Print and Visual Culture in Sixteenth-Century Europe*. London and New York: Routledge, 2007.

Index